SPOKEN TAMIL
FOR ABSOLUTE BEGINNERS

Sanjay D.

Expert in Language Training

INDIAN
Language Books

Book Title: Spoken Tamil for Absolute Beginners
Book Author: Sanjay D.
Published by Indian Language Books
Printed and bound by Amazon
This edition is published in: 2022
ISBN Print: 9789352912230
Copyright © Sanjay D 2019
Designed by Jacqueline Husse

For questions and Suggestions:
indianlanguages101@gmail.com

Acknowledgement and Dedications

I want to thank my mom Meenakshi and my wife Jacqueline for standing beside me throughout my career and helping me write this book. They have been the source of my inspiration and motivated me to continue improving my knowledge to write this book. They are my rock, and I dedicate this book to them. I would like to thank Jacqueline Husse for illustrating the book cover and interior designing. I also thank my Tamil students who encouraged and motivated me to write this book, especially Tricia Sutton 'She loves Tamil more than anybody I ever knew' and Edward. I also dedicate this book to all Tamil learners who want to connect with their loved ones and enjoy the beauty of the language that's being offered by the Beautiful and elegant Tamil. தமிழ் வாழ்க.

யாம் அறிந்த மொழியிலே தமிழ் மொழி போல் இனிதைக் காணோம்.

Of all the languages I knew, there is no language that's as sweet as Tamil.

By Subramania Bharati

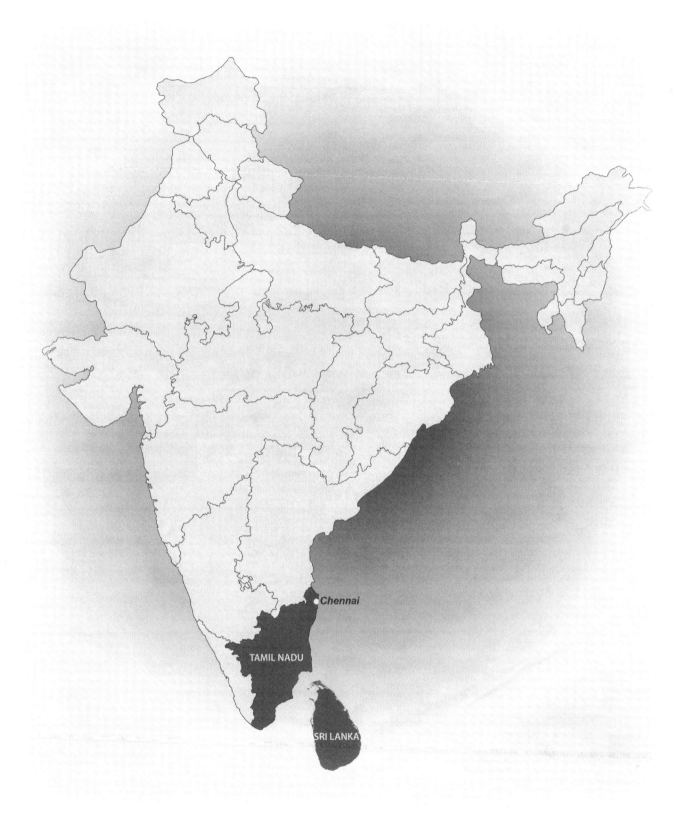

TABLE OF CONTENTS

INTRODUCTION

About Author:

Sanjay D was born and raised in Chennai, Tamil Nadu, the southern part of India. He is a passionate lover of the Tamil language and culture. He started teaching Tamil to many foreigners and gained lots of experience in understanding foreigners difficulty in learning the Tamil language. So, he prepared an organized and systematic course to help them learn and speak the language with ease and better pronunciation. This book is the ultimate result of years of experience in teaching Tamil to Indians and foreigners.

About Tamil:

Tamil is a Dravidian language spoken by over 70 million people worldwide. The two countries where Tamil is predominantly spoken are India and Sri Lanka. Tamil is the mother tongue of the Tamil Nadu people in India. In Sri Lanka, one-fourth of the inhabitants are Tamil speakers who migrated from Tamil Nadu many years ago. Tamil is the official language of Singapore and Sri Lanka. Over many years, Tamil speakers have migrated to other countries like Singapore, Malaysia, the USA, Canada, the UK, Germany, etc. Tamil is one of the longest-surviving classical languages in the world. It is also stated as 20th in the Ethnologue list of most-spoken languages worldwide. Tamil-Brahmi inscriptions from 500 BC have been found on Adichanallur and 2,200-year-old Tamil-Brahmi inscriptions on Samanamalai. It has been described as "the only language of contemporary India, which is recognizably continuous with a classical past". The variety and quality of classical Tamil literature have led to its being described as "one of the great classical traditions and literatures of the world". Tamil has a very rich culture and a visit to Tamil Nadu will provide you multiple opportunities to experience the beauty of the place and the language. Tamil Nadu has Mahabalipuram, a monolithic temple with rock sculptures carved in the seventh century.

About This Book:

1) The book is designed such that you do not need any previous knowledge before learning spoken Tamil. This book is for beginners and those looking to review, improve their Tamil fluency and understand the language better.

2) You will be provided with Transliteration in English for almost 80-90% of the Tamil scripts in the book. However, you are expected to learn Tamil letters and read them for the reasons below.

- Even if I give the transliteration for the Tamil script, the possibility that you read with the correct pronunciation is less. E.g. வணக்கம், (TL: vaNakkam), I am sure that five different people will read the transliteration 'vaNakkam' in five different ways depending on their English accent.

- The time taken to learn to read in Tamil is only approx. 10 hours.

- Learning Tamil scripts will enable you to pronounce Tamil letters easily and be more independent in learning Tamil.

Note:

Due to all the above reasons, I highly recommend you to learn to read the Tamil script. I have provided the first two lessons in video format as well. The link to access that playlist is "**www.tinyurl.com/readtamil**". You can use these videos to train yourself to learn to read in Tamil.

3) I do not expect you to learn to write in Tamil, but if you are interested, you are most welcome. It doesn't take much time to learn to write Tamil scripts.

4) Every Tamil script in this book is provided with the below mentioned for easy understanding:

Transliteration (tl) – This is the transliteration of the Tamil script. Simply put, this is how a Tamil pronunciation would be if it is written in Tamil.

Literally (lit) – Since the word order for many sentences is different from English, I have provided the literal translation of the Tamil script.

Translation (t) – This is the translation of the Tamil script into English. This gives you the end meaning of the sentence in English, no matter in which word order the sentence might be in.

5) I have created many Tamil courses in the website "**www.mylittlewordland.com**" to help you learn Tamil Alphabets, Vocabulary and useful Tamil phrases and sentences. A separate section is provided in page VIII to guide you in accessing those Tamil courses.

6) You are not expected to learn all the vocabulary before you begin. It is recommended to learn vocabulary little by little, but you are expected to learn and memorize pronouns and their suffixes, Verbs, and their conjugated forms as they are frequently used throughout the book.

7) Once you can read in Tamil, little by little, stop depending on the Transliteration I have given for the Tamil script. Please ignore them as much as possible.

8) Keys to most exercises are given at the end of each lesson.

9) Please try to understand every part given in the book, a lot of effort has been put into this book to explain in great detail with lots of examples. A concept or a part that is being mentioned in one chapter will not be repeated in another chapter. So, I expect you to put a lot of effort into understanding what's given in the book rather than memorizing the Tamil words.

What to Expect from the Book and How This Book is Designed.

Tamil's script, grammar, and other aspects differ from English. The language has a lot of rules and grammar. If you were to learn everything before speaking the language, it would take you a lifetime to learn it. So, I have taken some important key grammar topics, words, and suffixes required and explained them in great detail so that you can start speaking in Tamil.

Guarantee:

If you read this book with complete focus, motivation, and willingness to put effort into learning, understand the grammar given here and memorize words and suffixes; you will be able to make sentences in Tamil consisting of 3-6 words, using which you can make small talk with native speakers of Tamil.

This book is designed with a step-by-step practical approach to getting you to start speaking in Tamil.

After completing Lesson 1 and 2, you should be able to understand the Tamil letters, how they are combined, how to pronounce them, etc. and you should be able to read and pronounce the Tamil script with minimal struggle. To learn to read in Tamil should take approx. 10 hours.

Lesson 4 is all about helping you to speak in Tamil, it has no grammar explanations. Lesson 4A is to help you with vocabularies that you will come across in the following Lessons. Lesson 4B is to help you learn Tamil sentences which are used in day to day conversations. Lesson 4B Part 2 is to healp you to learn the vocabularies used in Lesson 4B Part 1. Lesson 4C is to help you practise role play scenarios (advanced Tamil learning)

After completing Lesson 5 and Lesson 6 you will be able to understand pronouns and their suffixes, how a letter may get inserted when you combine a word with suffix.

After completing Lesson 7, Lesson 8 and Lesson 9 you would have memorized 100 verbs and their conjugation in all three tense. Now you will be able to make 3 word sentences in Tamil using your Verb conjugation knowledge, use command and request. Now you have reached 25% of your goals in this book.

After completing Lesson 11 you will be able to effectively use the cases as per your needs and make much more sentences in Tamil, with cases in your arsenal you will be able to make sentences containing 4-5 words. Now you have reached 50% of your goals in this book.

After completing Lesson 12 you will be able to make sentences with adverbs and adjectives, with Lesson 13 and Lesson 14 you will be able to negate a sentence and you will be able to make much more sentences in Tamil. Now you have reached 100% of your goals in this book. You will be able to make a sentence in Tamil with 3-6 words.

Letters in Brackets

In this book, a few Tamil words, especially pronouns, have the last letter in brackets (e.g. நா(ன்)). This is because to speak easily and faster, many native Tamil speakers tend not to pronounce the last letter of some words, or they pronounce the last letter very softly that you can hardly hear them, specifically words that has the last letter (ன்), (ள்) and (ம்). Some words may end with the letter ன், ள், and ம், but you have to pronounce those last letters as well. That's why I have differentiated them by putting the ones you don't have to pronounce or to pronounce very softly in brackets.

Since these last letters are pronounced softly, the pronunciation sound of the letter before them changes a little. Since the change is minimal, one cannot simply put them in writing as you will require a whole new alphabet.

To overcome this problem, listen carefully to my audio recording of the Tamil words and sentences so you can mimic my pronunciation. There are very few words with the last letter in brackets, but some frequently used pronouns do; you will see them often.

For Example: பைய(ன்), அவ(ள்), முடியு(ம்)

Colloquial Tamil v/s Sentamil.

The spoken Tamil that we are speaking now (Colloquial) is slightly different from what we used to speak 30 – 40 years ago. There have been a lot of changes to speaking Tamil faster and pronouncing easier. Most native speakers nowadays will not pronounce the last letter of most Tamil words and change some letters in the Tamil words to make it easier for pronunciation.

Variation in Dialects

Similar to English (American vs. British vs. Australian English), Tamil also has various dialects. The Tamil spoken in Chennai differs from that in Sri Lanka. The Tamil spoken in different parts of Tamil Nadu (e.g., Coimbatore, Madurai, Tirunelveli, etc.) have their dialects, but basic Tamil is still the same. Any person who can speak Tamil fluently can understand any dialect.

This book is mainly focusing on 20th-century spoken Tamil from Chennai. To make it easier for you to learn Tamil, I've done my best to create grammar and a set of rules.

What else can you do apart from reading this book to boost your Tamil learning and becoming fluent in Tamil?

1) Book Classes from me: You can book classes with me through the link below, and I can help you become fluent in Tamil soon.

https://www.italki.com/teacher/3248724

2) Entertainment: Tamil Cinema is a very big entertainment industry. Every year around 300 plus movies get released, and we have movies of every genre: action, comedy, romance, thriller, etc. If you think that in Indian movies, all we do is dance and sing, then you are wrong. There are few movies that do that, but many movies showcase society and have a very good story.

To watch Tamil movies, you can register on the website below; they provide many Tamil movies with English subtitles.

https://www.einthusan.tv

Some movies that I would recommend:

Irudhi Suttru, Vil Ambu, Kadhalum Kadandhu Pogum, Thozha, 24, Oru Naal Koothu, Metro, Appa, Dhuruvangal Pathinaaru, Adhe Kangal, Thani oruvan, Kanavu Variyam, Kuttram 23, Maanagaram, 8 Thottakkal, Pa Paandi, Baahubali, Oru Kidayin Karunai Manu, Baahubali: The Conclusion, Maragadha Naanayam, Ivan Thanthiran, Meesaya Murukku, Vikram Vedha, Kootathil Oruthan, Taramani, Kurangu Bommai etc.

3) Music: The music of Tamil Nadu has a long tradition and history going back thousands of years. Music is a very important aspect of the culture of the Tamil people. The film music of Tamil Nadu is widely known for its innovation and eclecticism. The two most famous and acclaimed film composers of India, Ilaiyaraaja, and A. R. Rahman (Who won an Oscar award), are from Tamil Nadu. Other famous music composers are Harris Jayaraj, Yuvan Shankar Raja, Anirudh Ravichander, and Hip-hop Tamizha.

Here are some links below where you can listen to Tamil music;

http://gaana.com/playlist/shine-geo-mathews-arrahman-tamil-hits-004466

http://gaana.com/artist/iiaiyaraaja

https://www.saavn.com/tamil

http://gaana.com/album/tamil

https://www.youtube.com/watch?v=i4uXbSgVjZ8

4) Practice with your Tamil friends and family, if they have enough patience for it.

Guide on using the website "My little word land":

My little word land is a language learning website. It specializes in combining memory techniques like flash cards and spaced repetition to make language learning recreational.

Steps to Register and use "My little word land" in your browser.

Step 1:

a) Go to the link www.mylittlewordland.com

b) Click "register".

c) Provide your email address, username and native language and click "register".

d) A confirmation email will be sent to your email address. So, check your email and confirm the registration by clicking on the link and logging in.

Step 2:

a) Go to the below mentioned link and click the "Begin course" button.

Tamil Alphabets:

Note:

> This course is necessary for Lesson 1, in order to memorize Tamil scripts.

https://mylittlewordland.com/course/141738

https://tinyurl.com/tamil100

Lesson 4B Tamil Sentences for Conversation:

Note:

> This course is necessary if you want to memorize Lesson 4B.

https://mylittlewordland.com/course/295369

https://tinyurl.com/tamil101

VIII

Lesson 4B2 Vocabulary for Lesson 4B:

Note:

> This course is necessary if you want to memorize vocabularies used in Lesson 4B, I created this course for those who find it overwhelming to memorize big sentences.

https://mylittlewordland.com/course/295384

https://tinyurl.com/tamil102

Lesson 4A Vocabulary for lesson 5 to 14:

Note:

> This course is necessary if you want to memorize vocabularies used in Lesson 5 to 14.

https://mylittlewordland.com/course/141742

https://tinyurl.com/tamil103

How to use the courses in "My little word land":

Step 1: Once you click the "Begin course" button, those courses will be automatically added to your dashboard. In the dashboard click on the 'learn' button.

Step 2: You will be provided with three learning options.

Learning methods

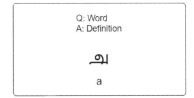 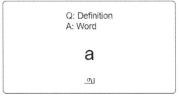 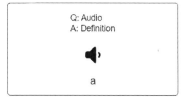

Option 1: I would highly recommend you to choose this option because this way you don't have to type the Tamil scripts and it will test your knowledge in the Tamil transliteration.

Option 2: This option is for those who wants to learn the other way around, you have to type the Tamil script and learn pronunciation from the Tamil script. This many not be suitable for many learners.

Option 3: This option is also good, it will strengthen your listening skill a lot.

Step 3: Once you choose your learning option, you will be taken to another page. Here, you can choose the test type based on whether you want to 'type' or have 'multiple choice'. I would suggest you to experiment on this and choose the one which suits your learning better. Then, you can choose the number of words and number of times that you want it to test you for those words. In the bottom of it, you can see the list of words that you will be learning as per what you choose. Then, click the "Begin test" button and that's it. You can start learning the course. The website will guide you.

The ultimate goal of this course is to let you decide on the speed of your learning and type of learning. Everything is customizable.

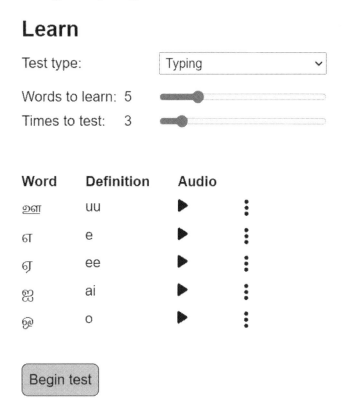

How to Write in Tamil on a Keyboard

There are multiple ways to use the Tamil keyboard on your computer. I have mentioned 2 different methods to use Tamil scripts on your computer, and you can use any one which suits your needs.

Method 1:

The details of this method is given as a pdf, and you can download them using the link below.

www.bit.ly/tamilwrite

Method 2:

This method is pretty straightforward, but you must have an internet connection and copy and paste the Tamil script every time.

Step 1: Go to the below-mentioned website:

www.tamil.changathi.com/

Step 2: You will see a screen where you can type the English transliteration as I did.

Step 3: Once you type the transliteration, press the spacebar, and the transliteration will get converted into a Tamil script.

Step 4: If this is not the desired Tamil script, then you can press the backspace key twice, and you will be provided with a drop-down to choose the desired Tamil script.

Step 5: You can copy and paste the Tamil script on Skype, MS word, or anywhere else.

Note:

> Using all the above two options, you can write in Tamil on your computer. Choose whichever you feel comfortable with. The first option may be a little difficult initially, but it will improve your typing speed. The second option is the easiest, but it will always slow you down because of the time to copy and paste, and sometimes, it will not show the desired word or Tamil script.

Learning to read in Tamil and book content in Video format

To make the learning experience more interactive, I have created two video playlists. Playlist 1: Specially designed for Lesson 1 and 2 of this book, Playlist 2: Myself explaining most of the content of the book. All you have to do is copy and paste the below links in your browser, and you will be taken to the YouTube video playlist, and you can watch the whole videos there.

Playlist 1: www.tinyurl.com/readtamil

Playlist 2: www.tinyurl.com/tamilvideos1

The content of these videos are the same as the content of this book. It's just when you listen to me explaining and pronuncing the Tamil words, It will be much more interactive.

The book contains all the lesson instructions you'll need to learn to speak Tamil fluently. It is not necessary that you watch the videos; you can follow the instructions and learn everything you need to communicate easily. But when you use the book and these videos as well, it will make it much more fun. This will also give you a student-teacher kind of experience.

If you need any further assistance you can email me at learntamilnow1@gmail.com.

TAMIL LETTERS

LESSON 1

Content:

- Vowels and Consonants
- Compound Letters
- Pronunciation Variation Guide
- Notes and Rules
- Exercises

LESSON 1:
TAMIL LETTERS

Attention!

Before continuing with the lessons, please read the following text.

I have created a video tutorial in YouTube explaining how to use the book and the content of the book in video format. So that it is much easier for you to understand and it will be more engaging to see me explain most of the contents in the book. Kindly go to the below link to access the YouTube playlist of me explaining everything in a video format.

www.tinyurl.com/tamilvideos1

1) Lesson 1 & lesson 2 are all about learning to read Tamil. Learning to read in Tamil is not mandatory as most of the Tamil scripts provided in the book have transliteration next to them. If you're not keen on learning to read Tamil, skip lesson 1 & 2.

Author's suggestion: I would highly recommend you to learn to read in Tamil before proceeding to the other lessons in the book because it takes you only a month or two to learn to read in Tamil and it helps you a lot with Tamil pronunciation.

2) Lesson 5 to lesson 14 is all about learning Tamil grammar and making Tamil sentences on your own. If you're not interested in Tamil grammar, you can skip these lessons.

Author's suggestion: It is recommended that learners do not concentrate on learning Tamil phrases before learning Tamil grammar in the book because Tamil grammar is slightly different from English grammar. I have given a detailed explanation about this in my introduction video in the playlist.

3) If you are not interested in Tamil grammar please go straight to lesson 4B and 4C at the end of the book or If you want to learn Tamil sentences simultaneously while learning Tamil grammar please focus on lesson 4B and lesson 5 to lesson 14.

The Tamil script has 12 vowels (உயிரெழுத்து; uyirezhuththu;"soul-letters"), 18 consonants (மெய்யெழுத்து; meyyezhuththu; "body-letters") and one special character, special character ∴ (ஆயுதஎழுத்து; aayudhaezhuththu) is not a vowel and we rarely use it. Therefore, the complete script consists of 31 letters in their independent form and 216 compound letters (a combination of 12 vowels and 18 consonants. 12*18 =216), (உயிர்மெய்யெழுத்து; uyirmeyyezhuhthu; "soul-body-letters"). So, in total, 247 letters are there in the Tamil script.

Vowels

There are 12 vowels in total; Short Vowels (குறில் kuRil), Long Vowels (நெடில் nedil) and Diphthongs. The following table lists the vowel letters with pronunciation.

Tamil Vowels	Pronunciation	Type of Vowel	Pronunciation equivalent in English
அ	a	Short Vowel	As sound of "a" in 'arrive', 'army', as sound of "u" in 'but', 'utter'.
ஆ	aa	Long Vowel	As sound of "aa" in 'aah', 'bazaar'.
இ	i	Short Vowel	As sound of "i" in 'kick', 'sick'.
ஈ	ii	Long Vowel	As sound of "ii" in 'skiing', as sound of "ee" in 'deep', 'sleep'.
உ	u	Short Vowel	As sound of "u" in 'put', 'pull'.
ஊ	uu	Long Vowel	As sound of "oo" in 'soon', 'moon', as sound of "u" in 'true', 'brute'.
எ	e	Short Vowel	As sound of "e" in 'entry', 'end', 'exit' or as sound of "a" in 'tame', 'cake'.
ஏ	ee	Long Vowel	As sound of "ae" in 'aeroplane' or as sound of "ay" in 'delay'.
ஐ	ai	Diphthongs	As sound of "i" in 'iron', 'item', 'idea'.
ஒ	o	Short Vowel	As sound of "o" in 'omit', 'slow'.
ஓ	oo	Long Vowel	As sound of "o" in 'pole', as sound of oa in 'coal'.
ஔ	au	Diphthongs	As sound of "ow" in cow, how, now.

Orthography:

1) Short vowels takes approx. 0.25 seconds, Long vowels takes approx. 0.50 seconds and Diphthongs take approx. 0.38 seconds to pronounce.

2) While pronouncing vowels, your tongue is positioned in different parts of your mouth without touching any part of the oral cavity.

Consonants

There are 18 consonants in Tamil; they are further divided into five stop sounds, six nasal sounds, two lateral sounds, three r sounds, and two glides

க்	ங்	ச்	ஞ்	ட்	ண்	த்	ந்	ப்	ம்	ய்	ர்	ல்	வ்	ழ்	ள்	ற்	ன்
k(g)	ng	s(ch)	nj	t(d)	N	th(dh)	<u>n</u>	p(b)	m	y	r	l	v	zh	L	R	n

Note:

- Please refer to the audio recording or video for pronouncing the consonants and compound letters. If you can pronounce the consonants and compound letters using the audio or video, then you are good. You don't have to practice the below pronunciation guide. If not, I recommend you read and practice the pronunciation guide below.

- From the above, you would have recognized that there are three different types of (ண் (N), ன் (n), ந் (<u>n</u>), two different types of ர் (r), ற் (R) and two different types of ல் (l), ள் (L). Of course, they are all pronounced differently, but in modern Tamil, nobody seems concerned about the difference anymore. So, as a Tamil learner if your goal is only read and speak in Tamil, then I would recommend you to treat all of them the same whether it's (n, N or <u>n</u>) (r, R) (l, L), it doesn't matter for you. I want to be technically right, so I differentiate them, but you don't have to do the same.

- In the above consonants, some consonants will have alternative pronunciations in the brackets. You can ignore them for now; they will be explained later.

Consonant Pronunciation Guide:

Kindly find the below diagram for reference in the pronunciation of Tamil consonants.

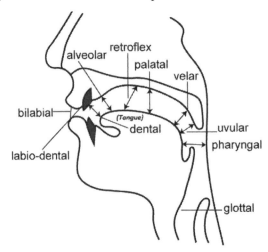

Glides:

There are two glides in Tamil ய் and வ்.

Tamil Consonants and their equivalent sound in English	Way to pronounce them
ய் (y) as sound of 'y' in 'toy'	As a palatal glide, ய் is pronounced by the middle part of your tongue sliding gently over the middle portion of the palate (top layer of your mouth) while you pronounce this letter.
வ் (v) as sound of "v" in 'van'	As labiodentals glide, வ் is pronounced with your lower lip sliding below or at the back of your upper portion of the teeth.

Stop Sounds:

They are called stop sounds because they are produced with an abrupt release of your tongue from a firm closure at some part of the mouth. For example, த் (th) a dental stop, is produced by pressing the front portion of the tongue firmly on the dental portion (back of your top teeth) of the mouth and releasing it abruptly. The below table explains the five stop consonants and how to pronounce them

Tamil Consonants and their equivalent sound in English	Way to pronounce them
க் (k) as sound of "ck" in 'brick', 'tick'.	As a velar stop, க் is pronounced at the very back portion of your mouth, without, moving your tongue much.
ச் (ch) as sound of "ch" in 'chin', 'detach'	As a palatal stop, ச் is pronounced by pressing your tongue in the middle portion of your mouth hard and releasing it immediately.
ட் (t) as sound of "t" in 'it', 'bit', 'sit'	As an alveolar retroflex stop, ட் is pronounced by pressing your tongue a little bit back of your teeth at the hard palate and bending your tongue a bit and releasing it immediately.
த் (th) as sound of "th" in 'cloth', 'thin'	As a dental stop, த் is pronounced by pressing the front portion of your tongue firmly on the dental portion (back of your top teeth) of the mouth and releasing it immediately.
ப் (p) as sound of "p" in 'pup', 'cup'	As a bilabial stop, ப் is pronounced by closing your lips slightly and releasing them immediately.

Nasal Sounds:

Nasal sounds are produced similarly to stop sounds, but the only exception here is that the air will be released through your nose instead of your mouth. There are six nasal consonants in Tamil, each produced in the same place where the corresponding stop sounds are produced.

Tamil Consonants and their equivalent sound in English	Way to pronounce them
ங (ng) as sound of "ng" in 'sing', 'ping'	As a velar nasal, ங is pronounced at the very back portion of your mouth, without moving your tongue much and the air being released through your nasal.
ஞ (nj) as sound of "nj" in 'brinjal'	As a palatal nasal, ஞ is pronounced by pressing your tongue in the middle portion of your mouth hard and releasing it immediately and the air is released through your nasal.
ண (N) as sound of "n" in 'inn'.	As a retroflex nasal; ண is pronounced by bending the tongue upwards and the tip of the tongue should touch the retroflex (which is almost in the middle portion of your mouth), Here the tongue curls up and retracts a lot.
ந (n) as sound of 'n' in 'month', 'enthusiasm'	ந as dental nasal, the tip of the tongue should touch the back portion of your teeth. Here, the tongue does not curl and retract much.
ன (n) as sound of "n" in chain, pain	ன as alveolar nasal; The tip of the tongue should touch the alveolar (which is simply a little bit more backside from the back of your teeth). Here, the tongue does not curl and retract much.

Note:

While pronouncing ண, ந, and ன, it sounds almost similar, one has to listen very carefully to notice the difference. Hence, I recommend you ignore the difference between these 3 consonants if your goal is only to learn to speak in Tamil, as these three consonants make a huge difference only in writing in Tamil.

Lateral Sounds:

Lateral sounds are produced when the tip of the tongue is touching the pre-alveolar portion of the mouth (a little bit to the back of your teeth), and the air is released through the sides of the tongue to make the lateral sound.

Tamil Consonants and their equivalent sound in English	Way to pronounce them
ல் (l) as sound of 'l' in 'fuel'.	As a alveolar lateral, the tip of your tongue curves back a little and moves further in front of the alveolar region of the mouth and is released.
ள் (L) Hard l, as sound of 'l' in 'temple', 'sample'	As a retroflex lateral, the tip of your tongue curves back a little and moves further back in the alveolar region of the mouth and is released.

Note:

While pronouncing ல் and ள் it sounds almost similar, one has to listen very carefully to notice the difference. Hence, I would recommend you to simply ignore the difference between these 2 consonants if your goal is to only learn to speak in Tamil as these three consonants makes a huge difference only in writing in Tamil.

Tap and Trilled R Sounds and ழ்:

While pronouncing the R sound, you will be making friction with your tongue and the upper portion of the palate (upper portion of your mouth). The sound is more or less similar to the sound of an engine or a motor. There are 3 R sounds in Tamil.

Tamil Consonants and their equivalent sound in English	Way to pronounce them
ர் (r) as the sound of "r" in 'river'	As flapped r, the tip of the tongue should tap the alveolar part of the mouth (middle of the mouth/palate),
ற் (R) Hard r as in 'mirror', 'error'	As trilled R, the tip of the tongue should tap the alveolar part of the mouth (middle of the mouth/palate), and little vibration is caused at the tip of your tongue while you pronounce the letter.

Note:

While pronouncing ŗ and ற் it sounds almost similar, one has to listen very carefully to notice the difference. Hence, I recommend you ignore the difference between these 2 consonants if your goal is only to learn to speak in Tamil, as these three consonants make a huge difference only in writing in Tamil.

Pronunciation of 'ழ' (zha):

Your tongue has to be folded upward completely and the tip of the folded tongue should be below the soft palate. The tip of the folded tongue should not touch anywhere inside the mouth and then you have to release your tongue, this is the best way to pronounce 'ழ'. If the tip of the tongue touches the soft palate, you will start pronouncing the Tamil letter 'ள'. Many of my students make mistakes here, and you have to be careful while pronouncing this letter. If you mispronounce it, then the meaning of the letter will change completely.

Example:

மழை (mazhai) (rain) vs. மலை (malai) (mountain)

Compound Letters

There are 216 Compound letters (Vowels-Consonants Combination).
Example of how compound letters are formed using the consonant 'க்' 'k':

Consonant + Vowel	Compound letter	Consonant + Vowel	Compound letter
க் + அ	க (ka)	க் + எ	கெ (ke)
க் + ஆ	கா (kaa)	க் + ஏ	கே (kee)
க் + இ	கி (ki)	க் + ஐ	கை (kai)
க் + ஈ	கீ (kii)	க் + ஒ	கொ (ko)
க் + உ	கு (ku)	க் + ஓ	கோ (koo)
க் + ஊ	கூ (kuu)	க் + ஔ	கௌ (kau)

As you have seen in the above table, some symbols need to be added along with the consonants. They are called diacritics. For example, க (ka) to make it as கா (kaa), simply add ா.

The dot above the consonant indicates that there is no vowel in it, ப் is a pure consonant.

You can easily obtain the compound letter for the other consonant + vowel combination using the below chart with Diacritics.

The compound letters are formed as per the below table

Consonant	Vowel	Diacritics	Compound letter
க்	அ	Remove the dot	க
க்	ஆ	ா	கா
க்	இ	ி	கி
க்	ஈ	ீ	கீ
க்	எ	ெ	கெ
க்	ஏ	ே	கே
க்	ஐ	ை	கை
க்	ஒ	ொ	கொ
க்	ஓ	ோ	கோ
க்	ஔ	ௌ	கௌ

However, for உ and ஊ, the Diacritics (symbols) can get irregular. Kindly find below complete list of உ and ஊ compound letters.

கு	ஙு	சு	ஞு	டு	ணு	து	நு	பு	மு	யு	ரு	லு	வு	ழு	ளு	று	னு
கூ	ஙூ	சூ	ஞூ	டூ	ணூ	தூ	நூ	பூ	மூ	யூ	ரூ	லூ	வூ	ழூ	ளூ	றூ	னூ

Compound Letters Chart

The following table lists vowel letters across the top and consonant letters along the side, the combination of which gives all Tamil compound (uyirmei) letters.

	அ a	ஆ aa	இ i	ஈ ii	உ u	ஊ uu	எ e	ஏ ee	ஐ ai	ஒ o	ஓ oo	ஔ au
க் k(g)	க ka	கா kaa	கி ki	கீ kii	கு ku	கூ kuu	கெ ke	கே kee	கை kai	கொ ko	கோ koo	கௌ kau
ங் ng	ங nga	ஙா ngaa	ஙி ngi	ஙீ ngii	ஙு ngu	ஙூ nguu	ஙெ nge	ஙே ngee	ஙை ngai	ஙொ ngo	ஙோ ngoo	ஙௌ ngau
ச் s(ch)	ச sa	சா saa	சி si	சீ sii	சு su	சூ suu	செ se	சே see	சை sai	சொ so	சோ soo	சௌ sau
ஞ் nj	ஞ nja	ஞா njaa	ஞி nji	ஞீ njii	ஞு nju	ஞூ njuu	ஞெ nje	ஞே njee	ஞை njai	ஞொ njo	ஞோ njoo	ஞௌ njau
ட் t(d)	ட ta	டா taa	டி ti	டீ tii	டு tu	டூ tuu	டெ te	டே tee	டை tai	டொ to	டோ too	டௌ tau
ண் N	ண Na	ணா Naa	ணி Ni	ணீ Nii	ணு Nu	ணூ Nuu	ணெ Ne	ணே Nee	ணை Nai	ணொ No	ணோ Noo	ணௌ Nau
த் th(dh)	த tha	தா thaa	தி thi	தீ thii	து thu	தூ thuu	தெ the	தே thee	தை thai	தொ tho	தோ thoo	தௌ thau
ந் n	ந na	நா naa	நி ni	நீ nii	நு nu	நூ nuu	நெ ne	நே nee	நை nai	நொ no	நோ noo	நௌ nau
ப் p(b)	ப pa	பா paa	பி pi	பீ pii	பு pu	பூ puu	பெ pe	பே pee	பை pai	பொ po	போ poo	பௌ pau
ம் m	ம ma	மா maa	மி mi	மீ mii	மு mu	மூ muu	மெ me	மே mee	மை mai	மொ mo	மோ moo	மௌ mau
ய் y	ய ya	யா yaa	யி yi	யீ yii	யு yu	யூ yuu	யெ ye	யே yee	யை yai	யொ yo	யோ yoo	யௌ yau

ந்	ர	ரா	ரி	ரீ	ரு	ரூ	ரெ	ரே	ரை	ரொ	ரோ	ரௌ
r	ra	raa	ri	rii	ru	ruu	re	ree	rai	ro	roo	rau
ல்	ல	லா	லி	லீ	லு	லூ	லெ	லே	லை	லொ	லோ	லௌ
l	la	laa	li	lii	lu	luu	le	lee	lai	lo	loo	lau
வ்	வ	வா	வி	வீ	வு	வூ	வெ	வே	வை	வொ	வோ	வௌ
v	va	vaa	vi	vii	vu	vuu	ve	vee	vai	vo	voo	vau
ழ்	ழ	ழா	ழி	ழீ	ழு	ழூ	ழெ	ழே	ழை	ழொ	ழோ	ழௌ
zh	zha	zhaa	zhi	zhii	zhu	zhuu	zhe	zhee	zhai	zho	zhoo	zhau
ள்	ள	ளா	ளி	ளீ	ளு	ளூ	ளெ	ளே	ளை	ளொ	ளோ	ளௌ
L	La	Laa	Li	Lii	Lu	Luu	Le	Lee	Lai	Lo	Loo	Lau
ற்	ற	றா	றி	றீ	று	றூ	றெ	றே	றை	றொ	றோ	றௌ
R	Ra	Raa	Ri	Rii	Ru	Ruu	Re	Ree	Rai	Ro	Roo	Rau
ன்	ன	னா	னி	னீ	னு	னூ	னெ	னே	னை	னொ	னோ	னௌ
n	na	naa	ni	nii	nu	nuu	ne	nee	nai	no	noo	nau

Grantha compound table

These six letters ஜ் ஷ் ஸ் ஹ் க்ஷ் ஸ்ரீ are used to accommodate Sanskrit words in Tamil writings.

ஜ்	ஜ	ஜா	ஜி	ஜீ	ஜு	ஜூ	ஜெ	ஜே	ஜை	ஜொ	ஜோ	ஜௌ
j	ja	jaa	ji	jii	ju	juu	je	jee	jai	jo	joo	jau
ஷ்	ஷ	ஷா	ஷி	ஷீ	ஷு	ஷூ	ஷெ	ஷே	ஷை	ஷொ	ஷோ	ஷௌ
sh	sha	shaa	shi	shii	shu	shuu	she	shee	shai	sho	shoo	shau
ஸ்	ஸ	ஸா	ஸி	ஸீ	ஸு	ஸூ	ஸெ	ஸே	ஸை	ஸொ	ஸோ	ஸௌ
S	Sa	Saa	Si	Sii	Su	Suu	Se	See	Sai	So	Soo	Sau
ஹ்	ஹ	ஹா	ஹி	ஹீ	ஹு	ஹூ	ஹெ	ஹே	ஹை	ஹொ	ஹோ	ஹௌ
h	ha	haa	hi	hii	hu	huu	he	hee	hai	ho	hoo	hau

The Grantha letters below are rarely used in Tamil.

க்ஷ்	க்ஷ	க்ஷா	க்ஷி	க்ஷீ	க்ஷூ	க்ஷூ	க்ஷெ	க்ஷே	க்ஷை	க்ஷொ	க்ஷோ	க்ஷௌ
ksh	ksha	ksha	kshi	kshii	kshu	kshuu	kshe	kshee	kshai	ksho	kshoo	kshau

11

Note:

ஸ்ரீ (srii) is a Symbolic Sanskrit character grantha letter. This is a rarely used one.

Orthography:

The compound letters are also classified as short (kuRil), long (nedil) and diphthong compound letters depending upon the vowels used to form these compound letters.

Example:

The short compound letters த (tha) and டு (tu) are formed by combining the short vowels அ (a) and உ (u), as explained below.

த் (th) + அ (a) = த (tha)

ட் (t) + உ (u) = டு (tu)

These are known as short compound letters because they are formed using the short vowels அ and உ, and these short compound letters take one maaththirai (approx. 0.25 sec) to pronounce. In total there are 90 short compound letters

The compound letters தா (thaa) and டூ (tuu) are formed by combining the long vowels ஆ (aa) and ஊ (uu) as explained below.

த் (th) + ஆ (aa) = தா (thaa)

ட் (t) + ஊ (uu) = டூ (tuu)

These are known as long compound letters because they are formed using the short vowels ஆ and ஊ and these long compound letters take two maaththirai (approx. 0.50 sec) to pronounce. In total, there are 90 long compound letters

The compound letter தை (thai) is formed by combining the diphthong ஐ (ai) as explained below.

த் (th) + ஐ (ai) = தை (thai)

These are known as diphthong compound letters, formed using the diphthong vowels ஐ and ஒள. These diphthong compound letters take 1.5 maaththirai (approx. 0.38 sec) to pronounce. In total there are 36 diphthong compound letters.

The below table for அ + consonants pronunciations:

Tamil Consonants	Pronunciation	Pronunciation equivalent in English
க	ka	As sound of 'ka' in 'karate'.
க	ga	As sound of 'gu' in 'gum', 'gun'.
ங	nga	Couldn't find an equivalent in English.
ச	cha	As sound of 'cha' in 'chance', 'charge'.
ச	sa	As sound of 'sa' in 'safari'.
ச	ja	As sound of 'ju' in justice, 'junk'.
ஞ	nja	As sound of 'ñ' in piñata.
ட	ta	As sound of 'ta' in 'tall'.
ட	da	As sound of 'da' in 'dark'.
ண	na	As sound of 'nna' in 'annoy'.
த	tha	As sound of 'th' in 'mother', 'brother'.
த	dha	As sound of 'dha' in 'dharma'.
ந	<u>na</u>	As sound of 'nu' in 'nut', 'null', 'nill'.
ப	pa	As sound of 'pu' in 'pun', 'punch'.
ப	ba	As sound of 'bu' in 'bun', 'bunch'.
ம	ma	As sound of 'ma' in 'mall'.
ய	ya	As sound of 'you' in 'young'.
ர	ra	As sound of 'ru' in 'run'.
ல	la	As sound of 'lu' in 'luck'.
வ	va	As sound of 'va' in 'vacation'.
ழ	zha	Couldn't find an equivalent in English.
ள	La	As sound of 'lu' in 'plum', 'plug'.
ற	Ra	As sound of 'ru' in 'crush', 'rush'.
ன	na	As sound of 'na' in 'tenant', 'penance'.

13

க், ச், ட் and த் Pronunciation Variation Guide

Pronunciation tips on combined letters with the consonant க், ச், ட் and த் as the base. Please note: these combined letters have a different sound when used in the beginning, middle, and next to a consonant, which will be explained in detail below.

Consonant	Sounds Like/Transliteration	Translation
க்	**k (beginning of the word or when preceded by க்)**	
	g (when it is not preceded by க்)	
கண்	kaN (we use 'k' here because it is the beginning of the word)	Eye
கால்	kaal	Leg
கடன்	kadan	Debt, credit
கடை	kadai	Shop
கதவு	kadhavu	Door
தூக்கம்	thuukkam (we use 'k' here because it is preceded by க்)	Sleep
துக்கம்	dhukkam	Sorrow
பக்கம்	pakkam	Side
மக்கள்	makkaL	People
மூக்கு	muukku	Nose
தாகம்	thaagam (we use 'g' here because it is not preceded by க்)	Thirst
அழகு	azhagu	Beauty
உலகம்	ulagam	World
தங்கம்	thanggam	Gold
மகன்	magan	Son
ச்	**ch (when preceded by ச்)**	
	s (when not preceded by ச்)	
	j (when preceded by ஞ்)	
காய்ச்சல்	kaayohchal (we use 'ch' here because it is preceded by ச்)	Fever
குச்சி	kuchchi	Stick
பச்சை	pachchai	Green
மூச்சு	muuchchu	Breath

14

பூச்சி	puuchchi	Insect
அரசு	arasu (we use 's' here because it is not preceded by ச்)	Government
காசு	kaasu	Coin
பாசம்	paasam	Affection
மேசை	meesai	Table
சத்தம்	saththam	Noise
அஞ்சு	anjju (we use 'j' here because it is preceded by (ஞ்)	Five
இஞ்சி	injji	Ginger
ஆரஞ்சு	aaranjju	Orange
மஞ்சள்	manjjaL	Yellow, turmeric
பஞ்சம்	panjjam	Famine
ட்	t (when preceded by ட்)	
	d (when not preceded by ட்)	
காட்டு	kaattu (we use 't' here because it is preceded by ட்)	Show
பட்டு	pattu	Silk
பாட்டு	paattu	Song
சட்டை	sattai	Shirt
தட்டு	thattu	Plate
காடு	kaadu (we use 'd' here because it is not preceded by ட்)	Forest
இடம்	idam	Place, location
இடது	idadhu	Left
எடை	edai	Weight
கடல்	kadal	Sea, ocean
த்	th (beginning of word or when preceded by த்)	
	dh (when not preceded by த்)	
தம்பி	thambi (we use 'th' here because it is the beginning of the word)	Younger brother
தலை	thalai	Head
தள்ளு	thaLLu	Push

15

தவறு	thavaRu	Wrong, mistake
தெரு	theru	Street
கத்தி	kaththi (we use 'th' here because it is preceded by த்)	Knife
அத்தை	aththai	Aunt
ஆபத்து	aabaththu (frequently used word)	Danger
கத்திரி	kaththiri	Scissor
தாத்தா	thaaththaa	Grand father
கதவு	kadhavu (we use 'dh' here because it is not preceded by த்)	Door
உதவி	udhavi	Help
காதல்	kaadhal	Love
பாதம்	paadham	Foot
மதியம்	madhiyam	Afternoon
ப்	p (beginning of the word or when preceded by ப்)	
	b (when not preceded by ப்)	
பால்	paal (we use 'p' here because it is the beginning of the word)	Milk
பசி	pasi	Hunger
பசு	pasu	Cow
பணம்	paNam	Money
பதில்	padhil	Answer
அப்பா	appaa (we use 'p' here because it is preceded by ப்)	Father
அப்படி	appadi	So, like that
உப்பு	uppu	Salt
கப்பல்	kappal	Ship
சீப்பு	siippu	Comb
பண்பாடு	paNbaadu (we use 'b' here because it is not preceded by ப்)	Culture
அபாயம்	abaayam (rarely used word)	Danger
ரூபாய்	ruubaay	Rupee
லாபம்	laabam	Profit
கம்பி	kambi	Wire

16

For reference please look at the below chart:

		அ	ஆ	இ	ஈ	உ	ஊ	எ	ஏ	ஐ	ஒ	ஓ	ஒள
		a	aa	i	ii	u	uu	e	ee	ai	o	oo	au
1a	க்	க	கா	கி	கீ	கு	கூ	கெ	கே	கை	கொ	கோ	கௌ
	k	ka	kaa	ki	kii	ku	kuu	ke	kee	kai	ko	koo	kau
1b	க்	க	கா	கி	கீ	கு	கூ	கெ	கே	கை	கொ	கோ	கௌ
	g	ga	gaa	gi	gii	gu	guu	ge	gee	gai	go	goo	gau
2a	ச்	ச	சா	சி	சீ	சு	சூ	செ	சே	சை	சொ	சோ	சௌ
	s	sa	saa	si	sii	su	suu	se	see	sai	so	soo	sau
2b	ச்	ச	சா	சி	சீ	சு	சூ	செ	சே	சை	சொ	சோ	சௌ
	ch	cha	chaa	chi	chii	chu	chuu	che	chee	chai	cho	choo	chau
3a	ட்	ட	டா	டி	டீ	டு	டூ	டெ	டே	டை	டொ	டோ	டௌ
	t	ta	taa	ti	tii	tu	tuu	te	tee	tai	to	too	tau
3b	ட்	ட	டா	டி	டீ	டு	டூ	டெ	டே	டை	டொ	டோ	டௌ
	d	da	daa	di	dii	du	duu	de	dee	dai	do	doo	dau
4a	த்	த	தா	தி	தீ	து	தூ	தெ	தே	தை	தொ	தோ	தௌ
	th	tha	thaa	thi	thii	thu	thuu	the	thee	thai	tho	thoo	thau
4b	த்	த	தா	தி	தீ	து	தூ	தெ	தே	தை	தொ	தோ	தௌ
	dh	dha	dhaa	dhi	dhii	dhu	dhuu	dhe	dhee	dhai	dho	dhoo	dhau
5a	ப்	ப	பா	பி	பீ	பு	பூ	பெ	பே	பை	பொ	போ	பௌ
	p	pa	paa	pi	pii	pu	puu	pe	pee	pai	po	poo	pau
5b	ப்	ப	பா	பி	பீ	பு	பூ	பெ	பே	பை	பொ	போ	பௌ
	b	ba	baa	bi	bii	bu	buu	be	bee	bai	bo	boo	bau

Spoken Tamil Pronunciation Tips:

Some word endings will be pronounced slightly differently in spoken Tamil when they don't have a suffix added. I have provided two such scenarios below.

<u>**Rule 1.**</u>

a. The word ends with a compound letter containing the vowel ஐ (ai) (eg. தை (thai), பை (pai), சை (sai) etc.) (த் (th) + ஐ (ai) = தை (thai)).

b. No suffix is added to this word.

If the rule has been satisfied, the vowel ஐ (ai) in the compound letter will be replaced with the vowel அ (a).

Example: கடை (kadai) (shop) will be pronounced as கட (kada) (shop) in spoken Tamil.

டை (dai) = ட் (d) + ஐ (ai).

ட (da) = ட் (d) + அ (a).

More examples:

With Suffix			Without Suffix		
பச்சை	(pachchai)	=	பச்ச	(pachcha)	Green
மேசை	(meesai)	=	மேச	(meesa)	Table
சட்டை	(chattai)	=	சட்ட	(chatta)	Shirt
எடை	(edai)	=	எட	(eda)	Weight
தலை	(thalai)	=	தல	(thala)	Head
அத்தை	(aththai)	=	அத்த	(aththa)	Aunt

<u>**Rule 2.**</u>

a. The word ends with a pure consonant ம்.

b. The letter preceding ம் is a compound letter containing the vowel அ (a).

c. No suffix is added to this word.

If the rule has been satisfied, then the pure consonant ம் will be removed and the preceding compound letter with the vowel அ (a) will be replaced with the vowel ஒ (o).

Example: தூக்கம் (thuukkam) (sleep) will be pronounced as தூக்கொ (thuukko) (sleep) in spoken Tamil. In the above example, I removed the letter ம் and replaced the letter க (ka) with கொ (ko). க் (k) + ஒ (o) = கொ (ko).

More examples:

With suffix			Without Suffix		
பக்கம்	(pakkam)	=	பக்கொ	(pakko)	Page
உலகம்	(ulagam)	=	உலகொ	(ulago)	World
தங்கம்	(thanggam)	=	தங்கொ	(thanggo)	Gold
சத்தம்	(saththam)	=	சத்தொ	(saththo)	Sound
பஞ்சம்	(panjjam)	=	பஞ்சொ	(panjjo)	Famine
இடம்	(idam)	=	இடொ	(ido)	Place
பாதம்	(paadham)	=	பாதொ	(paadho)	Foot
மதியம்	(madhiyam)	=	மதியொ	(madhiyo)	Afternoon
பணம்	(paNam)	=	பணொ	(paNo)	Money
லாபம்	(laabam)	=	லாபொ	(laabo)	Profit

Note:

You will pronounce the whole word when you add a suffix and nothing will change then, which applies to both Rule 1 and Rule 2.

Example:

புத்தகம் + ஆ (aa) ('Interrogative suffix') = புத்தகமா (puththagamaa) (is this a book?)

Some consonant cluster pronunciations are given below:

Tamil Consonants	Pronunciation	Pronunciation equivalent in English
ங்க	ngga	As sound of 'nga' in 'fungal'.
ஞ்ச	njja	As sound of 'nja' in 'benjamin'.
ன்ற	ndRa	As sound of 'ndra', in the name 'Kendra'.
ம்ப	mba	As sound of 'mba' in the word 'simba'.
ண்ட	Nda	As sound of 'nde' in the name 'Cinderella'.
ந்த	ndha	No equivalent in in english
ற்ற	tRRa	As sound of 'tra' in 'contra'

Vowel Consonant Combination:

This is a very important topic for learning Tamil as you must combine words with suffixes in Tamil. While doing so, letters may get combined, which may affect the pronunciation of the words.

As you have seen in the Compound letters chart, we combined vowels and consonants to form a combined letter. The same is applicable when a word is combined with suffixes.

C - Consonant; V - Vowel.

க் (C) + அ (V) = க (CV)

க் (C) + ஆ (V) = கா (CV)

Rule 1: Word ends with a pure consonant, and the suffix starts with a vowel, then you shall combine the letter to form a compound letter.

Example:

I will write 'I am good' in Tamil by combining nouns, adverbs, verbs, tenses and suffixes.

a) நா(ன்) நல்லா இருக்குறெ.

tl: naa(n) nallaa irukkuRe.

lit: I good am.

t: I am good.

Let's separate the words to understand how we formed this sentence in Tamil.

நா(ன்) (naa(n)) (I) நல்லா (nallaa) (good) (இரு (iru) (verb 'to be') + க்குற் (kkuR) (Present tense suffix) + எ (e) (Pronoun suffix for 'I' 'நா(ன்)'))

இரு + க்குற் + எ = இருக்குறெ

Here you would observe the letter ற் and எ is removed and the letter றெ is inserted because of the Vowels – Consonants Combination that you saw in the compound letters chart.

ற் (R) (C) + எ (e) (V) = றெ (Re) (CV)

Also, this satisfies the rule. It has a vowel எ in it. That's why you were able to combine and get றெ. Whereas in இரு and க்குற், இரு (iru) doesn't end with a vowel and க்குற் (kkuR) doesn't start with a vowel as well, hence this doesn't satisfy the rule, so we don't combine letters here.

b) எடுக்குறெ (edukkuRe) (I am taking)

எடு (edu) (verb 'to take') + க்குற் (kkuR) (Present tense suffix) + எ (e) (verb suffix)

Again, here the letter ற் and எ is removed and the letter றெ is inserted instead. This is because of the Vowels – Consonants as this satisfies the rule. It has a vowel எ in it. That's why you were able to combine and get றெ. Whereas in எடு and க்குற், எடு (edu) doesn't end with a vowel and க்குற் (kkuR) doesn't start with a vowel as well, hence this doesn't satisfy the rule, so we don't combine letter's here like the above example.

> **Rule 2:** If the word ends with a compound letter and the suffix starts with a vowel, then you will consider the base pure consonant of the compound letter and add it with the vowel of the suffix to form a new compound letter.

Example:

a) பாடு (paadu) (to sing) + அ (a) Infinitive suffix = பாட (paada) (sing) Infinitive.

Here the base consonant of டு which is ட் is added with the beginning of the suffix அ. Hence, we get the new compound letter ட. In detail: பாட் (paad) + அ (a) = பாட (paada).

b) ஓடு (oodu) + ஆம (aama) (negative form) = ஓடாம (oodaama) (without running)

Here, the base consonant of டு which is ட் is added to the beginning of the suffix ஆ hence we get the new compound letter டா.

In detail: ஓட் (ood) + ஆம (aama) = ஓடாம (oodaama).

The above 2 examples satisfy rule 2, because the word ending is a compound letter and the beginning of the suffix is a vowel. Hence, we take the pure consonant of the compound letter and combine it with the vowel.

Note:

> This combination is only possible when the suffix starts with a vowel. If the suffix begins with a pure consonant or a compound letter then no combination is possible.

Example:

a) பற (paRa) (to fly) + க்க (kka) Infinitive suffix = பறக்க (paRakka) (fly) Infinitive.

In the above example, the suffix starts with a pure consonant, so I didn't change the letters. I simply added a suffix to the word as it is. The same is applies if the suffix starts with a compound letter.

Note:

> In Tamil, a word always ends with a pure consonant or a compound letter.

EXERCISES:

A) Match the following Tamil syllables in the first column with the appropriate transliteration form in the second column. e.g. சி = si

1	சு		a	vee
2	வே		b	zha
3	யா		c	su
4	ஙெ		d	yaa
5	ழ		e	ka
6	க		f	nge

B) Write the Transliteration for the following words provided below. e.g. கடை = kadai.

கடை	பக்கம்	உலகம்	குச்சி	காசு	ஆரஞ்சு	பாட்டு
இடம்	தலை	தாத்தா	காதல்	பால்	உப்பு	லாபம்

C) Match the following compound letter in the first column with the appropriate vowel - consonant combination in the second column. e.g. க் + ஒ = கோ

1	ணி		a	ப் + ஊ
2	தீ		b	ல் + ஒ
3	நூ		c	ம் + எ
4	பூ		d	த் + ஈ
5	மெ		e	ர் + ஐ
6	யே		f	ண் + இ
7	ரை		g	ந் + உ
8	லொ		h	ழ் + ஒள
9	வோ		i	ய் + ஏ
10	ழௌ		j	வ் + ஒ

D) Match the following compound letter in the first column with the appropriate vowel - consonant combination in the second column. e.g. க் + ஒ = கோ

1	ழ	a	ழ் + எ	
2	ழா	b	ழ் + ஏ	
3	ழி	c	ழ் + அ	
4	ழீ	d	ழ் + ஆ	
5	ழு	e	ழ் + ஒ	
6	ழூ	f	ழ் + ஐ	
7	ழெ	g	ழ் + இ	
8	ழே	h	ழ் + ஓ	
9	ழை	i	ழ் + ஈ	
10	ழொ	j	ழ் + ஊ	
11	ழோ	k	ழ் + ஔ	
12	ழௌ	l	ழ் + உ	

E) Read the following letters. e.g. கை = kai

ஆ	கி	ஙீ	சு	ஞூ	டெ	ணே	தை	நொ	போ	மௌ
யோ	ரொ	லை	வே	ழெ	ளூ	று	னீ	ஐ	ஊ	சா
தீ	நூ	நே	யா	யெ	ரோ	ஙீ	மொ	யே	சோ	தே
றே	மை	ணெ	ஙி	ஞு	பொ	வி	ளோ	ம	ஙோ	யௌ
ட	வ	ள	ழ	ர	ப	ன	ய	ற	நே	நூ
ச	ஞு	ந	க	ம	த	ங	ண	ல	மொ	னா

F) Type the Tamil letter as per the English transliteration in computer. kaa = கா

ka	kaa	ngi	sii	nju	tuu	Ne	Nee	thai	tho	noo	pau
moo	yo	rai	lee	ve	zhuu	Lu	Rii	ni	Raa	La	zhaa
vi	Lii	ru	yuu	me	pee	nai	tho	Noo	tau	njoo	so
pe	nuu	thu	thii	Ni	taa	nga	oo	ii	e	kee	ngai

H) Write or type in the computer the appropriate vowel - consonant combination of the compound letters provided below. e.g. ந் + இ = நி

பெ	கி	ணை	சு	நூ	டெ	நீ	தை	நொ	போ	மௌ
யோ	ரொ	லூ	வே	பூ	ஞு	று	ணீ	தி	சீ	சா
தீ	நூ	ஞு	யா	யெ	ரோ	ஞீ	மோ	யே	சோ	தே
றே	மை	ணெ	ஙெ	ஞு	பொ	வி	ளோ	மூ	நோ	வெள
யீ	பீ	நா	லை	ழெ	த	ழீ	வா	ளா	நே	நூ
தூ	ஞு	நே	கு	கௌ	யௌ	றெ	ஞொ	ணெ	மொ	னா

I) Combine a word with a suffix using the Rules in Vowel Consonant Combination.

1 ஓடு   +   ஆம   _____
2 தொலை   +   க்க   _____
3 கத்து   +   அ   _____
4 டாம்   +   உக்கு   _____
5 அவன்   +   உக்கு   _____
6 அவள்   +   ஆ   _____
7 ராம்   +   ஓட   _____
8 சதீஷ்   +   ஆல   _____
9 குமார்   +   அ   _____
10 குமார்   +   கிட்ட   _____

SOLUTIONS

Lesson 1

Exercise A

1) c; 2) a; 3) d; 4) f; 5) b; 6) e.

Exercise B

kadai	pakkam	ulagam	kuchchi	kaasu	aaranjju	paattu
idam	thalai	thaaththaa	kaadhal	paal	uppu	laabam

Exercise C

1) f; 2) d; 3) g; 4) a; 5) c; 6) i; 7) e; 8) b; 9) j; 10) h.

Exercise D

1) c; 2) d; 3) g; 4) i; 5) l; 6) j; 7) a; 8) b; 9) f; 10) h; 11) e; 12) k.

Exercise F

க	கா	ஙி	சீ	னு	டு	ணெ	ணே	தை	தொ	னோ	பௌ
மோ	யொ	ரை	லே	வெ	மூ	ஞு	ரீ	னி	றா	எ	ழா
வி	லீ	ரு	யூ	மெ	பே	னை	தொ	ணோ	டௌ	ஞோ	சொ
பெ	னூ	து	தீ	ணி	டா	ங	ஒ	ஈ	எ	கே	னெ

Exercise I

1) ஓடாம. 2) தொலைக்க. 3) கத்த. 4) டாமுக்கு. 5) அவனுக்கு. 6) அவளா. 7) ராமோட.
8) சதீஷால. 9) குமார. 10) குமார்கிட்ட.

TL: 1) oodaama. 2) tholaikka. 3) kaththa. 4) taamukku. 5) avanukku. 6) avaLa.

7) raamooda. 8) sathiishaala. 9) kumaara. 10) kumaarkitta

LESSON 2

Content:

- Reading Practice 1 to 4
- Notes

LESSON 2:
READING PRACTICE

Note:

You have completed Lesson 1: Tamil Letter. By now, you should be able to read and pronounce Tamil letters individually and in some word form. Now you will have to improve your reading skills to read Tamil sentences and pronounce them properly. Please don't worry, it doesn't take much time to practice reading in Tamil, Initially, you may take much time to read the Tamil sentences, but after 2-3 attempts, you become faster in reading. The font size of this chapter is increased specifically for reading.

In this section, I am providing you with a Tamil story from Tenaali Raaman. You don't have to understand what's written there. Your primary focus should only be reading and pronouncing the sentences properly. I have provided my audio recording for the reading practice. You can listen to the audio recording when you need help or to check the correct pronunciation.

தெனாலி ராமன் கதைகள் – அரசியின் கொட்டாவி

Reading Practice 1:

திருமலாம்பாள் என்ற அம்மையார் கிருஷ்ண தேவராயர் துணைவியருள்

thirumalaambaaL endRa ammaiyaar kirushNa theevaraayar thuNaiviyaruL

ஒருவர். அவர் அடிக்கடி கொட்டாவி விட்டுக்கொண்டே இருப்பார். அது

oruvar. avar adikkadi kottaavi vittukkoNdee iruppaar. adhu

பழக்கமாகி விட்டது. ஆனால் அரசருக்கோ அது பிடிக்கவில்லை. அன்றிரவு

pazhakkamaagi vittadhu. aanaal arasarukkoo adhu pidikkavillai. andRiravu

அரசர் ஆசையோடு நெருங்கிசென்ற போதும் அவள் கொட்டாவி விட்டு

arasar aasaiyoodu nerungi. sendRa poodhum avaL kottaavi vittu

கொண்டே இருந்தாள். அப்போது அவள் முகத்தை பார்க்கவே மன்னருக்கு

koNdee irundhaaL. appoodhu avaL. mugaththai paarkkavee mannarukku

பிடிக்கவில்லை. அன்றிலிருந்து அவளிருக்கும் பக்கம் செல்வதையே

pidikkavillai. andRilirundhu avaLirukkum pakkam selvadhaiyee

மன்னர் தவிர்த்து வந்தார்.

mannar thavirththu vandhaar.

. . . .

Reading Practice 2:

அம்மயாருக்கு இது மிகுந்த வேதனையை தந்தது. மிகவும்
வருத்தத்துடன் இருந்த அம்மையாரை பார்த்த தெனாலிராமன் என்ன
நடந்தது என்று விசாரித்தார்.

அம்மையாரோ, நான் கொட்டாவி விடுவது பிடிக்காமல் மன்னர் எனது
இருப்பிடத்திற்கு வருவதையே நிறுத்திவிட்டார். எனக்கு என்ன செய்வதென்றே
தெரியவில்லை என்று வருந்தினாள்.

தெனாலிராமன் இப்பிரச்சனையை தீர்ப்பதாக அம்மையாருக்கு
வாக்குகொடுத்து சென்றான்.

. . . .

Reading Practice 3:

ஒரு நாள் அரசு அதிகாரிகள் சிலர் அரசரை காண வந்தனர். அப்போது
தெனாலிராமனும் அரசருடனிருந்தான். அந்த அதிகாரிகள் நாட்டில்
பயிர்வளத்தை எப்படி மேம்படுத்துவது என்பது பற்றி அரசருடன் விவாதித்துக்
கொண்டிருந்தனர்.

தெனாலி ராமனோ அவர்களது பேச்சினுள் புகுந்து "பயிர் நன்றாக வளர வேண்டுமானால் யாரும் கொட்டாவி விடக்கூடாது" என்றான்.

மன்னரும் மற்றவர்களும் தெனாலிராமனை வினோதமாகப்

பார்த்தனர். தெனாலிராமனோ விடாமல் "விவசாயம் செய்பவர்கள் யாரும் வாழ்நாள் முழுவதும் கொட்டாவி விடவே கூடாது. அப்போது தான் பயிர் நன்றாக வளரும்" என்றான்.

மன்னருக்கு கோபம் வந்துவிட்டது. "ராமா, இது என்ன வினோதம், விவசாயத்திற்காக வாழ்நாள் முழுவதும் கொட்டாவி விடாமல் இருக்கமுடியுமா?" என்றார்.

- -

Reading Practice 4:

This particular reading practice 4 is optional, you can try it if you want to.

"வேறென்ன மன்னா, உங்கள் முன்னால் கொட்டாவி விடும்போது

உங்களுக்கு கோபம் வருவதை போல, பயிர்கள் முன்னால் கொட்டாவி விட்டால் பயிர்கள் கோபித்துக்கொள்ளாதா? கேவலம் கொட்டாவியால் ஒருவர் வாழ்க்கை நாசம் ஆக வேண்டுமா?" என்று கூறிவிட்டு மன்னரை ஒரக்கண்ணா-ல் பார்த்தார் தெனாலி ராமன்.

மன்னருக்கு தெனாலிராமன் சூசகமாக் என்ன சொன்னார் என்று புரிந்து போனது. அப்போதே கேவலம் கொட்டாவிக்காக தன் மனைவியை கோபித்து கொண்டேனே என்று வருந்தினார். தெனாலி ராமன்

புத்திசாலித்தனமாக தகுந்த நேரத்தில் அதை புரியவைத்தான் என்பதையும் எண்ணி மகிழ்ந்தார்.

பின்னர் மகிழ்ச்சியில் திளைத்த அம்மையாரும் மன்னரும் சேர்ந்து தெனாலிராமனுக்கு பரிசுகளை பல அளித்து மகிழ்ந்தார்கள்.

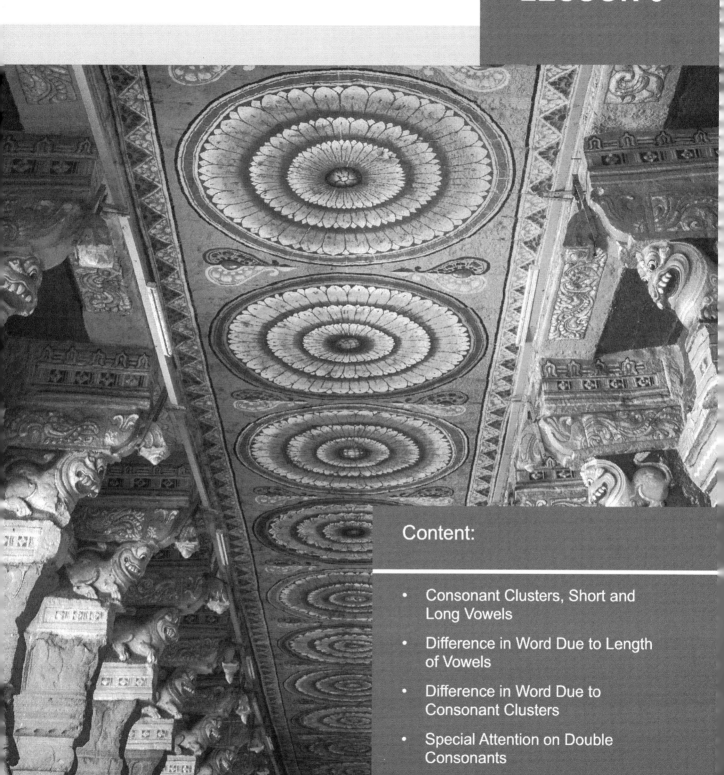

LESSON 3

Content:

- Consonant Clusters, Short and Long Vowels

- Difference in Word Due to Length of Vowels

- Difference in Word Due to Consonant Clusters

- Special Attention on Double Consonants

- And Short Versus Long Vowels

- Notes

LESSON 3:
FOR YOUR INFORMATION SECTION

Consonant Clusters, Short and Long Vowels

Double and Single Consonants

Sometimes, letters are doubled with the consonant sound preceding the letter and the consonant receives an extra emphasis when the word is pronounced.

Some single and double consonant words for your reference.

மாமா	maamaa	Uncle
அம்மா	ammaa	Mother
பயம்	payam	Fear
அய்யா	ayyaa	Sir
காலை	kaalai	Morning
கல்லூரி	kalluuri	College
அவ(ன்)	ava(n)	That guy
அவ்வளவு	avLavu	That much
புளி	puLi	Tamarind
பள்ளி	paLLi	School
ஒலி	oli	Sound
ஒல்லி	olli	Skinny
மறை	maRai	Hide
காற்று	kaatRtRu	Air, wind
பனி	pani	Snow
சின்ன	sinna	Little

Difference in Word Due to Length of Vowels

While pronouncing Tamil words, you must be careful with short vowels (kuril) and long vowels (nedil). If you make a mistake in this, the meaning will be changed.

Short Vowel				Long Vowel		
படு	padu	Lie down	Vs	பாடு	paadu	Sing
அடை	adai	Obtain	Vs	ஆடை	aadai	Clothes
படம்	padam	Picture	Vs	பாடம்	paadam	Lesson
பல்	pal	Tooth	Vs	பால்	paal	Milk
கல்	kal	Stone	Vs	கால்	kaal	Leg
பல	pala	Many	Vs	பலா	palaa	Jack fruit
விடு	vidu	Leave	Vs	வீடு	viidu	House
கொடு	kodu	Give	Vs	கோடு	koodu	Line
தொடு	thodu	Touch	vs	தோடு	thoodu	Earring
வலி	vali	Pain	vs	வாலி	vaali	Bucket
கலை	kalai	Art	vs	காலை	kaalai	Morning
சுடு	sudu	Shoot	vs	சூடு	suudu	Heat
முடி	mudi	Hair	vs	மூடி	muudi	Lid

Difference in Word Due to Consonant Clusters.

When a consonant occurs next to a secondary letter that belongs to the same base, it's called an identical consonant. These identical consonant pronunciations are usually subtle and need to be pronounced carefully.

Without identical consonant				With identical consonant		
இலை	ilai	Leaf	vs.	இல்லை	illai	No
பசை	pasai	Glue	vs.	பச்சை	pachchai	Green
குடை	kudai	Umbrella	vs.	குட்டை	kuttai	Small pond
காது	kaadhu	Ear	vs.	காத்து	kaaththu	Wind
குடி	kudi	Drink	vs.	குட்டி	kutti	Cub

33

Special Attention on Double Consonants And Short Versus Long Vowels

Many Tamil words differ from others by a small change in their sound. Such problems arise due to double consonants and short versus long vowels. A double consonant sounds different when it occurs on its own. A short vowel and a long vowel also differ when pronounced. For a long vowel, you should release air from your mouth for a slightly extended period compared to a short vowel. Learning to pronounce double consonants, short vowels and long vowels are very important for speaking in Tamil, as a mistake may change the meaning of the word/sentence completely.

For example: when you want to ask, 'is this a song' by saying இது பாட்டா? (idhu paattaa), but by mistake you might pronounce it as இது பட்டா? (idhu pattaa) which means 'is this a silk?'.

You wanted to ask 'Is this a tooth?' by saying இது பல்லா? (idhu pallaa) but when you mispronounce it, it might sound like இது பாலா? (idhu paalaa) (Is this milk?) Or you may even say இது பலா? (idhu palaa) (Is this a jackfruit?).

1. Practice pronouncing double consonants (e.g. ட்டு) and single consonants (e.g. ட்).

2. Practice pronouncing short vowels and long vowels.

Examples:

a) பாட்டு (paattu) (song) vs. பட்டு (pattu) (silk) vs. படு (padu) (lie down) vs. பாடு (paadu) (sing).

b) பத்து (paththu) (ten) vs. பாத்து (paaththu) (watch out) vs. படி (padi) (step) vs. பாதி (paadhi) (half).

c) கத்து (kaththu) (scream) vs. காத்து (kaaththu) (wind) vs. காது (kaadhu) (ear) vs. கதை (kadhai) (story).

d) மூக்கு (muukku) (nose) vs. முக்கு (mukku) (dip) vs. முகம் (mugam) (face) vs. மேகம் (meegam) (cloud).

Also, you need to focus your attention while pronouncing the letter ழ. Some times you might mispronounce it as ல, which may change the meaning of the word.

a) மழை (mazhai) (rain) vs. மலை (malai) (mountain).

b) பழம் (pazham) (fruit) vs. பலம் (palam) (strength).

34

Some More for Your Information:

1) While Using a. (ந, ன, ண) b. (ல, ள) c. (ர, ற).

As discussed earlier, while using the letters {a. (ந, ன, ண) b. (ல, ள) c. (ர, ற)},they may sound similar but they can change the meaning of the word when used in them, so you have to be careful when you are writing in Tamil.

Example:

வெல்லம்	(vellam)	(jaggery)	vs.	வெள்ளம்	(veLLam)	(flood)
ஒளி	(oLi)	(light)	vs.	ஒலி	(oli)	(sound)
மனம்	(manam)	(mind)	vs.	மணம்	(maNam)	(smell)
பள்ளி	(paLLi)	(school)	vs.	பல்லி	(palli)	(lizard)

Note:

This will be a problem only while you are writing in Tamil. When speaking in Tamil, it's quite difficult to notice such mistakes as the pronunciation is almost similar. So if you are practicing only spoken Tamil, I recommend you consider this and don't invest time in it.

2) Confusing ஒள (ou) with ஒ (o) and ள (La):

Sometimes you may get confused with the letter ஒள (ou) and (ஒ (o) and ள (La)). As seen in the vowels section the letter ஒள is a single letter, whereas the other is two letters ஒ (o) is a vowel and ள (La) is a compound letter. So, one must not get confused when ஒள (ou) is found in a word. However, there are no Tamil words containing ஒள (oLa). Therefore you don't have to face this confusion, whenever you see ஒள it should simply be pronounced as (ou).

The same goes for the compound letter கெள (kou) ஙெள (ngou) செள (sou) etc.; these are single compound letters and should not be confused with other compound letters when they come together.

Example: கெ (ke), ஙெ (nge), செ (se) together with the compound letter ள (La)

கெ (ke) + ள (La) should be pronounced as (keLa) instead of mispronouncing it as (kou). However, there are not many words in Tamil containing these compound letters (ஞெள டெள ணெள தெள நெள பெள மெள யெள ரெள லெள வெள ழெள ளெள றெள னெள ஜெள ஸெள ஷெள ஹெள) so, for example whenever you see a டெள in a Tamil word, it would most probably be the compound letter டெ (te) and ள (La) you should not mispronounce it as (tou)

Note:

- Tamil words will never begin with these letters ங, ண, ழ, ள, ற and ன.

- Tamil words will never end with the letters க, ச, ட, த, ப, ற, ங.

VOCABULARY , SENTENCES AND
ROLE PLAY SCENARIOS

LESSON 4

Content:

- Vocabulary, sentences and role play scenario overview

LESSON 4:
VOCABULARY, SENTENCES AND ROLE PLAY SCENARIOS

Note:

At the end of the book, this lesson will be divided into 4A, 4B - Part 1, 4B - Part 2, and 4C. My little word land courses have been created for the lessons 4A, 4B - Part 1 and 4B - Part 2, please refer to page number 'VIII' in the beginning of the book under the heading 'Guide on using the website "My little word land."

Lesson 4A: Tamil Vocabulary.

Here you can find tables with useful Tamil vocabularies used in lesson 5 to lesson 14 of this book. Lesson 5 to lesson 14 is all about Tamil grammar. Therefore, I recommend that you memorize these vocabularies only when you learn lesson 5 to lesson 14.

I would recommend you memorize these vocabularies in your free time either by using the website "my little word land" or by using the traditional method of reading and memorizing from the book. But don't spend too much time on it. Maybe around 15 minutes every day would be good.

The benefits of memorizing these vocabularies are:

1) You will be able to recall vocabulary during Lesson 5 to Lesson 14.

2) Your arsenal of vocabulary will allow you to create multiple sentences beyond the examples I have given you.

3) Much easier to do the exercises in the book, practice pronunciation, and many other things.

Lesson 4B – Part 1: Tamil sentences for conversation.

This lesson is dedicated to any of the learners below:

1) You have little or no interest in learning Tamil grammar. Your goal is to learn and memorize useful Tamil sentences and have a conversation with native Tamil speakers right away.

2) You want to learn Tamil sentences while learning Tamil grammar from Lesson 5 to Lesson 14.

3) You have already finished learning Tamil grammar from Lesson 5 to Lesson 14 and now you want to focus on learning Tamil sentences and making Tamil sentences on your own.

If you are one of the above three types of learners, then this lesson is for you. Lesson 4B – Part 1 contains 375 useful Tamil sentences. These Tamil sentences are categorized according to their use.

Lesson 4B – Part 2: Vocabulary for Tamil sentences.

This lesson contains most of the vocabularies used in 'Lesson 4B – Part 1: Tamil sentences for conversation'.

If you want to memorize vocabularies before you learn Tamil sentences in Lesson 4A – Part 1 or you have already learnt the sentences in the 'Lesson 4B – Part 1: Tamil sentences for conversation' and you want to know the meaning of specific words used in that lesson or memorize words used in that lesson, then 'Lesson 4B – Part 2' is for you.

Lesson 4C: Role play scenarios.

11 role play scenarios are included in this lesson.

The main agenda of this lesson is to give you a live experience of how an actual conversation with a native Tamil speaker would be like.

This lesson is dedicated to any of the learners below:

1) You have little or no interest in learning Tamil grammar. Your goal is to learn and memorize useful Tamil sentences and have a conversation with native Tamil speakers right away.

2) You want to learn Tamil sentences while learning Tamil grammar from Lesson 5 to Lesson 14.

3) You have already finished learning Tamil grammar in Lesson 5 to Lesson 14 and now you want to focus on learning Tamil sentences and making Tamil sentences on your own.

Authors' opinions and suggestions on lessons 4B and 4C.

It's recommended that learners don't focus on learning sentences before focusing on other lessons in this book, as Tamil grammar is slightly different from English grammar. It's difficult to comprehend Tamil sentences if you look at them before learning Tamil grammar. By learning Tamil grammar and then studying these sentences, you will be able to understand and learn the sentences well.

In my opinion, this is the best way to learn Tamil, and the statement above is just a suggestion. However, there are some exceptions as well.

1. You could also learn these Tamil sentences simultaneously along with lesson 4 to lesson 15, this would help you to understand Tamil grammar better, and at the same time, your Tamil vocabulary will improve.

2. Some of you might just want to learn a few sentences in the Tamil language to practice it with native Tamil speakers, and you might not be interested in Tamil grammar at all. These lessons are meant for you.

SUFFIXES IN TAMIL

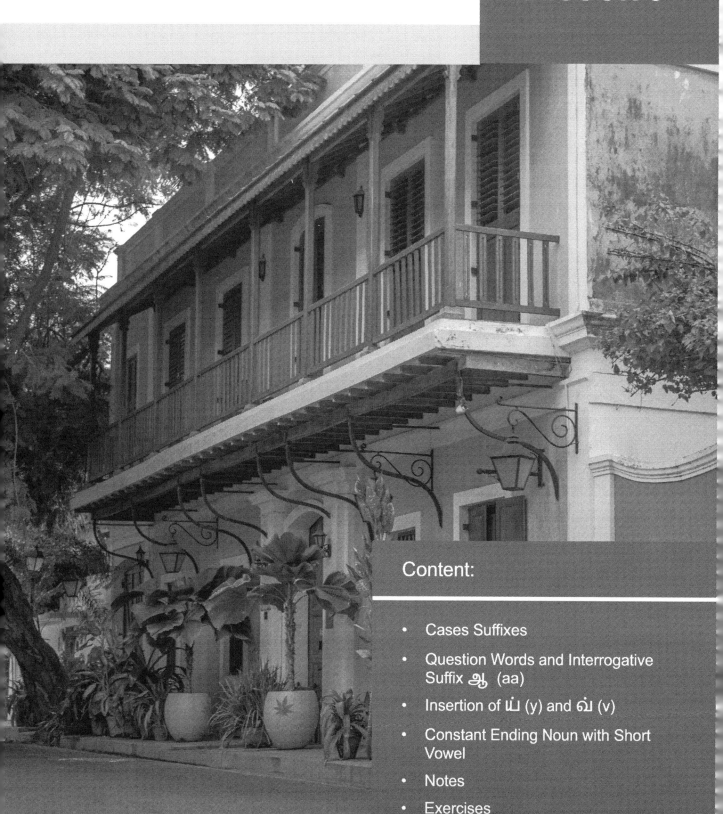

Content:

- Cases Suffixes
- Question Words and Interrogative Suffix ஆ (aa)
- Insertion of ய் (y) and வ் (v)
- Constant Ending Noun with Short Vowel
- Notes
- Exercises

LESSON 5: SUFFIXES IN TAMIL

The Tamil language comprises lots of suffixes that follow the Sandhi rules. These suffixes represent tenses, cases, pronouns, numbers, gender, adverbs, prepositions, etc. Suffixes are an important part of the Tamil language. When you master the suffixes, speaking Tamil becomes much easier. With these suffixes, you can form many many sentences in Tamil.

An example of suffix in English: In English, we use the suffix '-ist' to indicate 'the one who does', for instance: chemist, activist, alchemist, biologist, etc. Here we add the suffix '-ist' at the end of each profession to point out the person who does it.

Suffixes also serve the purpose of shortening some words and adding them to other words.

For example: -ணு(ம்) (-Nu(m)) this suffix is used to express the 'need' or 'obligation'.

When added to the infinitive form of a verb, it can have the sense of 'need' or 'obligation'.

Basically-ணு(ம்) is a short form of வேணு(ம்) (veeNu(m)) which means 'want', 'need'.

குடுக்க (kudukka) (give) + -ணு(ம்) = குடுக்கணு(ம்) (kudukkaNu(m)) (should give)

The above is a short form of குடுக்க வேணு(ம்) (kudukka veeNu(m)) which also means 'should give'.

When referring to an object in English, we usually add a preposition before the noun or a pronoun such as 'in the book', 'with him', 'in the office', 'for her', etc. Whereas in Tamil, we will add these prepositions as a suffix to the word itself (like a word ending). These are called case endings.

A small Introduction to cases in Tamil: Students who have already learned any European languages would already know what cases are. For English speakers: Case endings are added to nouns and pronouns, which will give them the ability to express grammatical relations (e.g. subject, direct object, possession etc.) also the prepositions that we use in English (e.g. 'in', 'to', 'for', 'from', etc.)

Note:

This is just a small introduction. Cases in Tamil will be explained later, and there are 8 case endings in Tamil. Kindly find below 4 case endings I would use as examples in other topics. You don't have to understand the cases now. I will explain it later.

Accusative Suffix: The object of the sentence. The suffix used in the accusative case is அ (a).

e.g.: அவன கூப்பிடு;

(அவ(ன்) (avan) (he) + அ (a) (accusative suffix) = அவன (avana) (him)

tl: avana kuuppidu.

lit: him call.

t: call him.

Genitive/Possessive Suffix: Similar to English 'of', 's. This indicates possession. The suffix used in the Genitive case is –ஓட (ooda).

e.g.: அவனோட புத்தகம்.

அவ(ன்) (ava(n)) (he) + ஓட (ooda) (genitive suffix) = அவனோட (avanooda) (his)

tl: avanooda puththagam.

lit/t: his book.

Sociative Suffix: Similar to English "Along with". This indicates the person or a thing in association with which something has happened. The suffix used in the Sociative case is also –ஓட (ooda).

e.g.: நா(ன்) அவனோட போனெ.

(அவ(ன்) (ava(n)) (he) + ஓட (ooda) (sociative suffix) = அவனோட (avanooda) (along with him)

tl: naa avanooda poone.

lit: I along with him went.

t: I went along with him.

Instrumental Suffix: Similar to English "by", "with", "because of". This indicates an instrument with which or a person by whom action was performed.

e.g. அவனால ஓட முடியல.

(அவ(ன்) (ava(n)) (he) + ஆல (aala) (Instrumental Suffix) = அவனால (avanaala) (he)

tl: avanaala ooda mudiyala.

lit: he run couldn't.

t: he couldn't run.

Question Words and Interrogative Suffix ஆ (aa)

To make a sentence as a question in Tamil, you can either add a questioner word like என்ன (enna) (what) or you can add an interrogative suffix to the end of the sentence or to any word (except modifier of a noun) questioned in the sentence.

Let's take a noun, for example புத்தகம் (puththagam) (book): to make this a question, all you have to do is add the Interrogative Suffix ஆ (aa) at the end of the noun.

புத்தகம் + ஆ (aa) ('Interrogative suffix') = புத்தகமா (puththagamaa) (is this a book?)

Let's take a pronoun, for example அவன் (avan) (he): to make this a question, all you have to do is add the Interrogative Suffix ஆ (aa) at the end of the pronoun.

அவ(ன்) + ஆ (aa) ('Interrogative suffix') = அவனா (avanaa) (is that him?)

Question words in Tamil can be placed in more than one position in a sentence. Most of the Question words start with the letter எ (e).

The following table will give you a list of Tamil question words.

Question words	English
என்ன (enna)	What?
ஏன் (een)	Why?
ஏது (eedhu)	How did you get?
யாரு (yaaru)	Who?
எங்கெ (engge) or எங்க (engga)	Where?
எப்போ (eppoo) or எப்ப (eppa)	When?
எது (edhu)	Which (noun)?
எந்த (endha)	Which (adjective)?
எப்படி (eppadi)	How?
எத்தன (eththana)	How many?
எவ்வளவு (evLavu)	How much?

Insertion of ய் (y) and வ் (v):

When a word ends with a vowel or a compound letter and a suffix that begins with a vowel are added together then either ய் (y) or வ் (v) is added in between them. Following are the rules for selecting which one to use based on the final letter of the word.

1) If the word ends in இ (i), ஈ (ii), எ (e), ஏ (ee), ஐ (ai) or a vowel - consonant combination that comes from these vowels as given below, then you should insert ய் (y) in between the word and suffix.

இ	ஈ	எ	ஏ	ஐ
கி	கீ	கெ	கே	கை
ஙி	ஙீ	ஙெ	ஙே	ஙை
சி	சீ	செ	சே	சை
ஞி	ஞீ	ஞெ	ஞே	ஞை
டி	டீ	டெ	டே	டை
ணி	ணீ	ணெ	ணே	ணை
தி	தீ	தெ	தே	தை
நி	நீ	நெ	நே	நை
பி	பீ	பெ	பே	பை
மி	மீ	மெ	மே	மை
யி	யீ	யெ	யே	யை
ரி	ரீ	ரெ	ரே	ரை
லி	லீ	லெ	லே	லை
வி	வீ	வெ	வே	வை
ழி	ழீ	ழெ	ழே	ழை
ளி	ளீ	ளெ	ளே	ளை
றி	றீ	றெ	றே	றை
னி	னீ	னெ	னே	னை

Examples:

ஐ Ending Words:

a) குடை (kudai) (umbrella) + ஆ (aa) ('Interrogative suffix') = குடையா? (kudaiyaa) (Is this an umbrella)?

So, what I did is I inserted the ய் in between the word 'குடை' and the suffix 'ஆ'.

Detail: குடை (kudai) + ய் (y) + ஆ (aa) = குடையா? (kudaiyaa).

b) புகை (pugai) (smoke) + ஆல (aala) ('Instrumental suffix') = புகையால (pugaiyaala) (because of the smoke).

Detail: புகை (pugai) + ய் (y) + ஆல (aala) = புகையால (pugaiyaala).

இ Ending Words:

a) பசி (pasi) (hungry) + ஆல (aala) ('Instrumental suffix') = பசியால (pasiyaala) (because of hunger).

Detail: பசி (pasi) + ய் (y) + ஆல (aala) = பசியால (pasiyaala).

b) தம்பி (thambi) (younger brother) + ஆல (aala) ('Instrumental suffix') = தம்பியால (thambiyaala) (because of/by younger brother).

Detail: தம்பி (thambi) + ய் (y) + ஆல (aala) = தம்பியால (thambiyaala).

c) தொப்பி (thoppi) (hat) + ஆ (aa) ('Interrogative suffix') = தொப்பியா? (thoppiyaa) (Is this hat?).

Detail: தொப்பி (thoppi) + ய் (y) + ஆ (aa) = தொப்பியா? (thoppiyaa).

ஈ Ending Words:

a) நீ (nii) (you) + ஆ (aa) ('Interrogative suffix') = நீயா (niiyaa) (is that you).

Detail: நீ (nii) + ய் (y) + ஆ (aa) = நீயா (niiyaa).

2) If the word ends in அ (a), ஆ (aa), உ (u), ஊ (uu), ஒ (o), ஓ (oo) or a compound letter which comes from these vowels as given below, then you should insert வ் (v) in between the word and suffix.

அ	ஆ	உ	ஊ	ஒ	ஓ
க	கா	கு	கூ	கொ	கோ
ங	ஙா	ஙு	ஙூ	ஙொ	ஙோ
ச	சா	சு	சூ	சொ	சோ
ஞ	ஞா	ஞு	ஞூ	ஞொ	ஞோ
ட	டா	டு	டூ	டொ	டோ
ண	ணா	ணு	ணூ	ணொ	ணோ
த	தா	து	தூ	தொ	தோ
ந	நா	நு	நூ	நொ	நோ
ப	பா	பு	பூ	பொ	போ
ம	மா	மு	மூ	மொ	மோ
ய	யா	யு	யூ	யொ	யோ
ர	ரா	ரு	ரூ	ரொ	ரோ
ல	லா	லு	லூ	லொ	லோ
வ	வா	வு	வூ	வொ	வோ
ழ	ழா	ழு	ழூ	ழொ	ழோ
ள	ளா	ளு	ளூ	ளொ	ளோ
ற	றா	று	றூ	றொ	றோ
ன	னா	னு	னூ	னொ	னோ

Examples:

அ Ending Words:

a) பேச (peesa) (speak) + ஆ (aa) ('Interrogative suffix') = பேசவா? (peesavaa) (Shall I speak?)

Detail: பேச (peesa) + வ் (v) + ஆ (aa) = பேசவா? (peesavaa).

47

ஆ Ending Words:

a) அம்மா (ammaa) (mother) + ஓட (ooda) ('sociative suffix') = அம்மாவோட (ammaavooda) (along with mother).

Detail: அம்மா (ammaa) + வ் (v) + ஓட (ooda) = அம்மாவோட (ammaavooda).

b) மாமா (maamaa) (uncle) + ஓட (ooda) ('sociative suffix') = மாமாவோட (maamaavooda) (with uncle).

Detail: மாமா (maamaa) + வ் (v) + ஓட (ooda) = மாமாவோட (maamaavooda).

உ Ending Words:

a) தெரு (theru) (street) +ஆ(aa) ('Interrogative suffix') = தெருவா (theruvaa) (is this a street).

Detail: தெரு (theru) + வ் (v) + ஆ (aa) ('Interrogative suffix') = தெருவா (theruvaa).

b) கொசு (kosu) (mosquito) + ஆ (aa) ('Interrogative suffix') = கொசுவா (kosuvaa) (is it a mosquito).

Detail: கொசு (kosu) + வ் (v) + ஆ (aa) ('Interrogative suffix') = கொசுவா (kosuvaa).

Note:

> There are many exceptional உ ending words where you shouldn't add the வ். For example: இது (idhu) (this), குரங்கு (kuranggu) (monkey), பட்டு (pattu) (silk) etc.

ஊ Ending Words:

a) பூ (puu) (flower) + ஓட (ooda) ('sociative suffix') = பூவோட (puuvooda) (along with flower).

Detail: பூ (flower) + வ் (v) + ஓட (ooda) ('sociative suffix') = பூவோட (puuvooda).

Constant Ending Noun with Short Vowel:

When a '2 Letter' consonant ending noun with word structure CVC (Consonant Vowel Consonant) or ('Short Compound letter' with 'Pure consonant') is added with any suffix, then the final consonant gets doubled.

Consonants: க், ங், ச், ஞ் etc; **Short vowels:** அ, இ, உ, எ, ஒ etc.

Example: கண், பல், கல், புல், புண் (puN) (sore), சொல் (sol) (Tell) etc.

Explanation of CVC Structure:

Let's split the word கண் (CVC) = க் (C) + அ (Short V) + ண் (C)

க் (C) + அ (Short V) = க (C Short V)

a) கண் (eye) (kaN) + அ (a) (accusative suffix) = கண்ண (kaNNa) (eye - object)

Detail: கண் (kaN) + ண் (N) + அ (a) = கண்ண (kaNNa)

b) கல் (kal) (stone) + அ (a) (accusative suffix) = கல்ல (kalla) (stone - object)

Detail: கல் (kal) + ல் (l) + அ (a) = கல்ல (kalla)

Note:

- As you see above, I have added an additional ல் because கல் fits the requirement; it has a CVC structure and a short vowel.

  c) புல் (pul) (grass) + உக்கு (ukku) (dative suffix) = புல்லுக்கு (pullukku) (for the grass)

  Detail: புல் (pul) + ல் (l) + உக்கு (ukku) = புல்லுக்கு (pullukku)

  d) பல் (pal) (tooth) + ஆ (aa) ('Interrogative suffix') = பல்லா? (pallaa) (Is this a tooth?)

  Detail: பல் (pal) + ல் (l) + ஆ (aa) = பல்லா? (pallaa)

- If the vowels are long, this rule will not apply even though the word is in CVC structure. That's why in the example below, the final ல் did not double because the vowels in that word were long.

Example:

a) கால் (kaal) (leg) + அ (a) (accusative suffix) = கால (kaala) (leg - object)

கா (kaa) = க் (k) (C) + ஆ (aa) (Long V) = கா (kaa) (C Long V) = rule doesn't apply.

b) பால் (paal) (milk) + அ (a) (accusative suffix) =பால (paala) (milk - object)

பா (paa) = ப் (p) (C) + ஆ (aa) (Long V) = பா (paa) (C Long V) = rule doesn't apply.

49

EXERCISES:

A) Change a noun into a question.

e.g. கதை (kadhai) to make it as a question, you will add the interrogative suffix ஆ (aa).
கதை (kadhai) + ய் (y) + ஆ (aa) = கதையா (kadhaiyaa) (is this story?).

1 தேன்   = _____ ? (Is this honey?)

2 தோல்   = _____ ? (Is this skin?)

3 இடம்   = _____ ? (Is this place?)

4 நிறுவனம் = _____ ? (Is this company?)

5 கேள்வி   = _____ ? (Is this question?)

6 வேலை   = _____ ? (Is this work?)

7 தண்ணி   = _____ ? (Is this water?)

8 அம்மா   = _____ ? (Is it mom?)

9 பணம்   = _____ ? (Is this money?)

10 உண்மை   = _____ ? (Is it true?)

B) Choose the correct answer by choosing the right combination of suffix.

e.g. கேள்வி using அ (a) (accusative suffix) = கேள்விய (right answer)
கேள்வ (wrong answer); detail: கேள்வி = கேள்வி + ய் + அ = கேள்விய (keeLviya)

1. வேலை (veelai) using உக்கு (ukku) (dative suffix)

    a. வேலைஉக்கு   b. வேலையுக்கு   c. வேலக்கு

2. தண்ணி (thaNNi) using ஆ (aa) ('Interrogative suffix')

    a. தண்ணா   b. தண்ணிஆ   c. தண்ணியா

3. அறை (aRai) using ஓட (ooda) ('genitive suffix')

    a. அறையோட   b. அறைஓட   c. ஆறோட

4. அம்மா (ammaa) using ஓட (ooda) ('sociative suffix')

    a. அம்மாவோட   b. அம்மாஓட   c. அம்மோட

5. கதை (kadhai) using ஆல (aala) ('Instrumental suffix')

    a. கதைஆல   b. கதையால   c. கதால

6. உண்மை (uNmai) using ஆ (aa) ('Interrogative suffix')

    a. உண்மா   b. உண்மைஆ   c. உண்மையா

7. நிறைய (niRaiya) using ஆ (aa) ('Interrogative suffix')

    a. நிறையவா   b. நிறையஆ   c. நிறையா

8. அப்பா (appaa) using உக்கு (ukku) (dative suffix)

    a. அப்பாவுக்கு   b. அப்பாஉக்கு   c. அப்பாக்கு

9. பூ (puu) using உக்கு (ukku) (dative suffix)

    a. பூ   b. பூஅ   c. பூவுக்கு

10. தெரு (theru) using உக்கு (ukku) (dative suffix)

    a. தெருஉக்கு   b. தெருவுக்கு   c. தெருக்கு

Lesson 5

Exercise A

1) தேனா. 2) தோலா. 3) இடமா. 4) நிறுவனமா. 5) கேள்வியா. 6) வேலையா 7) தண்ணியா. 8) அம்மாவா. 9) பணமா. 10) உண்மையா.

TL: 1) theenaa. 2) thoola. 3) idamaa. 4) n̲iRuvanamaa. 5) keeLviyaa. 6) veelaiyaa.

7) thaNNiyaa. 8) ammaavaa. 9) paNamaa. 10) uNmaiyaa.

Exercise B

1) b; 2) c; 3) a; 4) a; 5) b; 6) c; 7) a; 8) a; 9) c; 10) b.

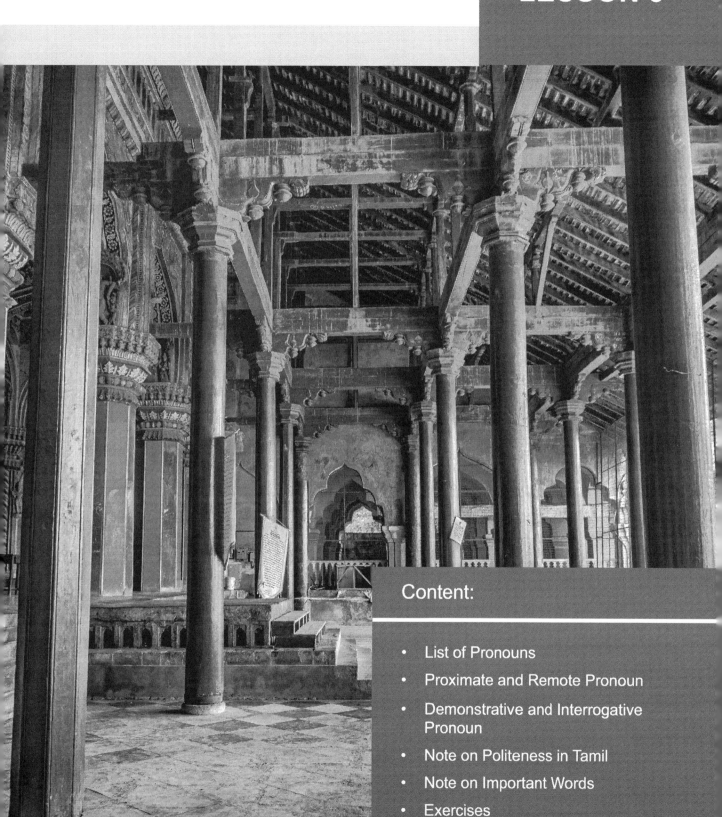

PRONOUNS

LESSON 6

Content:

LESSON 6: PRONOUNS

List of Pronouns:

	Singular		Plural	
	Nominative	**Other Case form**	**Nominative**	**Other Case form**
First person	நா(ன்) (naa(n)) (I)	எ(ன்) (e(n)) (my)	நாம (naama) (we) (listener included)	நம்ம (namma) (our) (listener included)
			நாங்க(ள்) (naangga(L)) (we) (listener not included)	எங்க(ள்) (engga(L)) (our) (listener not included)
Second person	நீ (nii) (you)	உ(ன்) (u(n)) (your)	நீங்க(ள்) (niingga(L)) (neengga) (you) (polite)	உங்க(ள்) (ungga(L)) (your) (polite)
	நீங்க(ள்) (niingga(L)) (you) (polite)	உங்க(ள்) (ungga(L)) (your) (polite)		
Third person	அவ(ன்) (ava(n)) (he)	அவ(ன்) (ava(n)) (his)	அவங்க(ள்) (avangga(L)) (they-human) (polite)	அவங்க(ள்) (avangga(L)) (their-human) (polite)
	அவரு (avaru) (he) (polite)	அவரு (avaru) (his) (polite)		
	அவ(ள்) (ava(L)) (she)	அவ(ள்) (ava(L)) (her)		
	அவங்க(ள்) (avangga(L)) (she) (polite)	அவங்க(ள்) (avangga(L)) (her) (polite)		
	அது (adhu) (that) இது (idhu) (this), both the word also means it.	அது (adhu) (that) இது (idhu) (this), both the word also means it.	அதுங்க(ள்) (adhungga(L)) (those) இதுங்க(ள்) (idhungga(L)) (these)	அதுங்க(ள்) (adhungga(L)) (those) இதுங்க(ள்) (idhungga(L)) (these)

Pronouns in Tamil are almost similar to English pronouns with some exceptions. Pronouns are divided into three people: the first person (the speaker), the second person (the listener) and the third person (the person spoken about). In Tamil, pronouns agree and represent Person, Number and Gender (PNG).

Person - First person or Second person or Third person; Number - Singular or Plural; Gender - Male or Female.

Case form: This form is always necessary when using a case suffix (which will be explained later in greater detail). This form differs from personal pronouns like I, you, we and it.

Nominative: It is the subject of the sentence and a basic noun form with no suffix being added to it. In Tamil nominative usually refers to an action. e.g. நா(ன்) சாப்பிடுறெ (naa(n) saappiduRe) (I am eating), நீ ஓடுறெ (nii ooduRe) (you are running), நா(ன்) வேலைக்கு வருவெ (naa(n) veelaikku varuve) (I will come to work.)

a) You will notice in the above chart that, Tamil unlike English has two forms of 'you', நீ (nii) which is an impolite 'you' and நீங்க (niingga) which is a polite 'you' and can be used for both singular and plural. When you are in doubt about which one to use, always use நீங்க (niingga) (polite ''you).

b) The third person pronoun is divided into three genders human masculine 'he', human feminine 'she' and neutral 'it'. We have polite forms for singular 'he' and 'she' in Tamil, the polite form for singular 'he' is அவரு (avaru) and the polite form for singular 'she' is அவங்க(ள்) (avangga(L)), அவங்க(ள்) (avangga(L)) is also used as 'they' plural form when you are referring to a group of people.

This polite form is usually used when referring to elders, superiors and strangers. The impolite form நீ (nii) (you), அவ(ன்) (ava(n)) (he) and அவ(ள்) (ava(L)) (she) are usually used when referring to someone younger than you and with someone whom you are very close with e.g. friends.

c) Unlike in English, we have two different corresponding pronouns for 'we' in Tamil,

One is நாம (nama) (we) (listener included), which includes the person whom you are speaking with as well.

Example: let's say, you are telling me நாம கடைக்கு போறோ(ம்) (naama kadaikku pooRoo(m)) (we are going to the shop) then it means that "yourself, myself and a bunch of others are going to the shop"

The other one is நாங்க(ள்) (naangga(L)) (we) (listener not included). This does not include the person with whom you are speaking to.

Example: let's say, you are telling me நாங்க(ள்) கடைக்கு போறோ(ம்) (naangga(L) kadaikku pooRoo(m)) (we are going to the beach) then it means that "yourself and a bunch of others are going to the beach"

d) The (ள்) (L) inside the bracket is optional. You can use the pronoun even without it, but when you are adding a suffix to this pronoun, it is mandatory to use (ள்) (L).

Example:

a) இது உங்க புத்தகம்.

tl: idhu ungga puththagam.

lit: This your book.

t: This is your book.

b) உங்களுக்கு இந்த புத்தகம் வேணு(ம்).

tl: ungaLukku indha puththagam veeNu(m).

lit: For you this book want.

t: You want this book.

As you see in the above example, for the example 'a' I didn't add the last letter (ள்) (L) since it doesn't have any suffix next to it, whereas in the example 'b' I added the last letter (ள்) (L) since it contains the suffix உக்கு (Dative suffix) next to it.

Proximate and Remote Pronoun (demonstrative pronouns):

In Tamil we use separate words when referring to a third person who is proximate (nearby) and remote (far away). These are also called demonstrative pronouns.

Example: அவ(ன்) டாம் (ava(n) taam) (he is Tom); here you are referring to the person 'Tom' who is far away from you (e.g. Tom is sitting a meter away from you). இவ(ன்) டாம் (iva(n) taam) (he is tom). Here you are referring to the person 'tom' who is nearby (e.g. Tom is sitting next to you). To make it easier for you to remember, if the word starts with (இ) (i), it means it is proximate. It is remote if the word starts with (அ) (a).

	Singular	Plural
	Nominative/case form	Nominative/case form
Third Person Proximate	இவ(ன்) (iva(n)) (he)	இவங்க(ள்) (ivangga(L)) (they)
	இவரு (ivaru) (he - polite)	
	இவ(ள்) (iva(L)) (she)	
	இவங்க(ள்) (ivangga(L) (she - polite)	
	இது (idhu) (this, it)	இதுங்க(ள்) (idhungga(L)) (these)
Third Person Remote	அவ(ன்) (ava(n)) (he)	அவங்க(ள்) (avangga(L)) (they)
	அவரு (avaru) (he - polite)	
	அவ(ள்) (ava(L)) (she)	
	அவங்க(ள்) (avangga(L)) (she - polite)	
	அது (adhu) (that, it)	அதுங்க(ள்) (adhungga(L) (those)

Demonstrative and Interrogative Pronoun:

There is another set of interrogative pronouns related to the above. The interrogative pronoun begins with the letter (எ) (e), which is used as a question word 'which' regarding a set of people mentioned, a thing or day etc. To ask 'who' in a more general sense, use யாரு (who).

	Demonstrative		Interrogative
	Proximate	Remote	
Masculine	இவ(ன்) (iva(n)) (he)	அவன் (ava(n)) (he)	யாரு? (yaaru) (Who?)
Feminine	இவ(ள்) (iva(L)) (she)	அவ(ள்) (ava(L)) (she)	யாரு? (yaaru) (Who?)
Masculine – polite	இவரு (ivaru) (he - polite)	அவரு (avaru) (he - polite)	யாரு? (yaaru) (Who?)
Feminine - polite	இவங்க(ள்) (ivangga(L) (she - polite)	அவங்க(ள்) (avangga(L) (she - polite)	யாரு? (yaaru) (Who?)
Plural	இவங்க(ள்) (ivangga(L) (they)	அவங்க(ள்) (ivangga(L)) (they)	யாரு? (yaaru) (Who?)
Things/ Animals	இது (idhu) (this - noun)	அது (adhu) (that - noun)	எது? (edhu) (Which? - noun)
Things/ Animals	இந்த (indha) (this - adjective)	அந்த (andha) (that - adjective)	எந்த? (endha) (Which? - adjective)
	இங்க (ingga) (here)	அங்க (angga) (there)	எங்க? (engga) (Where?)
	இப்போ (ippoo), இப்ப (ippa) (this time, now)	அப்போ (appoo), அப்ப (appa) (that time, then)	எப்போ (eppoo), எப்ப (eppa) ? (Which time?/ At what time?, When?)
	இவ்வளவு (ivLavu) (this much)	அவ்வளவு (avLavu) (that much)	எவ்வளவு? (evLavu) (How much?)
	இத்தன (iththana) (this many)	அத்தன (aththana) (that many)	எத்தன? (eththana) (How many?)
	இப்படி (ippadi) (like this, this way/manner)	அப்படி (appadi) (like that, that way/manner)	எப்படி? (eppadi) (Like how? in what way/manner?)

	இன்னிக்கு (innikku)/ இன்னைக்கு (innaikku), both means 'this day or today', it's just the difference in dialect	அன்னிக்கு (annikku)/ அன்னைக்கு (annaikku), both means 'that day, it's just the difference in dialect	என்னிக்கு? (ennikku)/ என்னைக்கு? (ennaikku) both means 'which day?', it's just the difference in dialect.

Here are a few more question words that were not included in the chart before.

Tamil form	English translation
என்ன (enna)	What?
ஏன் (een)	Why?
ஏது (eedhu)	How did you get?

Difference between இந்த (indha) (this - adjective), அந்த (andha) (that - adjective), எந்த? (endha) (which? - adjective) and இது (idhu) (this - noun) அது (adhu) (that - noun) ஏது? (edhu) (which? - noun):

As you have seen in the above table, இந்த and இது both means 'that', the difference here is, when you use இந்த an adjective should come next to it. When you use இது a noun should come next to it. இந்த is like "pointing at something (person or object)" whereas இது is like defining an object or a person.

Example:

a) இந்த புத்தகம் (indha puththagam) (this book) - here you are just pointing at a book which is nearby you. (For example: you are in a bookshop and you point your finger asking for a particular book)

b) இது புத்தகம் (idhu puththagam) (this is a book) - here you are explaining to someone (maybe a kid) that 'this is a book', which is also nearby you. (For example: you are explaining to a three year old kid that this is a book)

c) அந்த புத்தகம் (andha puththagam) (that book) - here you are just pointing at a book which is far from you. This is same as இந்த except that the one you are pointing at is far away from you.

d) அது புத்தகம் (adhu puththagam) (this is a book) - here you are explaining to someone (maybe a kid) that 'this is a book', which is also far away from you. This is the same as இது, except that the one you are explaining about/defining is far from you.

e) எந்த புத்தகம்? (endha puththagam) (Which book?) - here you are pointing to a bunch of books and questioning 'which book'. (For example: you are in a bookshop and the shopkeeper points to a bunch of books on his shelf and asks you which book you want?)

f) எது புத்தகம்? (edhu puththagam) (Which is a book?) - here you are pointing to a group of objects and questioning 'which is a book'. (For example: you are opening your friend's cupboard with lots of things in it and questioning him which one of these here is a book).

Note:

> Earlier, most interrogative pronouns have been provided under the heading "Question words and Interrogative Suffix ஆ (aa)".

Note on Politeness in Tamil:

The suffix -உங்க (ungga) brings politeness to the word. Whenever you add this suffix to a word or at the end of a sentence it brings politeness.

Example:

a) சொல் (sol) (say, tell)

சொல் (sol) + ல் (l) + உங்க (ungga) = சொல்லுங்க (sollungga) (please tell)

The suffix -ங்க/-உங்க when added in a word automatically includes please in a sentence.

b) குடு (kudu) (to give)

குடு (kudu) + உங்க (ungga) = குடுங்க (kudungga) (please give)

Note:

> In the word குடு it already has the உ (u) vowel in it because டு (du) = ட் (d) + உ (u), so we leave the டு (du) as it is and add ங்க (ngga) to it.

c) வேணு(ம்) (veeNu(m)) (want, need)

வேணு(ம்) + உங்க = வேணுமுங்க (veeNumungga) (it means "i want" in a polite manner).

There are other versions of politeness as well and they are optional.

In the state of Tamil Nadu in India, it is okay to address a person who is older than you as அண்ணா (aNNaa) (elder brother), அக்கா (akkaa) elder sister, அய்யா (ayyaa) (refers to a very elderly and respectable person) and அம்மா (ammaa) mother. You would usually use the shorter version of these words in the form of a suffix and add it to the suffix -உங்க (ungga), Using these suffixes brings additional politeness to the sentence as you give respect to the person you are talking to like you would give to your elder brother and sister or grandfather or mother.

There is no fixed rule regarding how older a person should be in terms of age, I have mentioned the criteria in the below table as per my assumption but it may change depending on the person and the place, I have seen some even call a 50 year old person as அண்ணா (aNNaa) (elder brother), so there are no fixed rules for it. The only ground rule here is that the person should be older than you.

The suffix/shorter version of அண்ணா is -ணா (Naa); அக்கா is -கா (kaa); அய்யா is -யா (yaa); அம்மா is -மா (maa). Whenever you see a male stranger, or a person you know who is older than you (age difference 1 to 20 years) it is advisable to use the suffix -ணா which represents அண்ணா (aNNaa) (elder brother). Be it a Taxi driver or a shopkeeper etc. You can use this suffix for any word, Usually it is added next to the suffix -உங்க, hence it brings additional politeness to your sentence.

Example:

a) சொல் (sol) (say, tell).

சொல் + ல் + உங்க + ணா = சொல்லுங்கணா (sollunggaNaa) (please tell me brother).

The suffix -ங்க/-உங்க (ngga/ungga), when added to a word, automatically includes the word 'please' in that word.

b) குடு (kudu) (to give).

குடு (kudu) + உங்க (ungga) + ணா (Naa) = குடுங்கணா (kudunggaNaa) (please give me brother).

c) சொல் (sol) (say, tell).

சொல் (sol) + ல் (l) + உங்க (ungga) + கா (kaa) = சொல்லுங்ககா (sollunggakaa) (please tell me sister).

d) குடு (kudu) (to give).

குடு (kudu) + உங்க (ungga) + கா (kaa) = குடுங்ககா (kudunggakaa) (please give me sister).

Note:

Addressing a stranger using the suffix -ணா, -கா, -யா, -மா is purely optional. You can always use the suffix –உங்க instead. The only difference here is when you use the suffix -ணா or -கா or -யா or –மா next to -உங்க, it brings additional politeness to your sentence. It is more like you are giving him respect on par with your elder brother or elder sister or grandfather or mother.

Suffix for politeness	Criteria	Full form of the suffix
-உங்க (ungga)	Should be older than you or superior in designation or a stranger.	
-ணா (Naa)	Should be a male and 1-20 years older than you	அண்ணா (aNNaa) elder brother
-கா (kaa)	Should be a female and 1-20 years older than you	அக்கா (akkaa) elder sister
-யா (yaa)	Should be a male and very elder to you, like your grandparents.	அய்யா (ayyaa), refers to a very elderly and respectable person
-மா (maa)	Should be a female and very elder to you, like your grandparents.	அம்மா (ammaa) mother

Note on Important Words இருந்துச்சு, இருக்கு, இருக்கும்.

These three words come from the root verb இரு (iru) (to be) and it indicates neutral (animals, things, etc.). Tamil's verb conjugation differs from English, which will be explained in detail in the chapter "Tenses".

Since these three words are important and we need them for the exercises, you will have to memorize these three words.

Neuter form of இரு	Meaning in English
அது இருந்துச்சு (adhu) (irundhuchchu)	It was
அது இருக்கு (adhu) (irukku)	It is
அது இருக்கு(ம்) (adhu) (irukku(m))	It will be

Note:

The word இருக்கு (irukku) is important and frequently used in Tamil. The word இருக்கு alone also gives you the meaning of 'Have' or 'it is there' or 'are there' etc., it is a multipurpose word and it is used in many sentence formations in Tamil.

	Multiple meanings in English
இருந்துச்சு (irundhuchchu)	Had
	Was available
	It was there
	Was there
	There was
இருக்கு (irukku)	Have
	Is available
	It is there, available
	Are there
	There are
	Is there
	There is
இருக்கு(ம்) (irukku(m))	Will have
	Will be available
	It will be there
	Will be there
	There will be

Example:

a) எங்கிட்ட பேனா இருக்கு.

tl: enggitta peenaa irukku.

lit: with me pen have.

t: i have pen with me.

b) அங்க பேனா இருக்கு.

tl: angga peenaa irukku.

lit: there pen is.

t: there is the pen.

c) Taxi Factoryல இருக்கு.

tl: Taxi Factoryla irukku.

lit: taxi in the factor is.

t: taxi is in the factory.

d) Taxi Factoryல இருக்கு(ம்).

tl: Taxi Factoryla irukku(m).

lit: taxi in the factor will be.

t: taxi will be in the factory.

Note:

Here 'Taxi' represents 'It' 'அது'.

e) Taxi Factoryல இருந்துச்சு.

tl: Taxi Factoryla irundhuchchu.

lit: taxi in the factor was.

t: taxi was in the factory.

f) எத்தன புத்தகங்கள் இருக்கு?

tl: eththana puththaganggaL irukku?

t/lit: how many books are there?.

g) அஞ்சு புத்தகங்கள் இருக்கு.

tl: anjju puththaganggaL irukku.

lit: five books there are.

t: there are five books.

h) தக்காளி இருக்கு.

tl: thakkaaLi irukku.

t/lit: tomato is available.

i) தக்காளி இருக்குமா?

t: is tomato available?.

EXERCISES:

A) Match the following Tamil pronoun in the first column with the appropriate English meaning in the second column.

1.	உங்க(ள்)	*(ungga(L))*	a.	I
2.	அவ(ன்)	*(ava(n))*	b.	you (informal)
3.	அவ(ள்)	*(ava(L))*	c.	you (polite) (singular)
4.	நாங்க(ள்)	*(naangga(L))*	d.	he
5.	அது	*(adhu)*	e.	she
6.	நா(ன்)	*(naa(n))*	f.	he (polite)
7.	அவங்க(ள்)	*(avangga(L))*	g.	she (polite)
8.	நம்ம	*(namma)*	h.	that
9.	நீங்க(ள்)	*(niingga(L))*	i.	this
10.	எங்க(ள்)	*(engga(L))*	j.	my
11.	அவரு	*(avaru)*	k.	your (informal)
12.	நீ	*(nii)*	l.	your (polite) (singular)
13.	என்(ன்)	*(e(n))*	m.	we (listener included)
14.	உ(ன்)	*(u(n))*	n.	we (listener excluded)
15.	இது	*(idhu)*	o.	our (listener included)
16.	நாம	*(naama)*	p.	our (listener excluded)

B) Choose the correct answer by choosing the right pronoun.

e.g. _____ Tom.

a.அவன்   b.அவள்   c.அது

The right answer is: **அவன்** Tom (he is Tom), since Tom is a male person name.

1. _____ Mary.

a. அவன்   b. அவள்   c.அது

2. _____ Dog.

a. அவன்   b. அவள்   c.அது

3. _____ (polite) Tom.

a. அவன்   b. அவள்   c. அவரு

4. _____ (polite) Mary.

a. அவங்க(ள்)   b. அவள்   c. அவரு

5. _____ பெரு (peru) (name) Jack.

a. என்   b. அது   c. அவள்

6. _____ பெரு Peter.

a. உன்   b. அது   c. அவள்

C) Now try to use the above exercise as reference and change the same sentence that you formed into a question

Example: my – என் பெரு ராஜா (en peru raajaa) (my name is raja)

Now change the above into a question: என் பெரு ராஜாவா? (en peru raajaavaa?) (Is my name raja?)

1. Your

2. Her

3. His

4. That's

5. Its

6. She (polite)

7. He (polite)

D) Use a pronoun to point to a person's name mentioned below.

Masculine: Raja, Ram, Ramesh; Feminine: Mala, Lakshmi, Akila.

Example: I -நா(ன்) ராஜா (naa(n) raajaa) (I am raja)

1. You

2. You (polite)

3. He

4. He (polite)

5. She

6. She (polite)

E) Introduce a person's name, using the word பெரு (peru) (name) and the case form of a pronoun.

Example: my – என் பெரு ராஜா (en peru raajaa) (my name is raja)

1. உங்க(ள்) (ungga(L)) (your)

2. அவ(ள்) (ava(L)) (her)

3. அவ(ன்) (ava(n)) (his)

4. அதோட (adhooda) (that's)

5. இதோட (idhooda) (it's)

6. அவங்க(ள்) (avangga(L)) (she (polite))

7. அவரு (avaru) (he (polite))

F) Translate the English Question into Tamil Question.

Example: who is this boy? – யாரு இந்த பையன்?

1. What is that?

2. What is this?

3. How many?

4. How much?

5. What time is it?

G) Choose the correct answer by choosing the right question word.

1. _____ தக்காளி (thakkaaLi) (tomato)?

a. எத்தன   b. எப்படி   c. என்னிக்கு

2. _____ போவீங்க (pooviingga) (you will go)?

a. என்னிக்கு   b. எது   c. எந்த

3. _____ போவீங்க (pooviingga) (you will go)?

a. இத்தன   b. எது   c. எப்படி

4. _____ போவீங்க (pooviingga) (you will go)?

a. எங்க   b. இவங்க(ள்)   c. இவரு

5. _____ ரூபாய் (ruubaay) (rupees)?

a. எவ்வளவு   b. எப்படி   c. என்னிக்கு

6. _____ போவீங்க (pooviingga) (you will go)?

a. எப்ப   h அந்த   c. இது

H) Translate the following from English to Tamil.

Example: Which is a head – எது தலை?

1. This is a boy.

2. This boy.

3. This a house.

4. Which house?

5. Which is a house?

6. Which boy?

7. That house.

8. Which vehicle?

9. That is a vehicle.

10 Which is a vehicle?

I) Translate the following from Tamil to English.

Example: இது தலை - This is a head.

1. இது வியாபாரம்.

2. இந்த வியாபாரம்.

3. எந்த வியாபாரம்.

4. எது வியாபாரம்.

5. அது வியாபாரம்.

6. அந்த வியாபாரம்.

J) Match the following Tamil question words in the first column with the appropriate English meaning in the second column.

1.	என்ன	*(enna)*	a.	How many?	
2.	ஏன்	*(een)*	b.	How did you get?	
3.	ஏது	*(eedhu)*	c.	Which (noun)?	
4.	யாரு	*(yaaru)*	d.	Which day?	
5.	எங்க	*(engga)*	e.	What?	
6.	எப்ப	*(eppa)*	f.	How?	
7.	எது	*(edhu)*	g.	Which (adjective)?	
8.	எந்த	*(endha)*	h.	Why?	
9.	எப்படி	*(eppadi)*	i.	When?	
10.	எத்தன	*(eththana)*	j.	How much?	
11.	எவ்வளவு	*(evLavu)*	k.	Who?	
12.	என்னிக்கு	*(ennikku)*	l.	Where?	

SOLUTIONS

Lesson 6

Exercise A

1) l; 2) d; 3) e; 4) n; 5) h; 6) a; 7) g; 8) o; 9) c; 10) p; 11) f; 12) b; 13) j; 14) k; 15) i; 16) m.

Exercise B

1) b; 2) c; 3) c; 4) a; 5) a; 6) a.

Note:

In Exercise C, D and E you can use random names, I used the names randomly that's all.

Exercise D

1) நீ ராஜா. 2) நீங்க(ள்) ராம். 3) அவ(ன்) ரமேஷ். 4) அவரு ராஜா. 5) அவ(ள்) மாலா. 6) அவங்க(ள்) அகிலா.

TL: 1) nii raajaa. 2) niingga(L) raam. 3) ava(n) rameesh. 4) avaru raajaa. 5) ava(L) maalaa. 6) avangga(L) agilaa.

Exercise C

1) உ(ன்) பெரு ராஜாவா? 2) அவ(ள்) பெரு மாலாவா? 3) அவ(ன்) பெரு ரமேஷா? 4) அது பெரு ராமா? 5) அது பெரு ரமேஷா? 6) அவங்களோட பெரு அகிலாவா? 7) அவரோட பெரு ராஜாவா?

TL: 1) un peru raajaavaa? 2) ava(L) peru maalaavaa? 3) ava(n) peru rameeshaa? 4) adhu peru raamaa? 5) adhu peru rameeshaa? 6) avanggaLooda peru agilaavaa? 7) avarooda peru raajaavaa?

Exercise E

1) உங்க(ள்) பெரு ராஜா. 2) அவ(ள்) பெரு மாலா. 3) அவ(ன்) பெரு ராஜா.

4) அதோட பெரு ராஜா. 5) இதோட பெரு ராஜா. 6) அவங்க(ள்) பெரு மாலா.

7) அவரு பெரு ராஜா.

TL: 1) ungga(L) peru raajaa 2) ava(L) peru maalaa 3) ava(n) peru raajaa 4) adhooda peru raajaa 5) adhooda peru raajaa 6) avangga(L) peru maalaa 7) avaru peru raajaa.

Exercise F

1) அது என்ன? 2) இது என்ன? 3) எத்தன? 4) எவ்வளவு? 5) மணி என்ன?

TL: 1) adhu enna? 2) idhu enna? 3) eththana? 4) evLavu? 5) maNi enna?

Exercise G

1) a; 2) a; 3) c; 4) a; 5) a; 6) a.

Exercise H

1) இது பையன். 2) இந்த பையன். 3) இந்த வீடு. 4) எந்த வீடு? 5) எது வீடு? 6) எந்த பையன்? 7) அந்த வீடு. 8) எந்த வண்டி? 9) அது வண்டி 10) எது வண்டி?

TL: 1) idhu paiyan. 2) indha paiyan. 3) indha viidu. 4) endha viidu? 5) edhu viidu?

6) endha paiyan? 7) andha viidu. 8) endha vaNdi? 9) adhu vaNdi. 10) edhu vaNdi?.

Exercise I

1) This is a business. 2) This business. 3) Which business? 4) What is a business? 5) That business. 6) That is a business.

Exercise J

1) e; 2) h; 3) b; 4) k; 5) l; 6) i; 7) c; 8) g; 9) f; 10) a; 11) j; 12) d

VERB CONJUGATION

LESSON 7

Content:

LESSON 7: VERB CONJUGATION

Verb conjugation refers to how a verb changes to show a different person, tense or number.

Review of Verb conjugation in English: In English, to conjugate a verb, the below form is necessary.

1. Person: In English, we have six different persons: first person singular (I), second person singular (you), third person singular (he/she/it/one) and we have to use them as it, a conjugated verb will always have a pronoun before it.

2. Tense: Verbs are also conjugated according to a tense: Verb tense indicates when the action in a sentence is happening or happened or will happen (e.g., in the present, future, or past). Regular verbs follow a standard pattern as mentioned in the table below and we have a few irregular verbs that don't follow a standard pattern.

	Simple present	Simple past	Simple future
Regular	Cook	Cooked	Will cook
Irregular	Eat	Ate	Will eat

Verb Conjugation in Tamil:

A conjugated verb in a sentence consists of three parts.

1. The root of the verb. e.g. ஓடு (oodu) (to run)

2. A suffix that indicates the tense, e.g. ன் (n) (class 3: Past tense)

3. Another suffix that indicates the PNG (Person-Number-Gender) e.g. எ (e) (verb suffix for நா(ன்))

ஓடு (oodu) + ன் (n) + எ (e) = ஓடுனெ (oodune) (I ran)

Note:

The root of the verb, e.g. ஓடு can occur on its own as an imperative form, simply to instruct someone to do something.

Verb conjugation in Tamil differs from English; the points listed below will explain those differences with examples.

1) Similar to English we use 'person' which comes before a conjugated verb, but this is optional because we use a verb suffix representing the PNG (Person Number Gender)

Example:

Let's take the Pronoun: நா(ன்) (naa(n)) (I), verb: ஓடு (oodu) (to run), Present tense suffix: ற் (R), Verb suffix for நா(ன்) (naa(n)) which is எ (e).

From the above, I can form a sentence "I run".

நா(ன்) (naa(n)) (pronoun 'I') + ஓடு (to run) + ற் (R) (Present tense suffix) + எ (e) (Verb suffix of 'I')

When you combine it all, we will get நா(ன்) ஓடுறெ (naa(n) ooduRe) (I run).

Since the verb suffix எ (e) already represents the pronoun நா(ன்) (naa(n)) (I), it is optional to use நா(ன்) in this sentence. நா(ன்) ஓடுறெ (naa(n) ooduRe) and ஓடுறெ (ooduRe) both means "I run". You should always use the verb suffix e.g. எ (e) when you conjugate a verb, it is mandatory, but when you do it, it is always optional to use the pronoun e.g. நா(ன்) (naa(n)).

2) In Tamil, we don't have a separate continuous tense. We use the same verb conjugation for both Simple and continuous tenses.

Example: நா(ன்) ஓடுறெ (ooduRe) can be translated into English as "I am running" or "I run" depending upon the context.

3) In Tamil, we don't use separate words like 'are', 'is', 'am', 'was', 'has', 'have', 'were' when conjugating a verb like in English, depending upon the 'person', 'tense' and 'context' it should be understood by the listener.

4) In Tamil, we use a suffix to represent whether the conjugated verb is in the past, present or future tense. The verbs are split into two categories: strong and weak verbs. The suffix changes depending on which category the verb belongs to, whether it is in a weak or a strong verb.

Note:

About the Strong and weak verb, tense and tense suffixes will be explained later in this chapter.

5) The 'verb root' is used while conjugating a verb and it is fixed. In a rare scenario when there is an irregular verb, the 'verb root' changes.

Note:

After this, you will come across some exercises where you would have to conjugate some verbs in different tenses. It would be easier to conjugate those verbs when you know which class those verbs belong to. The table below lists the verbs with their classes in those exercises.

Tamil Verb	Transliteration	English meaning	Tamil Verb	Transliteration	English meaning
Class 1					
செய்	sey	To Do			
Class 2					
ஒளி	oLi	To Hide	விழு	vizhu	To Fall down
வாழ்	vaazh	To Live			
Class 3					
ஓடு	oodu	To Run	வாங்கு	vaanggu	To Buy, take
பாடு	paadu	To Sing	விளையாடு	viLaiyaadu	To Play
பேசு	peesu	To Speak	ஆடு	aadu	To Dance
பூட்டு	puuttu	To Lock	கத்து	kaaththu	To Scream
தள்ளு	thaLLu	To Push	பன்னு	pannu	To Do
போ	poo	To Go			

Class 4					
தொடு	thodu	To Touch	போடு	poodu	To Put, wear
Class 6					
பிடி	pidi	To Hold	தெளி	theLi	To Spray
படி	padi	To Read, study	உடை/உடெ	udai/ude	To Break
கடி	kadi	To Bite	மடி	madi	To Fold
Class 7					
மற	maRa	To Forget	கல	kala	To Mix
திற	thiRa	To Open	இரு	iru	To Be

Verb Suffixes:

When a verb conjugation refers to a pronoun, a suffix will be added to the verb that matches up with the subject of the sentence. This is applicable only for the nominative case pronoun. As discussed earlier, a nominative case usually refers to an action. Each pronoun will be associated with a verb suffix. So, whenever a nominative case pronoun appears in a sentence, then its corresponding verb suffix is added to the end of the verb.

This verb suffix is also known as a PNG suffix (Person-Number-Gender), which agrees with all three of them.

The verb suffix table below shows the Nominative case pronoun and their corresponding verb suffixes

	Singular		Plural	
	Nominative	Suffix	Nominative	Suffix
First person	நா(ன்) (naa(n)) (I)	-எ (e) -ஏன்- (-een-)	நாம (nama) (we) (listener included)	-ஒ(ம்) (oo(m))
			நாங்க(ள்) (naangga(L)) (we) (listener not included)	-ஒ(ம்) (oo(m))
Second person	நீ (nii) (you)	-எ (e)	நீங்க(ள்) (niingga(L)) (neengga) (you) (polite)	-ஈங்க(ள்) (iingga(L))
	நீங்க(ள்) (niingga(L)) (you) (polite)	-ஈங்க(ள்) (iingga(L))		
Third person	அவ(ன்) (avan) (he)	-ஆ(ன்) (aa(n))	அவங்க(ள்) (avangga(L)) (they-human) (polite)	-ஆங்க(ள்) (aangga(L))
	அவரு (avaru) (he) (polite)	-ஆரு (aaru)		
	அவ(ள்) (avaL) (she)	-ஆ(ள்) (aa(L))		
	அவங்க(ள்) (avangga(L)) (she) (polite)	-ஆங்க(ள்) (aangga(L))		

Note:

The verb suffixes for "Person" given in the above will never change irrespective of which Tense you are using, but for neuter pronouns like இது (idhu) (this), அது (adhu) (that) அதுங்க (adhungga) (those) இதுங்க (idhungga) (these) etc. It will change depending on the tense and the type of verb (Strong or Weak verb). The neuter pronouns verb suffix will be provided in a different table later

Example: The below table shows the verb conjugation of ஓடு (oodu) (to run) in past tense with verb suffix.

Verb root	Past Tense Suffix	Verb Suffix	Suffix combination with the verb root	Past Tense	English Translation
ஓடு	-ன்-	--எ	ஓடு+ன்+எ	நா(ன்) ஓடுனெ	I ran
ஓடு	-ன்-	-எ	ஓடு+ன்+எ	நீ ஓடுனெ	you ran (informal/impolite)
ஓடு	-ன்-	-ஈங்க(ள்)	ஓடு+ன்+ஈங்க(ள்)	நீங்க(ள்) ஓடுனீங்க(ள்)	you ran (formal/polite)
ஓடு	-ன்-	-ஓ(ம்)	ஓடு+ன்+ஓ(ம்)	நாம/நாங்க ஓடுனோ(ம்)	we ran (Incl/Excl)
ஓடு	-ன்-	-ஆ(ன்)	ஓடு+ன்+ஆ(ன்)	அவ(ன்) ஓடுனா(ன்)	he ran (informal/impolite)
ஓடு	-ன்-	-ஆரு	ஓடு+ன்+ஆரு	அவரு ஓடுனாரு	he ran (formal/polite)
ஓடு	-ன்-	-ஆ(ள்)	ஓடு+ன்+ஆ(ள்)	அவ(ள்) ஓடுனா(ள்)	she ran (informal/impolite)
ஓடு	-ன்-	-ஆங்க(ள்)	ஓடு+ன்+ஆங்க(ள்)	அவங்க(ள்) ஓடுனாங்க(ள்)	she ran (formal/polite) / they ran

1. In the verb suffix table, for many verb suffixes you would have noticed that I have mentioned the last letter inside brackets at the end of the suffix. (e.g. ஈங்க(ள்) (iingga(L)), ஆ(ன்) (aa(n)), -ஆ(ள்) (aa(L)), -ஆங்க(ள்) (aangga(L)), -ஓ(ம்) (oo(m)), அவ(ன்)(avan), அவ(ள்).

This last letter is enclosed in brackets because it is only used and pronounced when a suffix is added to this verb suffix.

Example:

ஓடுனா (ava oodunaa) (she ran)

In the above example, I didn't add the last letter ள் (L) to the conjugated verb ஓடுனா (oodunaa) because we don't have any suffix next to this verb suffix.

a) அவ(ள்) ஓடுனா(ள்) + ஆ (interrogative suffix) = அவ(ள்) ஓடுனாளா? (ava(L) oodunaalaa) (Did she ran?)

Whereas, in the above example I added the last letter ள் (L) to the conjugated verb ஓடுனா (oodunaa) because we have an interrogative suffix next to this verb suffix.

b) நாம ஓடுனோமா? (naama oodunoomaa) (Did we run?)

Whereas, in the above example I added the last letter ம் (m) to the conjugated verb ஓடுனோ (oodunoo) because we have an interrogative suffix ஆ (aa) next to this verb suffix.

2. I have mentioned two verb suffixes for the pronoun நா(ன்) (naa(n)) (I). This is because of the below mentioned reason.

a) We will use the verb suffix - எ (e), when there is no other suffix being added next to this verb suffix.

Example: ஓடு (verb root) + ன் (past tense suffix) + எ (verb suffix of நா)
நா(ன்) ஓடுனெ (naa(n) oodune) (I ran)
I didn't use the verb suffix -ஏன்- (-een-) here because we don't have any suffix next to this verb suffix.

b) We will use the verb suffix -ஏன்- (-een-) when there is another suffix being added to this verb suffix.

Example: ஓடு (verb root) + ன் (past tense suffix) + ஏன் (verb suffix of நா(ன்)) + ஆ (interrogative suffix)
நா(ன்) ஓடுனேனா? (naa(n) ooduneenaa) (Did I ran?)

I didn't use the verb suffix எ (e) here because we have a suffix next to this verb suffix.

3. The verb suffix for both நா(ன்) (naa(n)) (I) and நீ (nii) (you) are the same (எ (e)).

You don't have to worry or get confused about recognizing the difference when both have the same suffix. There will be a slight variation in spoken Tamil when you pronounce this suffix for both the pronouns but it is impossible to put it in writing because the variation is very small.

80

Like I said earlier, do not worry about it because you will recognize which pronoun the suffix is referring to base on the context. You will eventually get the difference when you hear my pronunciation or start conversing with the native Tamil speakers.

4. I have mentioned the last letter of the pronoun அவ(ன்) (ava(n)) (he) and அவ(ள்) (ava(L)) (she) in the bracket, It is for the same reason that I have mentioned earlier that this last letter will be used and pronounced only when a suffix is being added to the pronoun.

Example:

அவ(ன்) (he) + ஆ (interrogative suffix) = அவனா? (Is he?)

அவ(ள்) (she) + ஆ (interrogative suffix) = அவளா? (Is she?)

In the above example, since I am adding a suffix to the pronoun, I have included the last letter from the bracket.

அவ ஓடுனா (ava oodunaa) (she ran)

அவ ஓடுனா (ava oodunaa) (he ran)

In the above example, since I am not adding any suffix to the pronoun, I have not included the last letter from the bracket.

5. In writing the pronoun and verb suffix for அவ(ன்) (ava(n)) (he) and அவ(ள்) (ava(L)) (she) is the same, then how would one recognize the difference between both of them?.

Answer: There is a small variation when a native speaker pronounces the above pronoun and their verb suffix. But, it is impossible to put it in writing because the variation is very small.

The below will explain the variation, but to fully understand and practice the pronunciation, you must listen to my audio when I pronounce these pronouns and their suffix or when speaking to a native Tamil speaker.

The below may help you pronounce அவ (ava) (he) and அவ (ava) (she) well.

a) When you are pronouncing அவ (ava) (he) - While pronouncing the letter வ you will have to fold your lower lip, place it below your upper teeth, and let the upper give light pressure to your lower lip and release your lower lip.

அவ (ava) (he) – This is similar to the pronunciation 'aveh' in English

b) When you are pronouncing அவ (ava) (she) - While pronouncing the letter வ you will have to let your upper teeth touch your lower lips gently and release them.

அவ (ava) (she) – This is similar to the pronunciation 'ava' in English but while pronouncing, the last letter 'a' is pronounced from the back of your throat

c) When you are pronouncing ஓடுணா (oodunaa) (she ran) - While pronouncing the letter ணா you will have to fold your tongue a bit backward to your mouth.

d) When you are pronouncing ஓடுனா (oodunaa) (he ran) - While pronouncing the letter னா you will have to touch the back of your upper teeth gently and release it.

Note:

Since it is difficult to display the difference in writing, I will always use அவ(ன்) and அவ(ள்) for 'he' and 'she', but in my audio recordings I will not pronounce the letter inside the bracket when there is no suffix added next to it.

EXERCISES:

A) Match the following Tamil Pronouns in the first column with the appropriate verb conjugation in the second column.

e.g.: அவ(ன்) = பாடுறா(ன்); The suffix for அவ(ன்) is ஆ(ன்)

பாடு + ற் + ஆ(ன்) = பாடுறா(ன்)

Note:

> You should ignore the tense and the verb in here, because the task is to find the right verb suffix.

1. அவரு (avaru)

2. அவ(ள்) (ava(L)

3. அவங்க(ள்) (avangga(L))

4. நீ (nii)

5. நீங்க(ள்) (niingga(L))

6. நா(ன்) (naa(n))

7. நாம/ நாங்க(ள்)

a. குளிக்குறாங்க(ள்) (kuLikkuRaangga(L))

b. கொடுக்குறெ (kodukkuRe)

c. எழுவீங்க(ள்) (ezhuviingga(L))

d. எடுத்தெ (eduththe)

e. கொடுக்குறாரு (kodukkuRaaru)

f. எடுக்குறோ(ம்) (edukkuRoo(m))

g. குளிக்குறா(ள்) (kuLikkuRaa(L)))

B) Choose the correct answer by choosing the right verb suffix.

e.g. அவ(ன்) = பாடு + ற் + ஆ(ன்) = பாடுறா(ன்) (right answer) பாடுறோம் (wrong answer)

Note:

You should ignore the tense and the verb in here, because the task is to find the right verb suffix.

1. அவ(ள்) _____ (she is singing).

a. பாடுறா(ன்)   b. பாடுறா(ள்)   c. பாடுறா

2. அவரு _____ (he (polite) is singing).

a. பாடுறாரு   b. பாடுறோ(ம்)   c. பாடுறாங்க

3. நா _____ (i am sleeping).

a. தூங்குறோ(ம்)   b.தூங்குறெ   c. தூங்குறாங்க

4. நீ _____ (you will dance).

a.ஆடுவா(ன்)   b. ஆடுவெ   c. ஆடுவா(ள்)

5. நாம _____ (we will dance).

a. ஆடுவோ(ம்)   b. ஆடுவா(ன்)   c. ஆடுவெ

6. அவங்க _____ (they will see).

a. படுப்பாங்க(ள்)   b. படுப்போ(ம்)   c. படுப்பேன்

7. நாங்க(ள்)   _____ (we will crouch).

a. குனிவா(ன்)   b. குனிவா(ள்)   c. குனிவோ(ம்)

Tense:

Similar to English, the Tenses are divided into three categories in Tamil.

1. Past Tense. (This relates to something that happened in the past)

2. Present Tense (This relates to something happening right now or in the near future)

3. Future Tense. (This relates to something which will happen in the future)

In the present tense, when I say near future, it means it will happen today, tomorrow or in a few days. We also have the same concept in English. For example: 'I am going to the shop on Sunday' or 'Tom arrives tomorrow morning at six'. We have both possibilities here. You can say 'I am going to the shop on Sunday' or 'I will go to the shop on Sunday', both indicate that you will go to the shop in the future but the tense can be present or future tense. The same is applicable in Tamil.

In Tamil, we use a suffix to indicate whether the conjugated verb (an action) will happen in the past, present or future. This suffix is called as tense marker. The verbs in Tamil are classified into two categories: Strong verbs and Weak verbs.

Note:

> There is no fixed rule which says why a verb is a strong verb or a weak verb, a verb is a weak verb or a strong verb because it is. However, I have designed a chart using the verb root form to which you can predict the strong and weak verbs (in few scenarios, which class a verb belongs to cannot be predicted only based on its form).

The verbs are further classified into seven classes:

Class 1-4: Weak verbs

Class 5: Irregular verbs

Class 6-7: Strong verbs

Class 1 is further categorized as Class 1a, Class 1b and Class 1c

Class 4 is further categorized as Class 4a, Class 4b

Note:

> There are hardly 10 commonly used irregular verbs in Tamil. Apart from them, everything else follows the standard pattern.

There are only 2 suffixes for present tense and future tense, one suffix for weak verbs and another suffix for strong verbs. These suffixes are much easier to predict because a verb with a strong verb, present tense suffix will always have a strong verb future tense suffix.

Type of verb	Present Tense	Future Tense
Weak verb	ற் (R)	வ் (v)
Strong verb	க்குற் (kkuR)	ப்ப் (pp)

Examples:

Class 1a Weak Verb:

செய் (sey) (To do)

Now, we will conjugate this verb into 'I am doing' and 'I will do'.

Present Tense: நா(ன்) செய் (sey) (verb root) + ற் (present tense suffix) + எ (e) (verb suffix) = நா(ன்) செய்றெ (naa(n) seyRe) (I am doing).

Future Tense: நா(ன்) செய் (sey) (verb root) + வ் (v) (future tense suffix) + எ (e) (verb suffix) = நா(ன்) செய்வெ (naa(n) seyve) (I will do).

As written above, all I did was to change the suffix ற் (R) to the suffix வ் (v) to change the conjugated verb from present tense into past tense.

Class 1c Weak Verb:

ஆள் (aaL) (to rule)

Now, we will conjugate this verb into 'i am ruling' and 'i will rule'.

Present Tense: ஆள் (aaL) + ற் (R) + எ (e) (verb suffix) = நா(ன்) ஆள்றெ (naa(n) aaLRe) (I am ruling).

Future Tense: ஆள் (aaL) + வ் (v) + எ (e) (verb suffix) = நா(ன்) ஆள்வெ (naa(n) aaLve) (I will rule).

Class 6 Strong Verb:

பார் (paar) (To see)

Now, we will conjugate this verb into 'I am seeing' and 'I will see'.

Present Tense: நா(ன்) (naa(n)) பார் (paar) (verb root) + க்குற் (kkuR) (present tense suffix) + எ (e) = நா(ன்) பார்க்குறெ (naa(n) paarkkuRe) (I am seeing).

Future Tense: நா(ன்) (naa(n)) பார் (paar) (verb root) + ப்ப் (pp) (future tense suffix) + எ (e) (verb suffix) = நா(ன்) பார்ப்பெ (naa(n) paarppe) (I will see).

As written above, all I did was to change the suffix க்குற் (kkuR) to the suffix ப்ப் (pp) to change the conjugated verb from present tense into past tense; since the verb is a strong verb we are using a different suffix here.

Class 7 Strong Verb:

நட (nada) (to walk), Now we will conjugate this verb into 'i am walking and 'i will walk.

Present Tense: நா(ன்) (naa(n)) நட (nada) + க்குற் (kkuR) (present tense suffix) + எ (e) (verb suffix) = நா(ன்) நடக்குறெ (naa(n) nadakkuRe) (i am walking).

Future Tense: நா(ன்) (naa(n)) நட (nada) + ப்ப் (pp) (future tense suffix) + எ (e) (verb suffix) = நா(ன்) நடப்பெ (naa(n) nadappe) (I will walk).

Verb Class Table

The following table lists the tense across the top and the verb root on the side.

Verb Root	Present Tense Verb Stem	Future Tense Verb Stem	Past Tense Verb Stem	Infinitive	Adverbial Participle (AvP)
1a பெய்	Root + ற் பெய்ற்	Root + வ் பெய்வ்	Root + த் பெய்த்	Root + அ பெய்ய	Past Stem + உ பெய்து
1b கொல்	கொல்ற்	கொல்வ்	ல் → ன்ற் கொன்ற	கொல்ல	கொன்று
1c ஆள்	ஆள்ற்	ஆள்வ்	ள் → ண்ட் ஆண்ட்	ஆள	ஆண்டு
2 வாழ்	வாழ்ற்	வாழ்வ	Root + ந்த் வாழ்ந்த்	வாழ	வாழ்ந்து
3 ஓடு	ஓடுற்	ஓடுவ்	Root + ன் ஓடுன்	ஓட	உ → இ ஓடி
4a பெறு	பெறுற்	பெறுவ்	று → த்த் பெத்த்	பெற	Past Stem + உ பெத்து
4b சுடு	சுடுற்	சுடுவ்	டு → ட்ட் சுட்ட்	சுட	சுட்டு
5 தின்	தின்ற்	Irregular	Irregular	தின்ன	Irregular
6 கடி	Root + க்குற் கடிக்குற்	Root + ப்ப் கடிப்ப்	Root + ச்ச் கடிச்ச்	Root + க்க கடிக்க	கடித்து
7 நட	நடக்குற்	நடப்ப்	Root + ந்த் நடந்த்	நடக்க	நடந்து

Pattern: We can recognize some verb classes based on their verb root endings. Class 1b verb ends in ல், Class 1c verb ends in ள், Class 3 verb ends in உ (also compound letters with vowel உ eg. டு), Class 4a verb ends in று, Class 4b verb ends in டு, Class 7 verb usually has only two letters and ends in அ or compound letter containing அ.

Note:

Few verbs in Class 6 will take the suffix த்த் for past tense instead of ச்ச்.

Meaning of verbs: பெய் (to rain), கொல் (to kill), ஆள் (to rule), வாழ் (to live), ஓடு (to run), பெறு (give birth), சுடு (to shoot), தின் (to eat (animals)), கடி (to bite), நட (to walk).

Important Note:

a) The suffix for each tense is called the **Tense marker**. There are a few exceptions in the verb class table, so one must not consider the verb class table as a golden rule and think that all Tamil verbs follow this rule. Some verbs don't follow this rule. The verb class table is prepared considering most Tamil verbs which follow a pattern.

The points listed below will explain the important aspects of the verb class table.

1. All three tenses given in the above table are applicable only for "Person" Pronouns like "I", "You", "He", "She", "We", and "They. For neuter pronouns like "This", "That", "These", "Those" their tense form and verb suffix will be given later in another table.

2. Verb root is the raw verb using which you conjugate, e.g. பெய், அழு etc.

3. For a few verb classes like class 1b, 1c, 3, 4a, 4b, and 7, it is possible to predict which class these verbs belong to depending on their verb endings. e.g. சாப்பிடு (saappidu) (to eat), this verb ends with the letter டு means that this verb belongs to the class 4b. Please note that I have mentioned this to some extent because there will be a few exceptions. e.g. பாடு (paadu) (to sing) also ends with the letter டு but it belongs to class 3.

4. The majority of the Tamil verbs come under class 6. When you doubt and cannot predict which class a verb belongs to, try using the class 6 Tense stem and infinitive rule because there is a higher possibility that the verb may belong to class 6 verbs.

5. Class 5 verbs are irregular; it is difficult to predict their past and future tense stem and adverbial participle. There are only 10 commonly used verbs under class 5 so I would recommend just learning them as it is.

6. There are only two present tense and future tense markers and the tenses are related. But there are many tense markers for past tense. Hence, you will have to put more effort into your past tense sentence formation.

EXERCISES:

C) Fill in the blanks by conjugating the verb given.

(Verb suffix: - எ, -எ, -ஈங்க(ள்), -ஆ(ன்), -ஆரு, -ஆ(ள்), -ஆங்க(ள்), -ஓ(ம்))

The format is: Verb Root + Tense marker (suffix) + Verb suffix

Example: எடு (edu) + ப்ப் (pp) (future tense marker) + எ (e) = எடுப்பெ (eduppe)

1. Verb: எடு (edu) (to take) (future)

எடு	+	ப்ப்	+	எ	= _____
எடு	+	ப்ப்	+	எ	= _____
எடு	+	ப்ப்	+	ஈங்க(ள்)	= _____
எடு	+	ப்ப்	+	ஆ(ன்)	= _____
எடு	+	ப்ப்	+	ஆரு	= _____
எடு	+	ப்ப்	+	ஆ(ள்)	= _____
எடு	+	ப்ப்	+	ஆங்க(ள்)	= _____
எடு	+	ப்ப்	+	ஓ(ம்)	= _____

2. Verb: எடு (edu) (to take) (past)

எடு	+	த்த்	+	எ	= _____
எடு	+	த்த்	+	எ	= _____
எடு	+	த்த்	+	ஈங்க(ள்)	= _____
எடு	+	த்த்	+	ஆ(ன்)	= _____
எடு	+	த்த்	+	ஆரு	= _____
எடு	+	த்த்	+	ஆ(ள்)	= _____
எடு	+	த்த்	+	ஆங்க(ள்)	= _____
எடு	+	த்த்	+	ஓ(ம்)	= _____

3. Verb: எடு (edu) (to take) (present)

எடு	+	க்குற்	+	எ	=	_____
எடு	+	க்குற்	+	எ	=	_____
எடு	+	க்குற்	+	ஈங்க(ள்)	=	_____
எடு	+	க்குற்	+	ஆ(ன்)	=	_____
எடு	+	க்குற்	+	ஆரு	=	_____
எடு	+	க்குற்	+	ஆ(ள்)	=	_____
எடு	+	க்குற்	+	ஆங்க(ள்)	=	_____
எடு	+	க்குற்	+	ஓ(ம்)	=	_____

4. Verb: நினை/நினெ (ninai/nine) (to think) (future)

நினெ	+	ப்ப்	+	எ	=	_____
நினெ	+	ப்ப்	+	எ	=	_____
நினெ	+	ப்ப்	+	ஈங்க(ள்)	=	_____
நினெ	+	ப்ப்	+	ஆ(ன்)	=	_____
நினெ	+	ப்ப்	+	ஆரு	=	_____
நினெ	+	ப்ப்	+	ஆ(ள்)	=	_____
நினெ	+	ப்ப்	+	ஆங்க(ள்)	=	_____
நினெ	+	ப்ப்	+	ஓ(ம்)	=	_____

5. Verb: நினை/நினெ (ninai/nine) (to think); (present)

நினெ	+	க்குற்	+	எ	=	_____
நினெ	+	க்குற்	+	எ	=	_____
நினெ	+	க்குற்	+	ஈங்க(ள்)	=	_____
நினெ	+	க்குற்	+	ஆ(ன்)	=	_____
நினெ	+	க்குற்	+	ஆரு	=	_____
நினெ	+	க்குற்	+	ஆ(ள்)	=	_____
நினெ	+	க்குற்	+	ஆங்க(ள்)	=	_____
நினெ	+	க்குற்	+	ஓ(ம்)	=	_____

6. Verb: நினை/நினெ (ninai/nine) (to think); (past)

நினெ	+	ச்ச்	+	எ	=	_____
நினெ	+	ச்ச்	+	எ	=	_____
நினெ	+	ச்ச்	+	ஈங்க(ள்)	=	_____
நினெ	+	ச்ச்	+	ஆ(ன்)	=	_____
நினெ	+	ச்ச்	+	ஆ(ரு	=	_____
நினெ	+	ச்ச்	+	ஆ(ள்)	=	_____
நினெ	+	ச்ச்	+	ஆங்க(ள்)	=	_____

7. Verb: உக்கார் (ukkaar) (to sit); (past)

உக்கார்	+	ந்த்	+	எ	=	_____
உக்கார்	+	ந்த்	+	எ	=	_____
உக்கார்	+	ந்த்	+	ஈங்க(ள்)	=	_____
உக்கார்	+	ந்த்	+	ஆ(ன்)	=	_____
உக்கார்	+	ந்த்	+	ஆ(ரு	=	_____
உக்கார்	+	ந்த்	+	ஆ(ள்)	=	_____
உக்கார்	+	ந்த்	+	ஆங்க(ள்)	=	_____
உக்கார்	+	ந்த்	+	ஓ(ம்)	=	_____

8. Verb: உக்கார் (ukkaar) (to sit); (present)

உக்கார்	+	ற்	+	எ	=	_____
உக்கார்	+	ற்	+	எ	=	_____
உக்கார்	+	ற்	+	ஈங்க(ள்)	=	_____
உக்கார்	+	ற்	+	ஆ(ன்)	=	_____
உக்கார்	+	ற்	+	ஆ(ரு	=	_____
உக்கார்	+	ற்	+	ஆ(ள்)	=	_____
உக்கார்	+	ற்	+	ஆங்கு(ள்)	=	_____
உக்கார்	+	ற்	+	ஓ(ம்)	=	_____

9. Verb: உக்கார் (ukkaar) (to sit); (future)

உக்கார்	+	வ்	+	எ	= _____
உக்கார்	+	வ்	+	எ	= _____
உக்கார்	+	வ்	+	ஈங்க(ள்)	= _____
உக்கார்	+	வ்	+	ஆ(ன்)	= _____
உக்கார்	+	வ்	+	ஆரு	= _____
உக்கார்	+	வ்	+	ஆ(ள்)	= _____
உக்கார்	+	வ்	+	ஆங்க(ள்)	= _____
உக்கார்	+	வ்	+	ஓ(ம்)	= _____

D) Fill in the blanks with the right verb conjugation in all three tenses for the pronoun நா(ன்) (naa(n)) (I).

Example: நா(ன்) _____ (நினெ) (to think)

நா(ன்) நினெக்குறெ (naa(n) ninekkuRe) (I am thinking); நா(ன்) நினெச்செ (naa(n) ninechche) (I thought); நா(ன்) நினெப்பெ (naa(n) nineppe) (I will think)

Verb	Past tense	Present Tense	Future Tense
1. ஓடு	நா(ன்) _____	நா(ன்) _____	நா(ன்) _____
2. குடி	நா(ன்) _____	நா(ன்) _____	நா(ன்) _____
3. பாடு	நா(ன்) _____	நா(ன்) _____	நா(ன்) _____
4. பேசு	நா(ன்) _____	நா(ன்) _____	நா(ன்) _____
5 செய்	நா(ன்) _____	நா(ன்) _____	நா(ன்) _____
6. பிடி	நா(ன்) _____	நா(ன்) _____	நா(ன்) _____
7. படி	நா(ன்) _____	நா(ன்) _____	நா(ன்) _____
8. கடி	நா(ன்) _____	நா(ன்) _____	நா(ன்) _____
9. தொடு	நா(ன்) _____	நா(ன்) _____	நா(ன்) _____
10. மற	நா(ன்) _____	நா(ன்) _____	நா(ன்) _____

Infinitive:

Usually, a verb when conjugated refers to a tense, be it past, present or future tense, so there is an end to it. But, when it comes to the infinitive of a verb, there is no indication when it will happen. It is similar to a noun, an infinitive should be supported by an another word or a verb. An infinitive will not give much meaning when it comes alone.

For example: In English, let's look at the sentences "I am going there" and "I go there" . Both sentences use the verb "go" referring to the present tense which means it is happening now or is going to happen in the near future. But when you look at this sentence "I must go there", here "I must" refers to the conjugation of the verb 'must' and "go" is an infinitive as it is similar to a noun and it doesn't say when it is going to happen.

In simple words: "An infinitive is a conversion of a verb to use it like a noun".

In Tamil, the infinitive is used in several aspects. You can add suffixes to it to expand their usage in a sentence etc. An infinitive may also be preceded by "to". e.g. போக (pooga) (go) or (to go) is an infinitive of the verb போ (to go)

Example:

a) "I am going there" or "I go there" = நா(ன்) அங்க போறெ (naa(n) angga pooRe).

Here, "must" is translated as வேணு(ம்) (veenu(m)) (want, need, must),

The suffix of வேணு(ம்) is '-ணு(ம்)'.

1. You should use "வேணு(ம்)" when it comes with a noun.

2. You should use the suffix "-ணு(ம்)" (Nu(m)) when it occurs with an infinitive of a verb.

b) போக (pooga) (go) or (to go) is an infinitive of the verb போ (to go)

"I must go there" - நா(ன்) அங்க போகணு(ம்) (naa(n) anga poogaNu(m));

lit: I there must go.

As you have seen in the above example we are using the infinitive of the verb போக (pooga) (go) or (to go) similar to the way we use it in English.

Similar to present tense and future tense, there are only 2 suffixes for changing a verb into an infinitive form அ (a) and க்க (kka). We use the suffix அ (a) for the weak verb to make it an infinitive and the suffix க்க (kka) to the root of the strong verb to make it an infinitive.

94

Examples:

Class 3 Weak Verb: காட்டு **(kaattu) (to show).**

காட்டு (kaattu) (to show) + அ (a) Infinitive suffix = காட்ட (kaatta) (show) Infinitive

Note:

Since the verb doesn't end with a consonant and the suffix is a vowel,, here you are considering the base consonant of டு (tu) which is ட் (t) to be added with the suffix அ (a). In detail: காட்ட் (kaatt) + அ (a) = காட்ட (kaatta).

Class 2 Weak Verb: எறி **(eRi) (to throw).**

எறி (eRi) (to throw) + அ (a) Infinitive suffix = எறிய (eRiya) (throw) Infinitive

In detail: எறி (eRi) + ய் (y) + அ (a) Infinitive suffix = எறிய (eRiya) (throw) Infinitive

Note:

If you are wondering why I inserted ய் in between, please refer to the topic "Insertion of ய் (y) and வ் (v)" in the chapter "suffixes in Tamil".

Class 4 Weak Verb: தொடு **(thodu) (to touch).**

தொடு (thodu) (to touch) + அ (a) Infinitive suffix = தொட (thoda) (touch) Infinitive

Class 6 Strong Verb: எடு **(edu) (to take).**

எடு (edu) (to take) + க்க் (kka) Infinitive suffix = எடுக்க (edukka) (take) Infinitive

Class 6 Strong Verb: துவை **(thuvai) (to wash).**

துவை (thuvai) (to wash) + க்க் (kka) Infinitive suffix = துவைக்க (thuvaikka) (wash) Infinitive

Class 6 Strong Verb: புதை **(pudhai) (to bury).**

புதை (pudhai) (to bury) + க்க் (kka) Infinitive suffix = புதைக்க (pudhaikka) (bury)

Class 7 Strong Verb: நட **(nada) (to walk); Verb:** போ **(poo) (to go)**

நா(ன்) நடக்க போறேன் (naa(n) nadakka pooReen) (i am going to walk);

EXERCISES:

E) Fill in the blanks with the infinitive form of the verb given on the left.

Example: குடி = குடிக்க

1. ஒளி = _____ _____ . (hide)
2. வாழ் = _____ . (live)
3. விழு = _____ . (fall)
4. பூட்டு = _____ . (lock)
5. போடு = _____ . (put down)
6. தெளி = _____ . (spray
7. உடை = _____ . (break)
8. மடி = _____ . (fold)
9. கல = _____ . (mix)
10. திற = _____ . (open)

F) Fill in the blanks with the right verb infinitive.

Example: நா(ன்) _____ (குடி) மாட்டெ

நா(ன்) குடிக்க மாட்டேன் (naa(n) kudikka maatteen) (I will not drink)

1. நா(ன்) _____ (ஓடு) மாட்டெ. (I will not run)

2. நா(ன்) _____ (குடி) போறெ. (I am going to drink)

3. நீ _____ (பாடு) கூடாது. (You should not sing)

4. நீ _____ (பேசு) கூடாது. (You should not speak)

5. அவ(ன்) _____ (செய்) கூடாது. (He should not do)

6. அவள _____ (பிடி) போறெ (I am going to catch her)

7. அவ(ள்) _____ (படி) போறா(ள்). (She is going to study)

8. அது _____ (கடி) போவுது. (That is going to bite)

96

Adverbial Participle (AvP):

Adverbial Participle (AvP) is used in complex sentences with more than one verb. AvP is used to create continuous and perfect tenses in Tamil. It conjoins actions that are carried out either simultaneously (e.g. "I went to the restaurant, ate breakfast, drank coffee and paid the bill") or sequentially (e.g. I am listening to music while sleeping). These actions must be casually related to each other. The first action will be in the past tense and only the last verb in the sequence will have the tense and verb suffix (PNG suffix). AvP is often translated as "having VERB".

Note:

As per the verb class table, to change a verb into AvP.

1. For verbs of all classes except class 3, take the past tense stem and add உ (u) to it.

2. For verb class 3, change the verb ending from உ (u) to இ (i). Class 3 verb ending is a compound letter (combination of vowel and consonant).

Example: The below table illustrates how to form an Adverbial Participle from a verb.

Class	Verb	Past Tense Stem + AvP	Adverbial Participle (AvP)
Class 6	புதை (pudhai) (to bury)	புதைச்ச் + உ	புதைச்சு (pudhaichchu) (having buried)
Class 6	உடை (udai) (to break)	உடைச்ச் + உ	உடைச்சு (udaichchu) (having broken)
Class 7	விய (viya) (to be surprised)	வியந்த் + உ	வியந்து (viyandhu) (having surprised)
Class 7	மற (maRa) (to forget)	மறந்த் + உ	மறந்து (maRandhu) (having forgotten)
Class 2	எழு (ezhu) (to get up, raise)	எழுந்த் + உ	எழுந்து (ezhundhu) (having gotten up)

The below table illustrates how to form an Adverbial Participle from a verb for Class 3 Verbs.

Class	Verb	change in verb ending	Adverbial Participle (AvP)
Class 3	ஒட்டு (oottu) (to drive)	உ (u) to இ (i)	ஒட்டி (ootti) (having driven)
Class 3	கட்டு (kattu) (to tie, build)	உ (u) to இ (i)	கட்டி (katti) (having built)
Class 3	காட்டு (kaattu) (to show)	உ (u) to இ (i)	காட்டி (kaatti) (having showed)

Note:

- The reason there is a difference in class 3 for AvP is simple; the verb ending of class 3 already contains உ, adding another உ next to it will not sound right.

- The use of AvP is not only limited to a verb. It is also used in the formation of compound verbs such as சொல்லிகொடு (sollikodu) (teach), கொண்டுபோ (koNdupoo) (take), கொண்டுவா (koNduvaa) (bring) etc., these compound verbs take the first part of the verb as an adverbial participle form.

Examples: Sequential Actions:

a) நா(ன்) கடைக்கு போயி காய்கறி வாங்கி சமெச்சு சாப்பிடுவெ.

tl: naa(n) kadaikku pooyi kaaygaRi vaanggi samechchu saappiduve.

lit: I to the shop go vegetable buy cook will eat.

t: I will go to shop, buy vegetable, cook and eat.

AvP: வாங்கி (vaanggi) (having bought), சமெச்சு (samechchu) (having cooked).

b) என் வீட்டுக்கு போயி கதவ திறந்து ராம கூப்பிட்டு அவன்கிட்ட பேசி இந்த பணத்த எண்ணி அவன்கிட்ட குடு.

tl: en viittukku pooyi kadhava thiRandhu raama kuuppittu avankitta peesi indha paNaththa eNNi avankitta kudu.

lit: my to house go door open ram call with him speak this money count with him give.

t: go to my house, open the door, call ram, speak to him, count this money and give it to him.

AvP: திறந்து (thiRandhu) (having opened), கூப்பிட்டு (kuuppittu) (having called), பேசி (peesi) (having spoken), எண்ணி (eNNi) (having counted).

Examples: Simultaneous Action:

a) நா(ன்) நடந்து போயி கடைல புத்தகம் வாங்குனெ.

tl: naa(n) nadandhu pooyi kadaila puththagam vaanggune.

lit: I walk go in the shop book bought.

t: I bought book from the shop walking.

AvP: நடந்து (nadandhu) (having walked).

b) நா(ன்) வேகமா ஓடி போட்டில பரிசு வென்றெ.

tl: naa(n) veegamaa oodi poottila parisu venRe.

lit: I fast walk in the competition prize won.

t: i won the prize in the competition by walking fast.

AvP: ஓடி (oodi) (having ran).

c) இந்த சாப்பாட சாப்பிட்டு பாருங்க(ள்).

tl: indha saappaada saappittu paarunggaL.

lit: this food eat and see.

t: Try this food.

AvP: சாப்பிட்டு (saappittu) (having ate).

Neuter Pronoun Verb Suffix

The following table lists the tense form for neuter pronoun.

Verb Root	Past Tense Verb Stem	Past Tense Neuter Pronoun	Present Tense Neuter Pronoun	Future Tense Neuter Pronoun
1a பெய்	Root + த் பெய்த்	Past Tense Stem + உச்சு or உது பெய்துச்சு	Root + உது பெய்யுது	Root + உ((ம்)) பெய்யு((ம்))
1b கொல்	ல் → ன்ற கொன்ற	கொன்றுச்சு	கொல்லுது	கொல்லு(ம்)
1c ஆள்	ள் → ண்ட் ஆண்ட்	ஆண்டுச்சு	ஆளுது	ஆளு(ம்)
2 வாழ்	Root + ந்த் வாழ்ந்த்	வாழ்ந்துச்சு	வாழுது	வாழு(ம்)
3 ஓடு	Root + ன் ஓடுன்	Root + ச்சு ஓடுச்சு	ஓடுது	ஓடு(ம்)
4a பெறு	று → த்த் பெத்த்	Past Tense Stem + உச்சு or உது பெத்துச்சு	பெறுது	பெறு(ம்)
4b சுடு	டு → ட்ட் சுட்ட்	சுட்டுச்சு	சுடுது	சுடு(ம்)
5 தின்	Irregular	தின்னுச்சு	தின்னுது	தின்னு(ம்)
6 கடி	Root + ச்ச் கடிச்ச்	கடிச்சுச்சு	Root + க்குது கடிக்குது	Root + க்கு(ம் கடிக்கு(ம்)
7 நட	Root + ந்த் நடந்த்	நடந்துச்சு	நடக்குது	நடக்கு(ம்)

Pattern. We can recognize some verb classes based on their root endings. Class 1b verb ends in ல், Class 1c verb ends in ள், Class 3 verb ends in உ (also compound letters with vowel உ eg. டு), Class 4a verb ends in று, Class 4b verb ends in டு, Class 7 verb usually has only two letters and ends in அ or compound letter containing அ.

The points listed below will explain the important aspects of the neuter pronoun suffix table.

1. We have a separate table for neuter pronouns because the way they are designed is completely different from "Person" pronouns.

2. The below table shows the Nominative case neuter pronoun. You should use the Neuter Pronoun verb suffix table for these neuter pronouns.

	Singular		Plural	
	Nominative	Suffix	Nominative	Suffix
Third person	அது (that) இது (this)	You should use the suffix as per the Neuter Pronoun verb suffix table	அதுங்க (those) இதுங்க (these)	You should use the suffix as per the Neuter Pronoun verb suffix table ,also add the suffix -ங்க (ngga) to it

Examples:

Verb: கடி (kadi) (to bite)

e.g. இது கடிக்குது (idhu kadikkudhu) (this is biting)

அது கடிக்குது (adhu kadikkudhu) (that is biting)

இதுங்க கடிக்குதுங்க (idhungga kadikkudhungga) (these are biting)

அதுங்க கடிக்குதுங்க (adhungga kadikkudhungga) (those are biting)

Note:

As you see in the above example, for the plural form all I did was add -ங்க (ngga) to the pronoun and verb conjugation.

3. We don't have a separate verb suffix for the Neuter pronoun; it is infused together with the tense.

Example:

Verb: ஓடு (oodu) (to run)

அது ஓடுது (adhu oodudhu) - It is running or that is running

அது ஓடு(ம்) (adhu oodu(m)) - it will run or that will run

அது ஓடுச்சு (adhu ooduchchu) - it ran or that ran

In the above example, I added one suffix to the verb root. This suffix includes the tense and verb suffix as well

4. Present Tense Neuter Pronoun: This Neuter Present tense is simple; it has only 2 suffixes, -உது (udhu) for weak verbs and -க்குது (kkudhu) for strong verbs.

Future Tense Neuter Pronoun: This Neuter Future tense is simple; it has only 2 suffixes, -உ(ம்) (u(m)) for weak verbs and –க்கு(ம்) (kku(m)) for strong verbs.

Past Tense Neuter Pronoun: This Neuter Future tense is also simple if you remember the Past tense stem, For the Past tense neuter you can add either the suffix உச்சு (uchchu) or உது (udhu) to the Past tense stem of the verb root from all classes except class 3. For class 3 verbs, add the suffix ச்சு (chchu) to the verb root.

5. While adding the root with neuter pronoun suffix or past tense stem with neuter pronoun suffix, you would have noticed that the letter உ (u) is getting infused; for some, it doesn't.

Example:

a) பெய் (pey) (to rain) + ய் (y) + உது (udhu) = பெய்யுது (peyyudhu) (it rains)

Here the உ (u) and ய் (y) combine together and you get the compound letter யு (yu).

b) ஓடு (oodu) (to run) + உது (udhu) = ஓடுது (oodudhu) (it runs)

Here we already have a compound letter டு and the base consonant of டு is ட். We combine the base consonant ட் with உ, and then we get the compound letter டு. This is how we formed ஓடுது (odudhu).

Note:

Always remember that nothing will change when the ending of a word has the same vowel as the beginning of the suffix that is to be combined with the word. All the verbs which belong to classes 1-4 either end with pure consonants like ய் or a compound letter that has the vowel உ in it like டு. In this case, all you have to do is when you see a pure consonant, then form a compound letter by combining it with the vowel உ. If it is a compound letter like டு which already has the vowel உ in it, then you can ignore the உ.

EXERCISES:

G) Fill in the blanks with the right verb conjugation in all three tenses for the pronoun அது (adhu) (that).

Example: அது _____ (நினை) (to think)

அது நினெக்குது (adhu ninekkudhu) (it is thinking); அது நினெச்சுச்சு (adhu ninechchuchchu) (It thought); அது நினெக்கு(ம்) (adhu ninekku(m)) (It will think)

Verb	Past tense	Present Tense	Future Tense
1. ஓடு	அது_____	அது_____	அது_____
2. குடி	அது_____	அது_____	அது_____
3. பாடு	அது_____	அது_____	அது_____
4. பேசு	அது_____	அது_____	அது_____
5. செய்	அது_____	அது_____	அது_____
6. பிடி	அது_____	அது_____	அது_____
7. படி	அது_____	அது_____	அது_____
8. கடி	அது_____	அது_____	அது_____
9. தொடு	அது_____	அது_____	அது_____
10. மற	அது_____	அது_____	அது_____

H) You will be provided with a series of examples of verbs in Past, Present and Future Tense for all pronouns, At the end of each example you will be provided with a verb similar to the example and you will have conjugate that verb as per the example.

The format is: Verb Root + Tense marker (suffix) + Verb suffix

Example: Verb: எடு (edu) (To take)

நா(ன்) (naa(n)) (I) எடு (edu) + ப்ப் (pp) (future tense marker) + எ (e) = எடுப்பெ (eduppe)

Note:

> You can fill in the blanks with either Tamil script or Transliteration of the same.

Past Tense Example:

The range of suffixes used in the past tense is large, as each class has its own tense suffix.

The below table is with Class 3 regular weak verb ஓடு (oodu) in past tense.

Verb root	Past Tense Suffix	Verb Suffix	Suffix combination with verb root	Past Tense	English Translation
ஓடு	-ன்-	-எ	ஓடு+ன்+எ	நா(ன்) ஓடுனெ	I ran
ஓடு	-ன்-	-எ	ஓடு+ன்+எ	நீ ஓடுனெ	you ran (informal)
ஓடு	-ன்-	-ஈங்க(ள்)	ஓடு+ன்+ஈங்க(ள்)	நீங்க(ள்) ஓடுனீங்க(ள்)	you ran (formal)
ஓடு	-ன்-	-ஓ(ம்)	ஓடு+ன்+ஓ(ம்)	நாம/நாங்க(ள்) ஓடுனோ(ம்)	we ran (Incl/Excl)
ஓடு	-ன்-	-ஆ(ன்)	ஓடு+ன்+ஆன்	அவ(ன்) ஓடுனா(ன்)	he ran (informal)
ஓடு	-ன்-	-ஆரு	ஓடு+ன்+ஆரு	அவரு ஓடுனாரு	he ran (formal)
ஓடு	-ன்-	-ஆ(ள்)	ஓடு+ன்+ஆள்	அவ(ள்) ஓடுனா(ள்)	she ran (informal)
ஓடு	-ன்-	-ஆங்க(ள்)	ஓடு+ன்+ஆங்க(ள்)	அவங்க(ள்) ஓடுனாங்க(ள்)	she / they ran
ஓடு		-ச்சு	ஓடு+ச்சு	அது ஓடுச்சு	it ran
ஓடு		-ச்சுங்க	ஓடு+ச்சுங்க	அதுங்க ஓடுச்சுங்க	those ran

1. Verb: ஓட்டு (oottu) (to drive) (Past) (Class 3)

Example: I drove = நா(ன்)ஒட்டுனெ (naa(n) oottune)

I drove	=	
You drove (informal/impolite)	=	
You drove (formal/polite)	=	
We drove (incl/excl)	=	
He drove (informal/impolite)	=	
He drove (formal/polite)	=	
She drove (informal/impolite)	=	
She drove (formal) / they drove	=	
It drove	=	
Those drove	=	

2. Verb: காட்டு (kaattu) (to show) (Past) (Class 3)

I showed	=	
You showed (informal/impolite)	=	
You showed (formal/polite)	=	
We showed (incl/excl)	=	
He showed (informal/impolite)	=	
He showed (formal/polite)	=	
She showed (informal/impolite)	=	
She showed (formal) / they showed	=	
It showed	=	
Those showed	=	

The below table with Class 6 regular strong verb குடி (kudi) in Past tense.

Verb root	Past Tense Suffix	Verb Suffix	Suffix combination with verb root	Past Tense	English Translation
குடி	-ச்ச்-	-எ	குடி+ச்ச்+எ	நா(ன்) குடிச்செ	I drank
குடி	-ச்ச்-	-எ	குடி+ச்ச்+எ	நீ குடிச்செ	you drank (informal)
குடி	-ச்ச்-	-ஈங்க(ள்)	குடி+ச்ச்+ஈங்க(ள்)	நீங்க(ள்) குடிச்சீங்க(ள்)	you drank (formal)
குடி	-ச்ச்-	-ஓ(ம்)	குடி+ச்ச்+ஓ(ம்)	நாம/நாங்க(ள்) குடிச்சோ(ம்)	we drank (Incl/Excl)
குடி	-ச்ச்-	-ஆ(ன்)	குடி+ச்ச்+ஆன்	அவ(ன்) குடிச்சா(ன்)	he drank (informal)
குடி	-ச்ச்-	-ஆரு	குடி+ச்ச்+ஆரு	அவரு குடிச்சாரு	he drank (formal)
குடி	-ச்ச்-	-ஆ(ள்)	குடி+ச்ச்+ஆள்	அவ(ள்) குடிச்சா(ள்)	she drank (informal/)
குடி	-ச்ச்-	ஆங்க(ள்)	குடி+ச்ச்+ஆங்க(ள்)	அவங்க(ள்) குடிச்சாங்க(ள்)	she drank (formal) / they drank
குடி	Past Tense Stem + உச்சு or உது	குடிச்ச் + உச்சு குடிச்ச் + உது	அது குடிச்சுச்சு (or) அது குடிச்சுது	it drank
குடி	Past Tense Stem + உச்சுங்க or உதுங்க	குடிச்ச் + உச்சுங்க குடிச்ச் + உதுங்க	அதுங்க குடிச்சுச்சுங்க அதுங்க குடிச்சுதுங்க	those drank

Present Tense Example:

There are only two suffixes which are used in present tense so it is easy to remember and use.

The below table with Class 3 regular weak verb ஓடு (oodu) in Present tense.

Verb root	Present Tense Suffix	Verb Suffix	Suffix combination with verb root	Present Tense	English Translation
ஓடு	-ற்-	-எ	ஓடு+ற்+எ	நா(ன்) ஓடுறெ	I am running
ஓடு	-ற்-	-எ	ஓடு+ற்+எ	நீ ஓடுறெ	you are running (informal)
ஓடு	-ற்-	-ஈங்க(ள்)	ஓடு+ற்+ஈங்க(ள்)	நீங்க(ள்) ஓடுறீங்க(ள்)	you are running (formal)
ஓடு	-ற்-	-ஒ(ம்)	ஓடு+ற்+ஒ(ம்)	நாம/நாங்க(ள்) ஓடுறோ(ம்)	we are running (Incl/Excl)
ஓடு	-ற்-	-ஆ(ன்)	ஓடு+ற்+ஆ(ன்)	அவ(ன்) ஓடுறா(ன்)	he is running (informal)
ஓடு	-ற்-	-ஆரு	ஓடு+ற்+ஆரு	அவரு ஓடுறாரு	he is running (formal)
ஓடு	-ற்-	-ஆ(ள்)	ஓடு+ற்+ஆ(ள்)	அவ(ள்) ஓடுறா(ள்)	she is running (informal)
ஓடு	-ற்-	ஆங்க(ள்)	ஓடு+ற்+ஆங்க(ள்)	அவங்க(ள்) ஓடுறாங்க(ள்)	she is running (formal) / they are running
ஓடு	-உது		ஓடு+து	அது ஓடுது	it is running
ஓடு	-உதுங்க		ஓடு+துங்க	அதுங்க ஓடுதுங்க	those are running

3. Verb: நம்பு (nambu) (to believe) (Present) (Class 3)

I am believing	=	
You are believing (informal)	=	
You are believing (formal/polite)	=	
We are believing (incl/excl)	=	
He is believing (informal/impolite)	=	
He is believing (formal/polite)	=	
She is believing (informal/impolite)	=	
She is believing (formal) / they are believing	=	
It is believing	=	
Those are believing	=	

4. Verb: உடை (udai) (to break) (Present) (Class 6), The example for உடை is given in the below table for குடி (kudi), please reference to that table before you do this one.

I am breaking	=	
You are breaking (informal/impolite)	=	
You are breaking (formal/polite)	=	
We are breaking (incl/excl)	=	
He is breaking (informal/impolite)	=	
He is breaking (formal/polite)	=	
She is breaking (informal/impolite)	=	
She is breaking (formal) / they are breaking	=	
It is breaking	—	
Those are breaking	=	

The below table with Class 6 regular strong verb குடி (kudi) in Present tense.

Verb root	Present Tense Suffix	Verb Suffix	Suffix combination with verb root	Present Tense	English Translation
குடி	-க்குற்-	-எ	குடி+க்குற்+எ	நா(ன்) குடிக்குறெ	I am drinking
குடி	-க்குற்-	-எ	குடி+க்குற்+எ	நீ குடிக்குறெ	you are drinking (informal)
குடி	-க்குற்-	-ஈங்க(ள்)	குடி+க்குற்+ஈங்க(ள்)	நீங்க(ள்) குடிக்குறீங்க(ள்)	you are drinking (formal)
குடி	-க்குற்-	-ஓ(ம்)	குடி+க்குற்+ஓ(ம்)	நாம/நாங்க(ள்) கு-டிக்குறோ(ம்)	we are drinking (Incl/Excl)
குடி	-க்குற்-	-ஆ(ன்)	குடி+க்குற்+ஆ(ன்)	அவ(ன்) குடிக்குறா(ன்)	he is drinking (informal)
குடி	-க்குற்-	-ஆரு	குடி+க்குற்+ஆரு	அவரு குடிக்குறாரு	he is drinking (formal/)
குடி	-க்குற்-	-ஆ(ள்)	குடி+க்குற்+ஆ(ள்)	அவ(ள்) குடிக்குறா(ள்)	she is drinking (informal)
குடி	-க்குற்-	ஆங்க(ள்)	குடி+க்குற்+ஆங்க(ள்)	அவங்க(ள்) குடிக்குறாங்க(ள்)	she is drinking (formal) / they are drinking
குடி	-க்குது		குடி+க்குது	அது குடிக்குது	it is drinking
குடி	-க்குதுங்க		குடி+க்குதுங்க	அதுங்க குடிக்குதுங்க	those are drinking

Future Tense Example:

There are only two suffixes which are used in the future tense so it is easy to remember.
The below table with Class 3 regular weak verb ஓடு (oodu) in Future tense.

Verb root	Future Tense Suffix	Verb Suffix	Suffix combination with verb root	Future Tense	English Translation
ஓடு	-வ்-	-எ	ஓடு+வ்+எ	நா(ன்) ஓடுவெ	I will run
ஓடு	-வ்-	-எ	ஓடு+வ்+எ	நீ ஓடுவெ	you will run (informal)
ஓடு	-வ்-	-ஈங்க(ள்)	ஓடு+வ்+ஈங்க(ள்)	நீங்க(ள்) ஓடுவீங்க(ள்)	you will run (formal)
ஓடு	-வ்-	-ஒ(ம்)	ஓடு+வ்+ஒ(ம்)	நாம/நாங்க(ள்) ஓடுவோ(ம்)	we will run (Incl/Excl)
ஓடு	-வ்-	-ஆ(ன்)	ஓடு+வ்+ஆ(ன்)	அவ(ன்) ஓடுவா(ன்)	he will run (informal)
ஓடு	-வ்-	-ஆரு	ஓடு+வ்+ஆரு	அவரு ஓடுவாரு	he will run (formal)
ஓடு	-வ்-	-ஆ(ள்)	ஓடு+வ்+ஆ(ள்)	அவ(ள்) ஓடுவா(ள்)	she will run (informal)
ஓடு	-வ்-	ஆங்க(ள்)	ஓடு+வ்+ஆங்க(ள்)	அவங்க(ள்) ஓடுவாங்க(ள்)	she will run (formal) / they will run
ஓடு	-உ(ம்)		ஓடு+உ(ம்)	அது ஓடு(ம்)	it will run
ஓடு	-உம்ங்க		ஓடு+உம்ங்க	அதுங்க ஓடும்ங்க	those will run

5. Verb: தேடு (theedu) (to search) (Future) (Class 3)

I will search	=	
You will search (informal/impolite)	=	
You will search (formal/polite)	=	
We will search (incl/excl)	=	
He will search (informal/impolite)	=	
He will search (formal/polite)	=	
She will search (informal/impolite)	=	
She will search (formal) / they will search	=	
It will search	=	
Those will search	=	

6. Verb: சமை/சமெ (samai/same) (to cook) (Future) (Class 6) The example for சமை is given in the below table for குடி (kudi), please reference to that table before you do this one.

I will cook	=	
You will cook (informal/impolite)	=	
You will cook (formal/polite)	=	
We will cook (incl/excl)	=	
He will cook (informal/impolite)	=	
He will cook (formal/polite)	=	
She will cook (informal/impolite)	=	
She will cook (formal) / they will cook	=	
It will cook	=	
Those will cook	=	

The below table with Class 6 regular strong verb குடி (kudi) in Future tense.

Verb root	Future Tense Suffix	Verb Suffix	Suffix combination with verb root	Future Tense	English Translation
குடி	-ப்ப்-	-எ	குடி+ப்ப்+எ	நா(ன்) குடிப்பெ	I will drink
குடி	-ப்ப்-	-எ	குடி+ப்ப்+எ	நீ குடிப்பெ	you will drink (informal)
குடி	-ப்ப்-	-ஈங்க(ள்)	குடி+ப்ப்+ஈங்க(ள்)	நீங்க(ள்) குடிப்பீங்க(ள்)	you will drink (formal)
குடி	-ப்ப்-	-ஓ(ம்)	குடி+ப்ப்+ஓ(ம்)	நாம/நாங்க(ள்) குடிப்போ(ம்)	we will drink (Incl/Excl)
குடி	-ப்ப்-	-ஆ(ன்)	குடி+ப்ப்+ஆ(ன்)	அவ(ன்) குடிப்பா(ன்)	he will drink (informal)
குடி	-ப்ப்-	-ஆரு	குடி+ப்ப்+ஆரு	அவரு குடிப்பாரு	he will drink (formal)
குடி	-ப்ப்-	-ஆ(ள்)	குடி+ப்ப்+ஆ(ள்)	அவ(ள்) குடிப்பா(ள்)	she will drink (informal)
குடி	-ப்ப்-	ஆங்க(ள்)	குடி+ப்ப்+ஆங்க(ள்)	அவங்க(ள்) குடிப்பாங்க(ள்)	she will drink (formal) / they will drink
குடி	-க்கு(ம்)		குடி+க்கு(ம்)	அது குடிக்கு(ம்)	they will drink
குடி	-க்கும்ங்க		குடி+க்கும்ங்க	அதுங்க குடிக்கும்ங்க	those will drink

The below table is transliteration for the verb ஓடு (oodu) in Past, Present and Future Tense.

ஓடு (oodu) (to run)		
Past Tense	**Present Tense**	**Future Tense**
நா(ன்) ஓடுனெ (naa(n) oodune)	நா(ன்) ஓடுறெ (naa(n) ooduRe)	நா(ன்) ஓடுவெ (naa(n) ooduve)
நீ ஓடுனெ (nii oodune)	நீ ஓடுறெ (nii ooduRe)	நீ ஓடுவெ (nii ooduve)
நீங்க(ள்) ஓடுனீங்க(ள்) (niinga(L) ooduniingga(L))	நீங்க(ள்) ஓடுறீங்க(ள்) (niinga(L) ooduRiingga(L))	நீங்க(ள்) ஓடுவீங்க(ள்) (niinga(L) ooduviingga(L))
நாம/நாங்க(ள்) ஓடுனோ(ம்) (naama/naangga(L) oodunoo(m))	நாம/நாங்க(ள்) ஓடுறோ(ம்) (naama/naangga(L) ooduRoo(m))	நாம/நாங்க(ள்) ஓடுவோ(ம்) (naama/naangga(L) ooduvoo(m))
அவ(ன்) ஓடுனா(ன்) (ava(n) oodunaa(n))	அவ(ன்) ஓடுறா(ன்) (ava(n) ooduRaa(n))	அவ(ன்) ஓடுவா(ன்) (ava(n) ooduvaa(n))
அவரு ஓடுனாரு (avaru oodunaaru)	அவரு ஓடுறாரு (avaru ooduRaaru)	அவரு ஓடுவாரு (avaru ooduvaaru)
அவ(ள்) ஓடுனா(ள்) (ava(L) oodunaa(L))	அவ(ள்) ஓடுறா(ள்) (ava(L) ooduRaa(L))	அவ(ள்) ஓடுவா(ள்) (ava(L) ooduvaa(L))
அவங்க(ள்) ஓடுனாங்க(ள்) (avangga(L) oodunaangga(L))	அவங்க(ள்) ஓடுறாங்க(ள்) (avangga(L) ooduRaangga(L))	அவங்க(ள்) ஓடுவாங்க(ள்) (avangga(L) ooduvaangga(L))
அது ஓடுச்சு (adhu ooduchchu)	அது ஓடுது (adhu oodudhu)	அது ஓடு(ம்) (adhu oodu(m))
அதுங்க ஓடுச்சுங்க (adhungga ooduchchungga)	அதுங்க ஓடுதுங்க (adhungga oodudhungga)	அதுங்க ஓடும்ங்க (adhungga oodumngga)

The below table is transliteration for the verb குடி (kudi) in Past, Present and Future Tense.

குடி (kudi) (to drink)		
Past Tense	**Present Tense**	**Future Tense**
நா(ன்) குடிச்செ (naa(n) kudichche)	நா(ன்) குடிக்குறெ (naa(n) kudikkuRe)	நா(ன்) குடிப்பெ (naa(n) kudippe)
நீ குடிச்செ (nii kudichche)	நீ குடிக்குறெ (nii kudikkuRe)	நீ குடிப்பெ (nii kudippe)
நீங்க(ள்) குடிச்சீங்க(ள்) (niinga(L) kudichchiingga(L))	நீங்க(ள்) குடிக்குறீங்க(ள்) (niinga(L) kudikkuRiingga(L))	நீங்க(ள்) குடிப்பீங்க(ள்) (niinga(L) kudippiingga(L))
நாம/நாங்க(ள்) குடிச்சோ(ம்) (naama/naangga(L) kudichchoo(m))	நாம/நாங்க(ள்) குடிக்குறோ(ம்) (naama/naangga(L) kudikkuRoo(m))	நாம/நாங்க(ள்) குடிப்போ(ம்) (naama/naangga(L) kudippoo(m))
அவ(ன்) குடிச்சா(ன்) (ava(n) kudichchaa(n))	அவ(ன்) குடிக்குறா(ன்) (ava(n) kudikkuRaa(n))	அவ(ன்) குடிப்பா(ன்) (ava(n) kudippaa(n))
அவரு குடிச்சாரு (avaru kudichchaaru)	அவரு குடிக்குறாரு (avaru kudikkuRaaru)	அவரு குடிப்பாரு (avaru kudippaaru)
அவ(ள்) குடிச்சா(ள்) (ava(L) kudichchaa(L))	அவ(ள்) குடிக்குறா(ள்) (ava(L) kudikkuRaa(L))	அவ(ள்) குடிப்பா(ள்) (ava(L) kudippaa(L))
அவங்க(ள்) குடிச்சாங்க(ள்) (avangga(L) kudichchaangga(L))	அவங்க(ள்) குடிக்குறாங்க(ள்) (avangga(L) kudikkuRaangga(L))	அவங்க(ள்) குடிப்பாங்க(ள்) (avangga(L) kudippaangga(L))
அது குடிச்சுச்சு (adhu kudichchuchchu)	அது குடிக்குது (adhu kudikkudhu)	அது குடிக்கு(ம்) (adhu kudikku(m))
அதுங்க குடிச்சுச்சுங்க (adhungga kudichchuchchungga)	அதுங்க குடிக்குதுங்க (adhungga kudikkudhungga)	அதுங்க குடிக்கும்ங்க (adhungga kudikkumngga)

The Important Verb இரு:

As mentioned earlier, the verb இரு is very important because it represents both 'To be' and 'To have', which is the frequently used of all verbs. Please try to memorize their verb conjugation of இரு and make sentences using them as it will come very handy while forming sentences. Since, இரு is frequently used. In colloquial spoken Tamil, the verb conjugation has been made much shorter so it doesn't follow the usual Class 7 rule.

Past Tense	English	Present Tense	English
நா(ன்) இருந்தெ	i was	நா(ன்) இருக்கெ	I am
நீ இருந்தெ	you was (informal)	நீ இருக்கெ	you are (informal)
நீங்க(ள்) இருந்தீங்க(ள்)	you was (formal)	நீங்க(ள்) இருக்கீங்க(ள்)	you are (formal)
நாம/நாங்க(ள்) இருந்தோ(ம்)	we were (incl/excl)	நாம/நாங்க(ள்) இருக்கோ(ம்)	we are (Incl/Excl)
அவ(ன்) இருந்தா(ன்)	he was (informal)	அவ(ன்) இருக்கா(ன்)	he is (informal)
அவரு இருந்தாரு	he was (formal)	அவரு இருக்காரு	he is (formal)
அவ(ள்) இருந்தா(ள்)	she was (informal)	அவ(ள்) இருக்கா(ள்)	she is (informal)
அவங்க(ள்) இருந்தாங்க(ள்)	she was (formal) / they were drinking	அவங்க(ள்) இருக்காங்க(ள்)	she is (formal) / they are drinking
அது இருந்துச்சு	that was drinking	அது இருக்குது	that is drinking (it)

Future Tense	English	Future Tense	English
நா(ன்) இருப்பெ	I will	அவ(ள்) இருப்பா(ள்)	she will (informal)
நீ இருப்பெ	you will (informal)	நாம/நாங்க(ள்) இருப்போ(ம்)	we will (Incl/Excl)
நீங்க(ள்) இருப்பிங்க(ள்)	you will (formal)	அவங்க(ள்) இருப்பாங்க(ள்)	she will (formal) / they will drink
அவ(ன்) இருப்பா(ன்)	he will (informal)	அது இருக்கு(ம்)	that will drink (it)
அவரு இருப்பாரு	he will (formal)		

Word Order in Tamil:

The standard word order in a sentence in Tamil is "Subject Object Verb" (SOV), which is opposite to the word order in English (SVO). There may be some sentences in Tamil where the word order is different, but it doesn't matter because in Tamil you have greater flexibility towards word order. You have all the freedom to change the word order to some extent.

In English, you don't have such freedom. You always have to follow the rule "Subject Verb Object"; otherwise, the whole sentence will be meaningless. But in Tamil, you can move them around. Most of the time, it will give you the same meaning. Sometimes, it may change the meaning of the sentence because while you reorder the sentences, you may give more importance to another word instead of the one you intend to.

Note:

- Not all Tamil sentences have subjects, verbs and objects.

- Word order in Tamil also has small rules like modifying words like adjectives and adverbs always precede the word they modify. However, an adverb that is not a modifier of an adjective or adverb can be reordered.

- In most Tamil sentences, the verb usually comes at the end.

Example:

a) I am in the shop. (The below two sentences mean the same in Tamil)

நா(ன்) கடைல இருக்குறெ (naa(n) kadaila irukkuRe) (lt: i am in the shop)

கடைல நா(ன்) இருக்குறெ (kadaila naa(n) irukkuRe) (lt: in the shop i am)

b) Shall we go to the shop? (The below two sentences mean the same in Tamil)

கடைக்கு போவோமா? (kadaikku poovoomaa) (lt: to the shop shall we go?)

போவோமா கடைக்கு? (poovoomaa kadaikku) (lt: shall we go to the shop)

c) When shall we go to the shop? (The below three sentences mean the same in Tamil).

கடைக்கு எப்ப போவோம்? (kadaikku eppa poovoom) (lt: to the shop when shall we go).

எப்ப போவோம் கடைக்கு? (eppa poovoom kadaikku) (lt: when shall we go to the shop).

எப்ப கடை க்கு போவோம்? (eppa kadaikku poovoom) (lit: when to the shop shall we go).

As you have seen in the above example, all of them are correct irrespective of their word order. However, as I have mentioned earlier, modifying words like adjectives and adverbs always precede the word they modify. But an adverb that is not a modifier of an adjective or adverb can be reordered.

Example:

நீ ஒரு அழகான பைய(ன்) (nii oru azhagaana paiya(n)) (you are a handsome boy) - Correct

Here அழகான (azhagaana) (handsome) is an Adjective of the noun பைய(ன்) (paiya(n)) (boy), so one should always use "அழகான பையன்" while forming a sentence, it should never change position.

நீ பையன் ஒரு அழகான - This sentence is wrong because you cannot split the adjective from the noun, hence it is wrong.

Important Note:

Verb Class Table in this chapter is simply a workaround for the indescribable weak and strong verbs because, in Tamil, a verb is considered weak or strong because they are and there is no other explanation for it.

Hence, we tried to find a pattern (like a pattern because of coincidence) and we were able to find a pattern for most of the classes and they were given in the form of a verb class table. Using this verb class table, you can figure out the present tense, past tense and future tense stem and Infinitive, Adverbial participle (AvP) of a verb. The chances of figuring it out right are approximately 70-80%, as we still have some exceptions.

It is a little difficult but present tense, past tense and future tense stem and Infinitive, Adverbial participle (AvP) of a verb are very important as we use them while creating almost every sentence in Tamil. So, you have to understand and form them; there is no other choice.

But you can follow one of the two methods I have given below to find the right tense, infinitive, AvP.

Method 1: You can use the Verb class table I provided in this chapter.

Advantages: This method is easier and less time consuming, as all you have to do is memorize the table and remember it whenever you need to form a sentence using tenses, infinitive and AvP, and then you are good.

Drawbacks: a. Since the table works only on some approx. 70-80% of verbs, there will be some verbs where you will have to memorize them.

b. As you are memorizing the verb class table, whenever you want to form a sentence in Tamil, you come across a tense or infinitive or AvP in that sentence. You will have to look into this table to find them, this will cause dependency on the table and you will also stammer while talking in Tamil as you have to do a lot of thinking while forming a sentence.

Method 2: In the next chapter, I will provide the top 100 frequently used verbs in Tamil and their verb conjugation with all three tenses and infinitive. You have to memorize all of them, practice using them in small sentences and know them by heart.

Advantages: a. This method is very traditional and effective; it will help you to form sentences using these verbs almost instantly, as you will know them by heart.

b. Similar to the Verb class table, all verbs have a pattern and that's how Tamil native speakers remember the tense stem and infinitive. Once you memorize these 100 Verbs and use them in sentences, you will be able to predict verbs that are not available in the 100 verbs list you have memorized.

Drawbacks: Time consuming.

Note:

> As a Tamil tutor, I recommend you go for method two. I know it's a lot of time- consuming, but it is the best way and will help you a lot to speak Tamil in the long run, but it's up to you. You can choose whichever method you feel comfortable with.

The Exceptional Verb வா:

The frequently used Class 2 verb வா (vaa) (to come) is an irregular verb when it comes to its base form, whereas the tense marker (suffix) follows the standard rule as per the verb class table.

The Verb root for each tense is given below; it is the same for both "person" and "neuter" pronouns.

Past tense verb root: வ (va)

Present tense verb root: வர் (var)

Future tense verb root: வரு (varu)

Example:

Past tense: வ (va) (verb root) + ந்த் (ndh) (Tense marker) + எ (e) (verb suffix for நா(ன்) (naa(n))

= நா(ன்) வந்தெ (naa(n) vandhe) (I came)

Present tense. வர் (var) + ற் (R) + எ (e) = நா(ன்) வர்றெ (naa(n) varRe) (I am coming)

Future tense: வரு (varu) + வ் (v) + எ (e) = நா(ன்) வருவெ (naa(n) varuve) (I came)

EXERCISES:

I) Form a question to ask if various people are going to the cinema.

Example: அவ(ன்): அவ(ன்) சினிமாவுக்கு போவானா? (Will he go to the cinema?)

போவானா (poovaanaa) (will he go?) = போ (poo) (to go) + வ் (v) (future tense suffix) + ஆ(ன்) (aa(n)) (verb suffix for அவ(ன்)) + ஆ (aa) Interrogative suffix

1.நா(ன்)

_____?

2.நீ

_____?

3.அவரு

_____?

4.அவ(ள்)

_____?

5.அவங்க(ள்)

_____?

6. Tom

_____?

7. Mary

_____?

8. உங்க(ள்) அப்பா (appa) (father)

_____?

9. எங்க(ள்) பேராசிரியர் (peeraasiriyar) (professor)

_____?

10. நாம

_____?

J) Form a question using the question words given below and conjugating the verb using tense marker and verb suffix.

Question word	Translation	Question word	Translation
என்ன (enna)	What?	எது (edhu)	Which (noun)?
ஏன் (eena)	Why?	எந்த (endha)	Which (adj)?
ஏது (eedhu)	How did you get?	எப்படி (eppadi)	How?
யாரு (yaaru)	Who?	எத்தன (eththana)	How many?
எப்போ (eppoo)	When?	எவ்வளவு (evLavu) How much?	
-ஆ - Interrogative suffix.		எங்கெ (engge)	Where?

Note:

You have multiple choices to form a question, try all of them. Hints are given next to every question to help you.

Example:

அவ(ன்) கல்லூரிக்கு _____ _____ (போ) (present)?

அவ(ன்) கல்லூரிக்கு ஏன் போறா(ன்)? (Why is he going to the college).

அவ(ன்) கல்லூரிக்கு எப்ப போறா(ன்)? (When is he going to the college).

அவ(ன்) கல்லூரிக்கு எப்படி போறா(ன்)? (How is he going to the college).

Note:

As you see in the above i am able to provide only 3 possible question because if i use any other question word in that sentence then the sentence wouldn't make any sense, similar to this for the below you should try to fill in the blanks using multiple possible questions, The first blank space (_____) is for question word and the second blank space is for verb conjugation, if there is only one blank space then it means you should use interrogative suffix.

1. நீ _____ _____ (இரு) (iru) (to be) (present tense)?

2. நீ _____ _____ (போ) (poo) (to go) (verb present tense)?

3. நீ _____ _____ (பன்னு) (pannu) (to do) (present tense)?

4. அவ(ன்) Ticket _____ (வாங்கு) (vaangu) (to buy) (future tense)?

Hint: use the Interrogative suffix to make it as a question.

5. அவ(ள்) _____ (போ)? (Past tense) (Interrogative suffix).

6. அவ(ள்) _____ (போ)? (Future tense) (Interrogative suffix).

7. _____ பேர் (peer) (people) _____ (வரு) (varu) (to come) (future tense)?

8. _____ பேர் (peer) _____ (வ) (va) (to come) (past tense)?

9. _____ வண்டிக(ள்) (vaNdigaL) (vehicles) _____ (வர்) (var) (to come)

(present)?

10. _____ வண்டிக(ள்) _____ (வரு) (var) (to come) (future)?

11. அவ(ன்) _____ (வாங்கு) (present tense)?

12. நீ _____ (பன்னு) (present tense)?

SOLUTIONS

Lesson 7

Exercise A

1) e; 2) g; 3) a; 4) b; 5) c; 6) d; 7) f.

Exercise B

1) b; 2) a; 3) b; 4) b; 5) a; 6) a; 7) c.

Exercise C

1. Verb: எடு (edu) (to take) (future)

எடுப்பெ	eduppe
எடுப்பெ	eduppe
எடுப்பீங்க(ள்)	eduppiingga(L)
எடுப்பா(ன்)	eduppaa(n)
எடுப்பாரு	eduppaaru
எடுப்பா(ள்)	eduppaa(L)
எடுப்பாங்க(ள்)	eduppaangga(L)
எடுப்போ(ம்)	eduppoo(m)

2. Verb: எடு (edu) (to take) (past)

எடுத்தெ	eduththe
எடுத்தெ	eduththe
எடுத்தீங்க(ள்)	eduththiingga(L)
எடுத்தா(ன்)	eduththaa(n)
எடுத்தாரு	eduththaaru
எடுத்தா(ள்)	eduththaa(L)
எடுத்தாங்க(ள்)	eduththaangga(L)

எடுத்தோ(ம்)	eduththoo(m)

3. Verb: எடு (edu) (to take) (present)

எடுக்குறெ	edukkuRe
எடுக்குறெ	edukkuRe
எடுக்குறீங்க(ள்)	edukkuRiingga(L)
எடுக்குறா(ன்)	edukkuRaa(n)
எடுக்குறாரு	edukkuRaaru
எடுக்கிறா(ள்)	edukkuRaa(L)
எடுக்குறாங்க(ள்)	edukkuRaangga(L)
எடுக்குறோ(ம்)	edukkuRoo(m)

4. Verb: நினை/நினெ (ninai/nine) (to think) (future)

நினெப்பெ	nineppe
நினெப்பெ	nineppe
நினெப்பீங்க(ள்)	nineppiingga(L)
நினெப்பா(ன்)	nineppaa(n)
நினெப்பாரு	nineppaaru
நினெப்பா(ள்)	nineppaa(L)
நினெப்பாங்கள்	nineppaanggaL
நினெப்போ(ம்)	nineppoo(m)

5. Verb: நினை/நினெ (ninai/nine) (to think); (present)

நினெக்குறெ	ninekkuRe
நினெக்குறெ	ninekkuRe
நினெக்குறீங்க(ள்)	ninekkuRiingga(L)
நினெக்கிறா(ன்)	ninekkuRaa(n)
நினெக்குறாரு	ninekkuRaaru
நினெக்கிறா(ள்)	ninekkuRaa(L)

| நினைக்குறாங்க(ள்) | ninekkuRaangga(L) |
| நினைக்கிறோ(ம்) | ninekkuRoo(m) |

6. Verb: நினை/நினெ (ninai/nine) (to think); (past)

நினெச்செ	ninechche
நினெச்செ	ninechche
நினெச்சீங்க(ள்)	ninechchiingga(L)
நினெச்சா(ன்)	ninechchaa(n)
நினெச்சாரு	ninechchaaru
நினெச்சா(ள்)	ninechchaa(L)
நினெச்சாங்க(ள்)	ninechchaangga(L)
நினெச்சோ(ம்)	ninechchoo(m)

7. Verb: உக்கார் (utkaar) (to sit); (past)

உக்கார்ந்தெ	ukkaarndhe
உக்கார்ந்தெ	ukkaarndhe
உக்கார்ந்தீங்க(ள்)	ukkaarndhiingga(L)
உக்கார்ந்தா(ன்)	ukkaarndhaa(n)
உக்கார்ந்தாரு	ukkaarndhaaru
உக்கார்ந்தா(ள்)	ukkaarndhaa(L)
உக்கார்ந்தாங்க(ள்)	ukkaarndhaangga(L)
உக்கார்ந்தோ(ம்)	ukkaarndhoo(m)

8. Verb: உக்கார் (utkaar) (to sit); (present)

உக்கார்றெ	ukkaarRe
உக்கார்றெ	ukkaarRe
உக்கார்ற்ங்க(ள்)	ukkaarRiingga(L)
உக்கார்றா(ன்)	ukkaarRaa(n)
உக்கார்றாரு	ukkaarRaaru

உக்கார்றா(ள்)	ukkaarRaa(L)
உக்கார்றாங்க(ள்)	ukkaarRaangga(L)
உக்கார்றோ(ம்)	ukkaarRoo(m)

9. Verb: உக்கார் (utkaar) (to sit); (future)

உக்கார்வெ	ukkaarve
உக்கார்வெ	ukkaarve
உக்கார்வீங்க(ள்)	ukkaarviingga(L)
உக்கார்வா(ன்)	ukkaarvaa(n)
உக்கார்வாரு	ukkaarvaaru
உக்கார்வா(ள்)	ukkaarvaa(L)
உக்கார்வாங்க(ள்)	ukkaarvaangga(L)
உக்கார்வோ(ம்)	ukkaarvoo(m)

Exercise D

Verb	Past tense	Present Tense	Future Tense
1. ஓடு	நா(ன்) ஓடுனெ	நா(ன்) ஓடுறெ	நா(ன்) ஓடுவெ
2. குடி	நா(ன்) குடிச்செ	நா(ன்) குடிக்குறெ	நா(ன்) குடிப்பெ
3. பாடு	நா(ன்) பாடுனெ	நா(ன்) பாடுறெ	நா(ன்) பாடுவெ
4. பேசு	நா(ன்) பேசுனெ	நா(ன்) பேசுறெ	நா(ன்) பேசவெ
5 செய்	நா(ன்) செய்தெ	நா(ன்) செய்றெ	நா(ன்) செய்வெ
6. பிடி	நா(ன்) பிடிச்செ	நா(ன்) பிடிக்குறெ	நா(ன்) பிடிப்பெ
7. படி	நா(ன்) படிச்செ	நா(ன்) படிக்குறெ	நா(ன்) படிப்பெ
8. கடி	நா(ன்) கடிச்செ	நா(ன்) கடிக்குறெ	நா(ன்) கடிப்பெ
9. தொடு	நா(ன்) தொட்டெ	நா(ன்) தொடுறெ	நா(ன்) தொடுவெ
10. மற	நா(ன்) மறந்தெ	நா(ன்) மறக்குறெ	நா(ன்) மறப்பெ

TL:

Verb	Past tense	Present Tense	Future Tense
1. oodu	<u>n</u>aa(n) oodune	<u>n</u>aa(n) ooduRe	<u>n</u>aa(n) ooduve
2. kudi	<u>n</u>aa(n) kudichche	<u>n</u>aa(n) kudikkuRe	<u>n</u>aa(n) kudippe
3. paadu	<u>n</u>aa(n) paadune	<u>n</u>aa(n) paaduRe	<u>n</u>aa(n) paaduve
4. peesu	<u>n</u>aa(n) peesune	<u>n</u>aa(n) peesuRe	<u>n</u>aa(n) peesuve
5 sey	<u>n</u>aa(n) seydhe	<u>n</u>aa(n) seyRe	<u>n</u>aa(n) seyve
6. pidi	<u>n</u>aa(n) pidichche	<u>n</u>aa(n) pidikkuRe	<u>n</u>aa(n) pidippe
7. padi	<u>n</u>aa(n) padichche	<u>n</u>aa(n) padikkuRe	<u>n</u>aa(n) padippe
8. kadi	<u>n</u>aa(n) kadichche	<u>n</u>aa(n) kadikkuRe	<u>n</u>aa(n) kadippe
9. thodu	<u>n</u>aa(n) thotte	<u>n</u>aa(n) thoduRe	<u>n</u>aa(n) thoduve
10. maRa	<u>n</u>aa(n) maRandhe	<u>n</u>aa(n) maRakkuRe	<u>n</u>aa maRappe

Exercise E

1) ஒளிய. 2) வாழ. 3) விழ. 4) பூட்ட. 5) போட. 6) தெளிக்க. 7) உடைக்க. 8) மடிக்க. 9) கலக்க. 10) திறக்க.

TL: 1) oLiya. 2) vaazha. 3) vizha. 4) puutta. 5) pooda. 6) theLikka. 7) udaikka. 8) madikka. 9) kalakka. 10) thiRakka.

Exercise F

1) ஓட. 2) குடிக்க. 3) பாட. 4) பேச. 5) செய்ய. 6) பிடிக்க. 7) படிக்க. 8) கடிக்க.

TL: 1) ooda. 2) kudikka. 3) paada. 4) peesa. 5) seyya. 6) pidikka. 7) padikka. 8) kadikka.

Exercise G

Verb	Past tense	Present Tense	Future Tense
1. ஓடு	அது ஓடுச்சு	அது ஓடுது	அது ஓடு(ம்)
2. குடி	அது குடித்துச்சு	அது குடிக்குது	அது குடிக்கு(ம்)
3. பாடு	அது பாடுச்சு	அது பாடுது	அது பாடு(ம்)
4. பேசு	அது பேசுச்சு	அது பேசுது	அது பேசு(ம்)
5 செய்	அது செய்துச்சு	அது செய்யுது	அது செய்யு(ம்)

6. பிடி	அது பிடித்துச்சு	அது பிடிக்குது	அது பிடிக்கு(ம்)
7. படி	அது படித்துச்சு	அது படிக்குது	அது படிக்கு(ம்)
8. கடி	அது கடித்துச்சு	அது கடிக்குது	அது கடிக்கு(ம்)
9. தொடு	அது தொட்டுச்சு	அது தொடுது	அது தொடு(ம்)
10. மற	அது மறந்துச்சு	அது மறக்குது	அது மறக்கு(ம்)

TL:

Verb	Past tense	Present Tense	Future Tense
1. oodu	adhu ooduchchu	adhu oodudhu	adhu oodu(m)
2. kudi	adhu kudiththuchchu	adhu kudikkudhu	adhu kudikku(m)
3. paadu	adhu paduchchu	adhu paadudhu	adhu paadu(m)
4. peesu	adhu pesuchchu	adhu peesudhu	adhu peesu(m)
5 sey	adhu seydhuchchu	adhu seyyudhu	adhu seyyu(m)
6. pidi	adhu pidiththuchchu	adhu pidikkudhu	adhu pidikku(m)
7. padi	adhu padiththuchchu	adhu padikkudhu	adhu padikku(m)
8. kadi	adhu kadiththuchchu	adhu kadikkudhu	adhu kadikku(m)
9. thodu	adhu thottuchchu	adhu thodudhu	adhu thodu(m)
10. maRa	adhu maRandhuchchu	adhu marakkudhu	adhu marakku(m)

Exercise H

1. Verb: ஓட்டு (oottu) (to drive) (Past) (Class 3)

I drove	=	நா(ன்) ஓட்டுனெ
You drove (informal/impolite)	=	நீ ஓட்டுனெ
You drove (formal/polite)	=	நீங்க(ள்) ஓட்டுனீங்க(ள்)
We drove (incl/excl)	=	நாம/நாங்க(ள்) ஓட்டுனோ(ம்)
He drove (informal/impolite)	=	அவ(ன்) ஓட்டுனா(ன்)
He drove (formal/polite)	=	அவரு ஓட்டுனாரு
She drove (informal/impolite)	=	அவ(ள்) ஓட்டுனா(ள்)

| She drove (formal) / they drove | = | அவங்க(ள்) ஓட்டுனாங்க(ள்) |
| It drove | = | அது ஓட்டுச்சு |

2. Verb: காட்டு (kaattu) (to show) (Past) (Class 3)

I showed	=	நா(ன்) காட்டுனெ
You showed (informal/impolite)	=	நீ காட்டுனெ
You showed (formal/polite)	=	நீங்க(ள்) காட்டுனீங்க(ள்)
We showed (incl/excl)	=	நாம/நாங்க(ள்) காட்டுனோ(ம்)
He showed (informal/impolite)	=	அவ(ன்) காட்டுனா(ன்)
He showed (formal/polite)	=	அவரு காட்டுனாரு
She showed (informal/impolite)	=	அவ(ள்) காட்டுனா(ள்)
She showed (formal) / they showed	=	அவங்க(ள்) காட்டுனாங்க(ள்)
It showed	=	அது காட்டுச்சு
Those showed	=	அது காட்டுச்சுங்க

3. Verb: நம்பு (nambu) (to believe) (Present) (Class 3)

I am believing	=	நா(ன்) நம்புறெ
You are believing (informal)	=	நீ நம்புறெ
You are believing (formal/polite)	=	நீங்க(ள்) நம்புறீங்க(ள்)
We are believing (incl/excl)	=	நாம/நாங்க(ள்) நம்புறோ(ம்)
He is believing (informal/impolite)	=	அவ(ன்) நம்புறா(ன்)
He is believing (formal/polite)	=	அவரு நம்புறாரு
She is believing (informal/impolite)	=	அவ(ள்) நம்புறா(ள்)
She is believing (formal) / they are believing	=	அவங்க(ள்) நம்புறாங்க(ள்)
It is believing	=	அது நம்புது

Those are believing	=	அதுங்க நம்புதுங்க

4. Verb: உடை (udai) (to break) (Present) (Class 6)

I am breaking	=	நா(ன்) உடைக்குறெ
You are breaking (informal/impolite)	=	நீ உடைக்குறெ
You are breaking (formal/polite)	=	நீங்க(ள்) உடைக்குறீங்க(ள்)
We are breaking (incl/excl)	=	நாம/நாங்க(ள்) உடைக்குறோ(ம்)
He is breaking (informal/impolite)	=	அவ(ன்) உடைக்குறா(ன்)
He is breaking (formal/polite)	=	அவரு உடைக்குறாரு
She is breaking (informal/impolite)	=	அவ(ள்) உடைக்குறா(ள்)
She is breaking (formal) / they are breaking	=	அவங்க(ள்) உடைக்குறாங்க(ள்)
It is breaking	=	அது உடைக்குது
Those are breaking	=	அதுங்க உடைக்குதுங்க

5. Verb: தேடு (theedu) (to search) (Future) (Class 3)

I will search	=	நா(ன்) தேடுவெ
You will search (informal/impolite)	=	நீ தேடுவெ
You will search (formal/polite)	=	நீங்க(ள்) தேடுவீங்க(ள்)
We will search (incl/excl)	=	நாம/நாங்க(ள்) தேடுவோ(ம்)
He will search (informal/impolite)	=	அவ(ன்) தேடுவா(ன்)
He will search (formal/polite)	=	அவரு தேடுவாரு
She will search (informal/impolite)	=	அவ(ள்) தேடுவா(ள்)
She will search (formal) / they will search	=	அவங்க(ள்) தேடுவாங்க(ள்)
It will search	=	அது தேடு(ம்)

6. Verb: சமை/சமெ (samai/same) (to cook) (Future) (Class 6)

I will cook	=	நா(ன்) சமெப்பெ
You will cook (informal/impolite)	=	நீ சமெப்பெ
You will cook (formal/polite)	=	நீங்க(ள்) சமெப்பீங்க(ள்)
We will cook (incl/excl)	=	நாம/நாங்க(ள்) சமெப்போம்(ம்)
He will cook (informal/impolite)	=	அவ(ன்) சமெப்பா(ன்)
He will cook (formal/polite)	=	அவரு சமெப்பாரு
She will cook (informal/impolite)	=	அவ(ள்) சமெப்பா(ள்)
She will cook (formal) / they will cook	=	அவங்க(ள்) சமெப்பாங்க(ள்)
It will cook	=	அது சமெக்கு(ம்)
Those will cook	=	அதுங்க சமெக்கும்ங்க

Exercise I

1) நா(ன்) சினிமாவுக்கு போவேனா? 2) நீ சினிமாவுக்கு போவியா? 3) அவரு சினிமாவுக்கு போவாரா? 4) அவ(ள்) சினிமாவுக்கு போவாளா? 5) அவங்க(ள்) சினிமாவுக்கு போவாங்களா? 6) Tom சினிமாவுக்கு போவானா? 7) Mary சினிமாவுக்கு போவாளா? 8) உங்க(ள்) அப்பா சினிமாவுக்கு போவாரா? 9) எங்க(ள்) பேராசிரியர் சினிமாவுக்கு போவாரா? 10) நாம சினிமாவுக்கு போவோமா?

TL: 1) naa(n) sinimaavukku pooveenaa? 2) nii sinimaavukku pooviyaa? 3) avaru sinimaavukku poovaaraa? 4) ava(L) sinimaavukku poovaaLaa? 5) avangga(L) sinimaavukku poovaanggaLaa? 6) Tom sinimaavukku poovaanaa? 7) Mary sinimaavukku poovaaLaa? 8) ungga(L) appaa sinimaavukku poovaaraa? 9) engga(L) peeraasiriyar sinimaavukku poovaaraa? 10) naama sinimaavukku poovoomaa?

Content:

- Verb classes 1 to 7

- Verb Conjugation and Infinitive of Top 100 Verbs

- Commonly Used Verb with Same meaning

- Exercises

LESSON 8: **FREQUENTLY USED TAMIL VERBS**

Like every other languages there are more than 100 verbs in Tamil. It will be difficult to memorize all of their verb conjugations. Instead of doing that, I have two simple steps for you to follow.

Step 1: Memorize the '20 frequently used Tamil verbs for conversations' table and their verb conjugation given below that table.

20 Frequently used Tamil verbs for conversations

	Tamil Verb	Transliteration (TL)	English
1	செய்	sey	To Do
2	பண்ணு	paNNu	To Do, Make
3	எழு	ezhu	To Raise, Get up
4	வா	vaa	To Come
5	ஆ / ஆகு	aa / aagu	To Become, Happen
6	பேசு	peesu	To Speak
7	போ	poo	To Go
8	வாங்கு	vaanggu	To Buy, Get
9	சொல்	sol	To Say, Tell
10	போடு	poodu	To Put, Wear
11	சாப்பிடு	saappidu	To Eat
12	எடு	edu	To Take

13	பார்	paar	To See
14	படி	padi	To Study, read
15	இரு	iru	To Be
16	தூங்கு	thuunggu	To Sleep
17	வை / வெ	vai, ve	To Put (placing something gently)
18	நினை, நினெ	ninai, nine	To Wonder, Think
19	குடு	kudu	To Give
20	கேள்	keeL	To Ask, Listen

1) செய் (sey) (To Do, Make) (Class 1)

	நா(ன்) (naa(n)) (I)	English	அது (adhu) (that) (it)	English
Past Tense	செய் + த் + எ	I did	செய்த் + உது	It did
	செய்தெ (seydhe)		செய்துது (seydhudhu)	
Present Tense	செய் + ற் + எ	I am doing	செய் + ய் + உது	It is doing
	செய்றெ (seyRe)		செய்யுது (seyyudhu)	
Future Tense	செய் + வ் + எ	I will do	செய் + ய் + உ(ம்)	It will do
	செய்வெ (seyve)		செய்யு(ம்) (seyyu(m))	
Infinitive	செய் + ய் + அ		Do, Make	
	செய்ய (seyya)			

Important Note:

1. While conjugating a verb, only the verb suffix will change depending on the pronoun, but the Tense marker (suffix) will be the same. It will not change, so I am providing the verb conjugation only for the pronoun நா(ன்) (naa(n)) (I). All you have to do for the rest of the pronoun is change the verb suffix as per the required pronoun.

Example:

நா(ன்) (naa(n)) (I) செய் (sey) + த் (th) + எ (e) (verb suffix) = நா(ன்) செய்தெ (naa(n) seydhe) (I did)

அவ(ன்) (ava(n)) (he) செய் (sey) + த் (th) + ஆ(ன்) (aa(n)) (verb suffix) = அவ(ன்) செய்தா(ன்) (ava(n) seydhaa(n)) (he did)

In the above example, I changed the verb suffix from எ (e) to ஆ(ன்) (aa(n)). The rest of the form is still the same. Similarly, you can change the verb suffix for the rest of the pronouns.

2. Detailed Explanation of the verb conjugation in the table below.

Tense	Detailed Explanation
Past Tense	செய் + த் (Past Tense Marker) + எ (Verb Suffix of நா(ன்) (I))
Present Tense	செய் + ற் (Present Tense Marker + எ (Verb Suffix of நா(ன்) (I))
Future Tense	செய் + வ் (Future Tense Marker) + எ (Verb Suffix of நா(ன்) (I))
Neuter Past Tense	செய்த் (Past tense Stem) + உது (Neuter Past Tense suffix for அது (that))
Neuter Present Tense	செய் + ய் + உது (Neuter Present Tense suffix for அது (that))
Neuter Future Tense	செய் + ப் + உ(ம்) (Neuter Future Tense suffix for அது (that))
Infinitive	செய் + ய் + அ (Infinitive suffix)

Example: In the below table, I have used the past tense of நா(ன்) as a base to create the whole verb conjugation of செய் (sey) (to do). You can replicate the same for all the verbs tables provided in this lesson.

Verb root	Past Tense	Verb Suffix	Past Tense	English Translation
செய்	த்	-எ	நா(ன்) செய்தெ	I ran
செய்	த்	-எ	நீ செய்தெ	you ran (informal)
செய்	த்	-ஈங்க(ள்)	நீங்க(ள்) செய்தீங்க(ள்)	you ran (formal)
செய்	த்	-ஓ(ம்)	நாம/நாங்க செய்தோ(ம்)	we ran (Incl/Excl)
செய்	த்	-ஆ(ன்)	அவ(ன்) செய்தா(ன்)	he ran (informal)
செய்	த்	-ஆரு	அவரு செய்தாரு	he ran (formal)
செய்	த்	-ஆ(ள்)	அவ(ள்) செய்தா(ள்)	she ran (informal)
செய்	த்	-ஆங்கள்	அவங்க(ள்) செய்தாங்க(ள்)	they/she ran (formal/)

2) பண்ணு (paNNu) (To Do, Make) (Class 3)

	நா(ன்) (naa(n)) (I)	English	அது (adhu) (that) (it)	English
Past Tense	பண்ணு + ன் + எ பண்னெ (paNune)	I did, made	பண்ணு + ச்சு பண்ணுச்சு (paNNuchchu)	It did
Present Tense	பண்ணு + ற் + எ பண்றெ (paNdRe)	I am doing	பண்ணு + உது பண்ணுது (paNNudhu)	It is doing
Future Tense	பண்ணு + வ் + எ பண்ணுவெ paNNuve)	I will do	பண்ணு + உ(ம்) பண்ணு(ம்) (paNNum)	It will do
Infinitive	பண்ணு + அ பண்ண (paNNa)		Do, Make	

3) எழு (ezhu) (To Raise, To Get Up)

	நா(ன்) (naa(n)) (I)	English	அது (adhu) (that) (it)	English
Past Tense	எழு + ந்த் + எ எழுந்தெ (ezhundhe)	I got up	எழுந்த் + உது எழுந்துது (ezhundhudhu)	It got up
Present Tense	எழு + ற் + எ எழுறெ (ezhuRe)	I am getting up	எழு + உது எழுது (ezhudhu)	It is getting up
Future Tense	எழு + வ் + எ எழுவெ (ozhuve)	I will get up	எழு + உ(ம்) எழு(ம்) (ezhum)	It will get up
Infinitive	எழு + அ எழ (ezha)		Raise, Get Up	

4)வா (vaa) (To Come)

	நா(ன்) (naa(n)) (I)	English	அது (adhu) (that) (it)	English
Past Tense	வ + ந்த் + எ வந்தெ (vandhe)	I came	வந்த் + உது வந்துது (vandhudhu)	It came
Present Tense	வர் + ற் + எ வர்றெ (varRe)	I am coming	வர் + உது வருது (varudhu)	It is coming
Future Tense	வரு + வ் + எ வருவெ (varuve)	I will come	வர் + உ(ம்) வரு(ம்) (varum)	It will come
Infinitive	வர (vara)		Come	

5) ஆ / ஆகு (aa / aagu) (To Become)

	நா(ன்) (naa(n)) (I)	English	அது (adhu) (that) (it)	English
Past Tense	ஆ / ஆகு + ன் + எ ஆனெ / ஆகுனெ	I became	ஆ + ச்சு ஆச்சு	It became
Present Tense	ஆ / ஆகு + ற் + எ ஆறெ / ஆகுறெ	I am becoming	ஆகு + உது ஆகுது	It is becoming
Future Tense	ஆ / ஆகு + வ் + எ ஆவெ / ஆகுவெ	I will become	ஆகு + உ(ம்) ஆகு(ம்)	It will become
Infinitive	ஆகு + அ ஆக		Become	

6) பேசு (peesu) (To Speak)

	நா(ன்) (naa(n)) (I)	English	அது (adhu) (that) (it)	English
Past Tense	பேசு + ன் + எ பேசுனெ (peesune)	I spoke	பேசு + ச்சு பேசுச்சு (peesuchchu)	It spoke
Present Tense	பேசு + ற் + எ பேசுறெ (peesuRe)	I am speaking	பேசு + உது பேசுது (peesudhu)	It is speaking
Future Tense	பேசு + வ் + எ பேசுவெ (peesuve)	I will speak	பேசு + உ(ம்) பேசு(ம்) (peesum)	It will speak
Infinitive	பேசு + அ பேச (peesa)		Speak	

7) போ (poo) (To Go)

	நா(ன்) (naa(n)) (I)	English	அது (adhu) (that) (it)	English
Past Tense	போ + ன் + எ போனெ (poone)	I went	போ + ச்சு போச்சு (poochchu)	It went
Present Tense	போ + ற் + எ போறெ (pooRe)	I am going	போ + உது போவுது (poovudhu)	It is going
Future Tense	போ + வ் + எ போவெ (poove)	I will go	போ + உ(ம்) போவு(ம்) (poovum)	It will go
Infinitive	போக (pooga)		Go	

8) வாங்கு (vaanggu) (To Buy, Take)

	நா(ன்) (naa(n)) (I)	English	அது (adhu) (that) (it)	English
Past Tense	வாங்கு + ன் + எ வாங்குனெ (vaanggune)	I bought	வாங்கு + ச்சு வாங்குச்சு (vaangguchchu)	It bought
Present Tense	வாங்கு + ற் + எ வாங்குறெ (vaangguRe)	I am buying	வாங்கு + உது வாங்குது (vaanggudhu)	It is buying
Future Tense	வாங்கு + வ் + எ வாங்குவெ (vaangguve)	I will buy	வாங்கு + உ(ம்) வாங்கு(ம்) (vaanggum)	It will buy
Infinitive	வாங்கு + அ வாங்க (vaangga)		Buy	

9) சொல் (sol) (To Say, Tell)

	நா(ன்) (naa(n)) (I)	English	அது (adhu) (that) (it)	English
Past Tense	சொன் + ன் + எ சொன்னெ (sonne)	I said	சொன் + அது சொன்னது (sonnadhu)	It said
Present Tense	சொல் + ற் + எ சொல்றெ (soldRe)	I am saying	சொல் + ல் + உது சொல்லுது (solludhu)	It is saying
Future Tense	சொல் + வ் + எ சொல்வெ (solve)	I will say	சொல் + ல் + உ(ம்) சொல்லு(ம்) (sollum)	It will say
Infinitive	சொல் + ல் + அ சொல்ல (solla)		Say, Tell	

10) போடு (poodu) (To Put, Wear (Shirt, Pant))

	நா(ன்) (naa(n)) (I)	English	அது (adhu) (that) (it)	English
Past Tense	போ + ட்ட் + எ போட்டெ (pootte)	I wore	போட்ட் + உது போட்டுது (poottudhu)	It wore
Present Tense	போடு + ற் + எ போடுறெ (pooduRe)	I am wearing	போடு + உது போடுது (poodudhu)	It is wearing
Future Tense	போடு + வ் + எ போடுவெ (pooduve)	I will wear	போடு + உ(ம்) போடு(ம்) (poodum)	It will wear
Infinitive	போடு + அ போட (pooda)		Put, wear	

11) சாப்பிடு (saappidu) (To Eat)

	நா(ன்) (naa(n)) (I)	English	அது (adhu) (that) (it)	English
Past Tense	சாப்பி + ட்ட் + எ சாப்பிட்டெ (saappitte)	I ate	சாப்பிட்ட் + உது சாப்பிட்டுது (saappittudhu)	It ate
Present Tense	சாப்பிடு + ற் + எ சாப்பிடுறெ (saappiduRe)	I am eating	சாப்பிடு + உது சாப்பிடுது (saappidudhu)	It is eating
Future Tense	சாப்பிடு + வ் + எ சாப்பிடுவெ (saappiduve)	I will eat	சாப்பிடு + உ(ம்) சாப்பிடு(ம்) (saappidum)	It will eat
Infinitive	சாப்பிடு + அ சாப்பிட (saappida)		Eat	

140

12) எடு (edu) (To Take)

	நா(ன்) (naa(n)) (I)	English	அது (adhu) (that) (it)	English
Past Tense	எடு + த்த் + எ எடுத்தெ (eduththe)	I took	எடுத்த் + உது எடுத்துது (eduththudhu)	It took
Present Tense	எடு + க்குற் + எ எடுக்குறெ (edukkuRe)	I am taking	எடு + க்குது எடுக்குது (edukkudhu)	It is taking
Future Tense	எடு + ப்ப் + எ எடுப்பெ (eduppe)	I will take	எடு + க்கு(ம்) எடுக்கு(ம்) (edukkum)	It will take
Infinitive	எடு + க்க எடுக்க (edukka)		Take	

13) பார் (paar) (To See)

	நா(ன்) (naa(n)) (I)	English	அது (adhu) (that) (it)	English
Past Tense	பார் + த்த் + எ பார்த்தெ (paarththe)	I saw	பார்த்த் + உது பார்த்துது (paarththudhu)	It saw
Present Tense	பார் + க்குற் + எ பார்க்குறெ (paarkkuRe)	I am seeing	பார் + க்குது பார்க்குது (paarkkudhu)	It is seeing
Future Tense	பார் + ப்ப் + எ பார்ப்பெ (paarppe)	I will see	பார் + க்கு(ம்) பார்க்கு(ம்) (paarkkum)	It will see
Infinitive	பார் + க்க பார்க்க (paarkka)		See	

14) படி (padi) (To Study, Read)

	நா(ன்) (naa(n)) (I)	English	அது (adhu) (that) (it)	English
Past Tense	படி + ச்ச் + எ படிச்செ (padichche)	I studied	படிச்ச் + உது படிச்சுது (pidichchudhu)	It studied
Present Tense	படி + க்குற் + எ படிக்குறெ (padikkuRe)	I am studying	படி + க்குது படிக்குது (padikkudhu)	It is studying
Future Tense	படி + ப்ப் + எ படிப்பெ (padippe)	I will study	படி + க்கு(ம்) படிக்கு(ம்) (padikkum)	It will study
Infinitive	படி + க்க படிக்க (padikka)		Study, Read	

15) இரு (iru) (To Be)

	நா(ன்) (naa(n)) (I)	English	அது (adhu) (that) (it)	English
Past Tense	இரு + ந்த் + எ இருந்தெ (irundhe)	I was	இருந்த் + உது இருந்துது (irundhudhu)	It was
Present Tense	இருக்கெ (irukke)	I am	இரு + க்குது இருக்குது (irukkudhu)	It is
Future Tense	இரு + ப்ப் + எ இருப்பெ (iruppe)	I will be	இரு + க்கு(ம்) இருக்கு(ம்) (irukkum)	It will be
Infinitive	இரு + க்க இருக்க (irukka)		Be	

142

16) தூங்கு (thuunggu) (To Sleep)

	நா(ன்) (naa(n)) (I)	English	அது (adhu) (that) (it)	English
Past Tense	தூங்கு + ன் + எ	I slept	தூங்கு + ச்சு	It slept
	தூங்குனெ (thuunggune)		தூங்குச்சு (thuungguchchu)	
Present Tense	தூங்கு + ற் + எ	I am sleeping	தூங்கு + உது	It is sleeping
	தூங்குறெ (thuungguRe)		தூங்குது (thuungudhu)	
Future Tense	தூங்கு + வ் + எ	I will sleep	தூங்கு + உ(ம்)	It will sleep
	தூங்குவெ (thuungguve)		தூங்கு(ம்) (thuunggum)	
Infinitive	தூங்கு + அ		Sleep	
	தூங்க (thuungga)			

17) வை/வெ (vai/ve) (To Put, To Have)

	நா(ன்) (naa(n)) (I)	English	அது (adhu) (that) (it)	English
Past Tense	வெ + ச்ச் + எ	I put	வெச்ச் + உது	It put
	வெச்செ (vechche)		வெச்சுது (vechchudhu)	
Present Tense	வெ + க்குற் + எ	I am putting	வெ + க்குது	It is putting
	வெக்குறெ (vekkuRe)		வெக்குது (vekkudhu)	
Future Tense	வெ + ப்ப் + எ	I will put	வெ + க்கு(ம்)	It will put
	வெப்பெ (veppe)		வெக்கு(ம்) (vekkum)	
Infinitive	வெ + க்க		Put, Have	
	வெக்க (vekka)			

18) நினை/நினெ (ṉinai/ṉine) (To Wonder, Think)

	நா(ன்) (naa(n)) (I)	English	அது (adhu) (that) (it)	English
Past Tense	நினெ + ச்ச் + எ நினெச்செ (ṉinechche)	I thought	நினெச்ச் + உது நினெச்சுது (ṉinechchudhu)	It thought
Present Tense	நினெ + க்குற் + எ நினெக்குறெ (ṉinekkuRe)	I am thinking	நினெ + க்குது நினெக்குது (ṉinekkudhu)	It is thinking
Future Tense	நினெ + ப்ப் + எ நினெப்பெ (ṉineppe)	I will think	நினெ + க்கு(ம்) நினெக்கு(ம்) (ṉinekkum)	It will think
Infinitive	நினெ + க்க நினெக்க (ṉinekka)		Think, Remember, Assume	

19) குடு (kudu) (To Give)

	நா(ன்) (naa(n)) (I)	English	அது (adhu) (that) (it)	English
Past Tense	குடு + த்த் + எ குடுத்தெ (kuduththe)	I thought	குடுத்த் + உது குடுத்துது (kuduththudhu)	It thought
Present Tense	குடு + க்குற் + எ குடுக்குறெ (kudukkuRe)	I am thinking	குடு + க்குது குடுக்குது (kudukkudhu)	It is thinking
Future Tense	குடு + ப்ப் + எ குடுப்பெ (kuduppe)	I will think	குடு + க்கு(ம்) குடுக்கு(ம்) (kudukkum)	It will think
Infinitive	குடு + க்க குடுக்க (kudukka)		Give	

20) கேள் (keeL) (To Ask, Listen)

	நா(ன்) (naa(n)) (I)	English	அது (adhu) (that) (it)	English
Past Tense	கே + ட்ட் + எ கேட்டெ (keette)	I asked	கேட்ட் + உது கேட்டுது (keettudhu)	It asked
Present Tense	கே + க்குற் + எ கேக்குறெ (keekkuRe)	I am asking	கே + க்குது கேக்குது (keekkudhu)	It is asking
Future Tense	கே + ப்ப் + எ கேப்பெ (keeppe)	I will ask	கே + க்கு(ம்) கேக்கு(ம்) (keekkum)	It will ask
Infinitive	கே + க்க கேக்க (keekka)		Ask, Listen	

145

Step 2 (optional): If possible, please memorize the 100 verbs given below. Memorizing these 100 verbs will be very handy when you want to make sentences on your own in Tamil. This will broaden your vocabulary, and you can have a solid conversation in Tamil. This is optional, you can very well skip this and move on to the next lesson if you want to.

Class 1:

TL: Transliteration

Tamil Verb	TL	English	Tamil Verb	TL	English
அழு	azhu	To Cry	கொல்	kol	To Kill
கொள்	koL	To do to oneself (reflexive)	செய்	sey	To Do
பெய்	pey	To Rain			

Class 2:

Tamil Verb	TL	English	Tamil Verb	TL	English
விழு	vizhu	To Fall	ஒளி	oLi	To Hide
அலை	alai	To Wander	குனி	guni	To Crouch
உக்கார்	ukkaar	To Sit	வா	vaa	To Come
உணர்	uNar	To Feel	வாழ்	vaazh	To Live
எழு	ezhu	To Raise, get up	எறி	eRi	To Throw

Class 3:

Tamil Verb	TL	English	Tamil Verb	TL	English
ஆ / ஆகு	aa / aagu	To Become	திருத்து	thiruththu	To Correct
ஆடு	aadu	To Dance	திருப்பு	thiruppu	To Turn
ஊத்து	uuththu	To Pour	தேடு	theedu	To Search
எழுது	ezhudhu	To Write	நம்பு	nambu	To Believe
ஓடு	oodu	To Run	நிறுத்து	niRuththu	To Stop
ஓட்டு	oottu	To Drive	பயன்படுத்து	payanpaduth-thu	To Use
கட்டு	kattu	To Build, tie on	பாடு	paadu	To Sing
கத்து	kaththu	To Scream	பேசு	peesu	To Speak
கழுவு	kazhuvu	To Clean	போ	poo	To Go
கழட்டு	kazhattu	To Remove	மாத்து	maaththu	To Change
சப்பு	sappu	To Suck	மூடு	muudu	To Close
சிந்து	sindhu	To Spill	திருடு	thirudu	To steal
சீவு	siivu	To Comb	தள்ளு	thaLLu	To Push
விரட்டு	virattu	To Chase away	விளையாடு	viLaiyaadu	To Play
திட்டு	thittu	To Scold	வீசு	viisu	To Throw
வாங்கு	vaanggu	To Buy, take	வெட்டு	vettu	To Cut

Class 4:

Tamil Verb	TL	English	Tamil Verb	TL	English
கூப்பிடு	kuuppidu	To Call	சொல்	sol	To Say
கெடு	kedu	To go bad/rot	தொடு	thodu	To Touch
கோபப்படு	koobappadu	To get angry	போடு	poodu	To Put,Wear
சாப்பிடு	saappidu	To Eat	விடு	vidu	To Leave (something)
சுடு	sudu	To Shoot			

Class 5:

Tamil Verb	TL	English	Tamil Verb	TL	English
கேள்	keel	To Ask	வில்	vil	To Sell
நில்	nil	To Stand			

Class 6:

Tamil Verb	TL	English	Tamil Verb	TL	English
மிதி	midhi	To Step on, Pedal	முடி	mudi	To finish
கவனி	kavani	To listen, look after	குளி	kuLi	To Bathe
சிரி	siri	To Smile, laugh	எரி	eri	To Burn
வை / வெ	vai, ve	To Put, Have	தெளி	theLi	To Spray
உடை/உடெ	udai /ude	To Break	எடு	edu	To Take
புதை/புதெ	pudhai/pudhe	To Bury	பிடி	pidi	To Catch, hold
துவை/துவெ	thuvai/thuve	To Wash	மடி	madi	To Fold
தை/தெ	thai/the	To Sew, stitch	கிழி	kizhi	To Tear, rip
தொலை/ தொலெ	tholai / thole	To Lose	துடை/ துடெ	thidai / thude	To Wipe
சொல்லி கொடு	solli kodu	To Teach	பார்	paar	To See
சமை/சமெ	samai/same	To Cook	அடி	adi	To Hit
பறி	paRi	To Pluck.	கடி	kadi	To Bite
அழி	azhi	To Erase, destroy	குடி	kudi	To Drink
கண்டுபிடி	kaNdubidi	To Find	தேய்	theey	To Iron, rub
படி	padi	To Study, read			

Class 7:

Tamil Verb	TL	English	Tamil Verb	TL	English
இரு	iru	To Be	பிற	piRa	To be born
நட	nada	To Walk	பற	paRa	To Fly
மற	maRa	To Forget	இற	iRa	To Die
தொற	thoRa	To Open	கல	kala	To Mix
எழுந்திரு	ezhundhiru	To get up			

Some commonly used verbs which has the same meaning:

Tamil Verb	TL	English	Class
காட்டு	kaattu	Show	class 3
காமி	kaami	Show	class 6
யோசி	yoosi	Think, remember	class 6
நினை, நினெ	ninai, nine	Think, remember, assume	class 6
தா	thaa	Give	class 2
குடு	kudu	Give	class 6
செய்	sey	Do, make	class 1
பண்ணு	paNNu	Do, make	class 3

Note:

1) In the before table, I have given two verbs with the same meaning because Tamil speakers use both forms daily, it is better to learn both the verbs even though they mean the same thing.

2) As you have seen in the tables of class 6, some of the verbs have two forms to pronounce these verbs easily.

Sentamil and written: வை, உடை, புதை, துவை, சமை, தை, துடை, தொலை, நினை

Spoken version: வெ, உடெ, புதெ, துவெ, சமெ, தெ, துடெ, தொலெ, நினெ.

3) There are two more verbs that have the same meaning, but are used for different purposes:

a) வாங்கு (vaanggu) (To buy, to take) = you will use the verb வாங்கு as 'To take' when you are borrowing something from someone and you will return it afterwards, so you will need permission for it. The Verb வாங்கு can be used for both 'To buy' and 'To take'.

b) எடு (edu) (To take) = you will use the verb எடு as 'To take' when you are just taking something, so you will not need any permission for it.

Example:

a) நா(ன்) அவள்கிட்டேருந்து பேனா வாங்குனெ

tl: naa(n) avaLkitteerundhu peenaa vaanggune

lit: He from him pen took

t: I took the pen from him

In the above example, he took the pen from another person to the other person's knowledge, e.g. let's think of an exam room and you don't have a pen, so you borrowed a pen from your friend, you ask him "do you have a pen?" and he gives you the pen. Now, someone comes to you and asks you "who did you get this pen from?" and you would say "நா(ன்) அவள்கிட்டேருந்து பேனா வாங்குனெ" (I took the pen from him), Here you shouldn't use the verb எடு, you should use the verb வாங்கு because you took the pen from another person in his knowledge.

151

Note:

b) நா(ன்) அவள்கிட்டேருந்து பேனா எடுத்தெ

tl: naa(n) avaLkitteerundhu peenaa eduththe

lit: I from him pen took

t: I took the pen from him

In the above example, he took the pen from another person without the other person's knowledge. Let's use the same classroom scenario, you don't have a pen and your friend wouldn't lend you one either, so you take his pen without his knowledge when looking away. Now, if someone comes to you and asks you "who did you get this pen from?" and you would say "நா(ன்) அவள்கிட்டேருந்து பேனா எடுத்தெ" (I took the pen from him), Here you shouldn't use the verb வாங்கு, you should use the verb எடு because you took the pen from another person without his knowledge

---

IMPORTANT !

I have created a pdf document with verb conjugation for the 100 verbs and exercises for you to practice. This is advanced and for serious Tamil learners. If you are a serious Tamil learner and you want to improve your conversational ability by expanding your knowledge on verb conjugation, then please use the below links to download the pdf document to learn more verb conjugations.

Google drive link:

https://bit.ly/100tamilverbs

Drop box link:

https://bit.ly/100tamilverbs2

EXERCISES:

A) Match the following Verb in the first column with the appropriate meaning in the second column.
e.g. எடு = To take

1.	பண்ணு	a.	To Become, Happen
2.	எழு	b.	To Say, Tell
3.	வா	c.	To Put, Wear
4.	ஆ / ஆகு	d.	To Raise, Get up
5.	பேசு	e.	To Come
6.	போ	f.	To Go
7.	வாங்கு	g.	To Do, Make
8.	சொல்	h.	To Buy, Get
9.	போடு	i.	To Eat
10.	சாப்பிடு	j.	To Take

B) Fill in the blanks with the right verb conjugation in all three tenses for the given verb. Example: The first line for the pronoun நா have been filled as an example for you, you are supposed to fill the consecutive lines as such for the respective pronoun.

1) பேசு (peesu) (To Speak)

Pronoun	Past tense	Present Tense	Future Tense
நா(ன்)	பேசினெ	பேசுறெ	பேசுவெ
நீ			
நீங்க(ள்)			

153

அவ(ன்)			
அவரு			
அவ(ள்)			
அவங்க(ள்)			
நாம/நாங்க(ள்)			
அது/இது			

2) எழுது (ezhudhu) (To Write)

Pronoun	Past tense	Present Tense	Future Tense
நா(ன்)	எழுதுனெ	எழுதுறெ	எழுதுவெ
நீ			
நீங்க(ள்)			
அவ(ன்)			
அவரு			
அவ(ள்)			
அவங்க(ள்)			
நாம/நாங்க(ள்)			
அது/இது			
அதுங்க			

3) போ (poo) (To Go)

Pronoun	Past tense	Present Tense	Future Tense
நா(ன்)			
நீ			
நீங்க(ள்)			
அவ(ன்)			
அவரு			
அவ(ள்)			
அவங்க(ள்)			
நாம/நாங்க(ள்)			
அது/இது			
அதுங்க			

4) குடு (kudu) (To Give)

Pronoun	Past tense	Present Tense	Future Tense
நா(ன்)			
நீ			
நீங்க(ள்)			
அவ(ன்)			
அவரு			
அவ(ள்)			

அவங்க(ள்)			
நாம/நாங்க(ள்)			
அது/இது			
அதுங்க			

5) பண்ணு (paNNu) (To Do)

Pronoun	Past tense	Present Tense	Future Tense
நா(ன்)			
நீ			
நீங்க(ள்)			
அவ(ன்)			
அவரு			
அவ(ள்)			
அவங்க(ள்)			
நாம/நாங்க(ள்)			
அது/இது			
அதுங்க			

SOLUTIONS

Lesson 8

Exercise A

1) g; 2) d; 3) e; 4) a; 5) j; 6) f; 7) h; 8) b; 9) c; 10) i.

Exercise B

1) பேசு (peesu) (To Speak)

Pronoun	Past tense	Present Tense	Future Tense
நா(ன்)	பேசினெ	பேசுறெ	பேசுவெ
நீ	பேசினெ	பேசுறெ	பேசுவெ
நீங்க(ள்)	பேசினீங்க(ள்)	பேசுறீங்க(ள்)	பேசுவீங்க(ள்)
அவ(ன்)	பேசினா(ன்)	பேசுறா(ன்)	பேசுவா(ன்)
அவரு	பேசினாரு	பேசுறாரு	பேசுவாரு
அவ(ள்)	பேசினா(ள்)	பேசுறா(ள்)	பேசுவா(ள்)
அவங்க(ள்)	பேசினாங்க(ள்)	பேசுறாங்க(ள்)	பேசுவாங்க(ள்)
நாம/நாங்க(ள்)	பேசினோ(ம்)	பேசுறோ(ம்)	பேசுவோ(ம்)
அது/இது	பேசுச்சு	பேசுது	பேசு(ம்)

2) எழுது (ezhudhu) (To Write)

Pronoun	Past tense	Present Tense	Future Tense
நா(ன்)	எழுதுனெ	எழுதுறெ	எழுதுவெ
நீ	எழுதுனெ	எழுதுறெ	எழுதுவெ
நீங்க(ள்)	எழுதுனீங்க(ள்)	எழுதுறீங்க(ள்)	எழுதுவீங்க(ள்)
அவ(ன்)	எழுதுனா(ன்)	எழுதுறா(ன்)	எழுதுவா(ன்)
அவரு	எழுதுனாரு	எழுதுறாரு	எழுதுவாரு
அவ(ள்)	எழுதுனா(ள்)	எழுதுறா(ள்)	எழுதுவா(ள்)

அவங்க(ள்)	எழுதுனாங்க(ள்)	எழுதுறாங்க(ள்)	எழுதுவாங்க(ள்)
நாம/நாங்க(ள்)	எழுதுனோ(ம்)	எழுதுறோ(ம்)	எழுதுவோ(ம்)
அது/இது	எழுதுச்சு	எழுதுது	எழுது(ம்)
அதுங்க	எழுதுச்சுங்க	எழுதுதுங்க	எழுதும்ங்க

3) போ (poo) (To Go)

Pronoun	Past tense	Present Tense	Future Tense
நா(ன்)	போனெ	போறெ	போவெ
நீ	போனெ	போறெ	போவெ
நீங்க(ள்)	போனீங்க(ள்)	போறீங்க(ள்)	போவீங்க(ள்)
அவ(ன்)	போனா(ன்)	போறா(ன்)	போவா(ன்)
அவரு	போனாரு	போறாரு	போவாரு
அவ(ள்)	போனா(ள்)	போறா(ள்)	போவா(ள்)
அவங்க(ள்)	போனாங்க(ள்)	போறாங்க(ள்)	போவாங்க(ள்)
நாம/நாங்க(ள்)	போனோ(ம்)	போறோ(ம்)	போவோ(ம்)
அது/இது	போச்சு	போவுது	போவு(ம்)
அதுங்க	போச்சுங்க	போவுங்க	போவும்ங்க

4) குடு (kudu) (To Give)

Pronoun	Past tense	Present Tense	Future Tense
நா(ன்)	குடுத்தெ	குடுக்குறெ	குடுப்பெ
நீ	குடுத்தெ	குடுக்குறெ	குடுப்பெ
நீங்க(ள்)	குடுத்தீங்க(ள்)	குடுக்குறீங்க(ள்)	குடுப்பீங்க(ள்)
அவ(ன்)	குடுத்தா(ன்)	குடுக்குறா(ன்)	குடுப்பா(ன்)
அவரு	குடுத்தாரு	குடுக்குறாரு	குடுப்பாரு
அவ(ள்)	குடுத்தா(ள்)	குடுக்குறா(ள்)	குடுப்பா(ள்)
அவங்க(ள்)	குடுத்தாங்க(ள்)	குடுக்குறாங்க(ள்)	குடுப்பாங்க(ள்)
நாம/நாங்க(ள்)	குடுத்தோ(ம்)	கொடுக்குறோ(ம்)	குடிப்போ(ம்)

| அது/இது | குடுத்துச்சு | குடுக்குது | குடுக்கு(ம்) |
| அதுங்க | குடுத்துச்சுங்க | குடுக்குதுங்க | குடுக்கும்ங்க |

5) பண்ணு (paNNu) (To Do)

Pronoun	Past tense	Present Tense	Future Tense
நா(ன்)	பண்ணுனெ	பண்ணுறெ	பண்ணுவெ
நீ	பண்ணுனெ	பண்ணுறெ	பண்ணுவெ
நீங்க(ள்)	பண்ணுனீங்க(ள்)	பண்ணுறீங்க(ள்)	பண்ணுவீங்க(ள்)
அவ(ன்)	பண்ணுனா(ன்)	பண்ணுறா(ன்)	பண்ணுவா(ன்)
அவரு	பண்ணுனாரு	பண்ணுறாரு	பண்ணுவாரு
அவ(ள்)	பண்ணுனா(ள்)	பண்ணுறா(ள்)	பண்ணுவா(ள்)
அவங்க(ள்)	பண்ணுனாங்க(ள்)	பண்ணுறாங்க(ள்)	பண்ணுவாங்க(ள்)
நாம/நாங்க(ள்)	பண்ணுனோ(ம்)	பண்ணுறோ(ம்)	பண்ணுவோ(ம்)
அது/இது	பண்ணுச்சு	பண்ணுது	பண்ணு(ம்)
அதுங்க	பண்ணுச்சுங்க	பண்ணுங்க	பண்ணும்ங்க

Content:

- Imperative
- Informal Imperative

LESSON 9: IMPERATIVE

Imperative: In Tamil, the imperative form of a verb is used to make requests, give orders or simply ask someone to do something. Hence, there are two types of imperatives:

1. Informal imperative (Similar to an order).

2. Polite of Formal Imperative (Similar to a request)

Informal Imperative:

Informal imperatives are used only for addressing someone younger than your age, children and servants. Please never use the Informal imperative form with elders and people higher in position. This will offend them and put you in a very embarrassing situation.

An Informal imperative is just the root form of a verb you have already memorized.

For example: You are a secretary for the general manager and you and your general manager are in a meeting. In the middle of the meeting, he looks at you and says எழுது (write). It means he is instructing you to write down what's being told in the meeting.

Example:

Class 6:

Tamil Verb	TL	English (Like an Instruction)
கவனி	kavain	listen (Singular)
சிரி	siri	Smile, laugh (Singular)
வை	vai, ve	Put (Singular)
உடை/உடெ	udai /ude	Break (Singular)
புதை/புதெ	pudhai/pudhe	Bury (Singular)
துவை/துவெ	thuvai/thuve	Wash (Singular)
பாரு	paaru	See (Singular)
சொல்லி கொடு	solli kodu	Teach (Singular)
சமை/சமெ	samai/same	Cook (Singular)
எழுது	ezhudhu	Write (Singular)

Polite of Formal Imperative: Formal Imperative is used when addressing a stranger, someone older than you and someone higher in position. When using the Formal Imperative the word 'Please' automatically adds to your formal imperative. You don't have to use a separate word to say 'Please' here. Formal Imperative can be used to politely issue a command to one or more people (plural).

The suffix to make a verb root a Formal Imperative is given below:

1. If the verb root ends with a consonant letter (e.g. க், ங், ச், ட், த், ப் etc) then you should add the suffix –உங்க to it to make it Formal Imperative.

Example:

பார் (paar) (to see) + உங்க (ungga) = பாருங்க (paarungga) (Please see)

நில் (nil) (to stand) + ல் (l) + உங்க (ungga) = நில்லுங்க (nillunga) (Please stand)

2. For the rest of the verb roots, add the suffix –ங்க to it to make it Formal Imperative.

Example:

குடு (kudu) (to give) + ங்க (ngga) = குடுங்க (kudungga) (Please give)

எடு (edu) (to take) + ங்க (ngga) = எடுங்க (edungga) (Please take)

Note:

> As you have seen in the above example, the word 'Please' get automatically added to the sentence. In Tamil we hardly use a separate word for 'Please'; it is usually added in a sentence when you have a suffix that denotes formal or politeness.

Adding additional politeness to a Formal Imperative: It is possible to add even more politeness to a Formal Imperative using the word கொஞ்சம் (konjjam) (some, little).

Example:

கொஞ்சம் தண்ணி குடுங்க (konjjam thaNNi kudungga) (Please) give me water (little).

The above example is more polite than saying 'தண்ணி குடுங்க'. In the above example the word கொஞ்சம் denotes the additional politeness. It does not give the meaning 'little' to the sentence. For example: when you go to a stranger's house and say கொஞ்சம் தண்ணி குடுங்க, then it means that you are asking for water in a very polite manner, it does not mean that you are asking for 'little water'.

NUMBERS AND TIME

LESSON 10

Content:

LESSON 10: NUMBERS AND TIME

Numbers:

Numbers in Tamil are almost similar to English with some variations.

From 1 to 19:

Numbers 1 to 10 are unique words, so you must memorize them; the numbers 11 to 19 start with the prefix பதி.

Tamil	TL	English	Tamil	TL	English
ஒண்ணு	oNNu	One	பதினொன்னு	padhinonnu	Eleven
ரெண்டு	reNdu	Two	பன்னெண்டு	panneNdu	Twelve
மூணு	muuNu	Three	பதிமூணு	padhimuunu	Thirteen
நாலு	naalu	Four	பதிநாலு	padhinaalu	Fourteen
அஞ்சு	anjju	Five	பதினஞ்சு	padhinanjju	Fifteen
ஆறு	aaRu	Six	பதினாறு	padhinaaRu	Sixteen
ஏழு	eezhu	Seven	பதினேழு	padhineezhu	Seventeen
எட்டு	ettu	Eight	பதினெட்டு	padhinettu	Eighteen
ஒன்பது	onbadhu	Nine	பத்தொம்பது	paththombadhu	Nineteen
பத்து	paththu	Ten			

Note:

The number 'nineteen', 'ninety', 'nine hundred' are the defective form of numbers in Tamil. **For example:** தொன்னூறு (thonnuuRu) (ninety) is a defective hundred and தொள்ளாயிரம் (thoLLaayiram) (nine hundred) is a defective thousand. So the numbers which contain 'nine' will not follow the same pattern most of the time.

When you are referring to the number 'one' then you should use 'ஒண்ணு'. The rest of the time use 'ஒரு' (oru) ('a', 'an') and when you say numbers like one thousand, one lakh etc.

From 20 to 99:

Here, memorize only the ten's form (e.g. Twenty, Thirty, Forty etc.), Then the rest of them will follow the pattern.

Tamil	TL	English
இருவது	iruvadhu	Twenty
இருவத்தி ஒண்ணு	iruvaththi oNNu	Twenty-one
இருவத்தி ரெண்டு	iruvaththi reNdu	Twenty-two
முப்பது	muppadhu	Thirty
முப்பத்தி ஒண்ணு	muppaththi oNNu	Thirty-one
நாப்பது	naappadhu	Forty
நாப்பத்தி ஒண்ணு	naappaththi oNNu	Forty-one
அம்பது	ambadhu	Fifty
அம்பத்தி ஒண்ணு	ambaththi oNNu	Fifty-one
அறுவது	aRuvadhu	Sixty
அறுவத்தி ஒண்ணு	aRuvaththi oNNu	Sixty-one
எழுவது	ezhuvadhu	Seventy
எழுவத்தி ஒண்ணு	ezhuvaththi oNNu	Seventy-one
எண்பது	eNbadhu	Eighty
எண்பத்தி ஒண்ணு	eNbaththi oNNu	Eighty-one
தொன்னூறு	thonnuuRu	Ninety
தொன்னூத்தி ஒண்ணு	thonnuuththi oNNu	Ninety-one

As you see in the above table, I just replaced the letter து with த்தி and added ஒண்ணு, ரெண்டு and so on. All you have to do is memorize the ten's form and how to replace the letter; the rest of the things are similar to English.

இருவத்தி ஒண்ணு, இருவத்தி ரெண்டு, இருவத்தி மூணு, இருவத்தி நாலு, இருவத்தி அஞ்சு.

From 100 to 999:

Tamil	TL	English
நூறு	nuuRu	Hundred
நூத்தி ஒண்ணு	nuuththi oNNu	Hundred and one
எரநூறு	eranuuRu	Two hundred
எரநூத்தி ஒண்ணு	eranuuththu oNNu	Two hundred and one
முன்னூறு	munnuuRu	Three hundred
முன்னூத்தி ஒண்ணு	munnuuththi oNNu	Three hundred and one
நானூறு	naanuRu	Four hundred
நானூத்தி ஒண்ணு	naanuththi oNNu	Four hundred and one
ஐநூறு	ainuuRu	Five hundred
ஐநூத்தி ஒண்ணு	ainuuththi oNNu	Five hundred and one
அறநூறு	aRanuuRu	Six hundred
அறநூத்தி ஒண்ணு	aRanuuththi oNNu	Six hundred and one
எழுநூறு	ezhunuuRu	Seven hundred
எழுநூத்தி ஒண்ணு	ezhunuuththi oNNu	Seven hundred and one
எட்நூறு	etnuuRu	Eight hundred
எட்நூத்தி ஒண்ணு	etnuuththi oNNu	Eight hundred and one
தொள்ளாயிரம்	thoLLaayiram	Nine hundred
தொள்ளாயிரத்தி ஒண்ணு	thoLLaayiraththi oNNu	Nine hundred and one

Similar to the previous one, memorize the hundred's form and how to replace the last letter று with த்தி and add ஒண்ணு, ரெண்டு and so on. The only exception here is தொள்ளாயிரம் (nine hundred). As mentioned earlier this is a defective thousand.

From 1,000 to 99,999:

Tamil	TL	English
ஆயிரம்	aayiram	Thousand
ஆயிரத்தி ஒண்ணு	aayiraththi oNNu	Thousand and one
ரெண்டாயிரம்	reNdaayiram	Two Thousand
ரெண்டாயிரத்தி ஒண்ணு	reNdaayiraththi oNNu	Two hundred and one
மூனாயிரம்	muunaayiram	Three Thousand
மூனாயிரத்தி ஒண்ணு	muunaayiraththi oNNu	Three Thousand and one
நாலாயிரம்	naalaayiram	Four Thousand
நாலாயிரத்தி ஒண்ணு	naalaayiraththi oNNu	Four Thousand and one
அஞ்சாயிரம்	anjjaayiram	Five Thousand
அஞ்சாயிரத்தி ஒண்ணு	anjjaayiraththi oNNu	Five Thousand and one
ஆறாயிரம்	aaRaayiram	Six Thousand
ஆறாயிரத்தி ஒண்ணு	aaRaayiraththi oNNu	Six Thousand and one
ஏழாயிரம்	eezhaayiram	Seven Thousand
ஏழாயிரத்தி ஒண்ணு	eezhaayiraththi oNNu	Seven Thousand and one
எட்டாயிரம்	ettaayiram	Eight Thousand
எட்டாயிரத்தி ஒண்ணு	ettaayiraththi oNNu	Eight Thousand and one
ஒன்பதாயிரம்	onbathaayiram	Nine Thousand
ஒன்பதாயிரத்தி ஒண்ணு	onbathaayiraththi oNNu	Nine Thousand and one
பத்தாயிரம்	paththaayiram	Ten Thousand
பத்தாயிரத்தி ஒண்ணு	paththaayiraththi oNNu	Ten Thousand and one
பதினொன்னாயிரம்	padhinonnaayiram	Eleven Thousand

Here, to change a single digit number to a thousand all you have to do is add the suffix ஆயிரம் to it. For example: ரெண்டு (Two) + ஆயிரம் = ரெண்டாயிரம் (Two thousand)

And similar to the last time replace the last letter ம் with த்தி and add ஒண்ணு, ரெண்டு and so on.

169

Example:

Method 1:

One thousand nine hundred and sixty nine (1969).

ஆயிரத்தி தொள்ளாயிரத்து அறுபத்தி ஒம்பது (1969).

Method 2:

Nineteen sixty nine (1969).

பத்தொாம்பது அறுபத்தி ஒம்பது (1969).

Lakhs and Crore:

In India, we use lakhs and crores instead of billions and millions.

a) லட்சம் (latcham) (a lakh) (one hundred thousand)

b) கோடி (koodi) (a crore) (ten million)

Note:

100 Lakhs = 1 Crore; 100 லட்சம் = 1 கோடி.

The same rule as the previous one applies here too, but it is more complicated for someone from America and other countries because the Indian numbering system is different.

Example:

a) One Hundred thousand five hundred and five (100,505). (American number system)

One Lakh five hundred and five (1,00,505). (Indian number system)

ஒரு லட்சத்தி ஐநூற்றி அஞ்சு (1,00,505).

b) Eighteen million one hundred and fifty thousand (18,150,000). (American number system)

One crore and eighty one lakhs and fifty thousand (1,81,50,000). (Indian number system)

ஒரு கொடியே எண்பத்தி ஒரு லட்சத்தி அம்பதாயிரம் (1,81,50,000).

Ordinal Numbers in Tamil:

Ordinal numbers in Tamil are similar to –th (e.g. Fifth, Sixth) in English, To create an ordinal number, add either the suffix –ஆம் (aam) or –ஆவது (aavadhu) to the number. An exception here is ஒண்ணு, The alternative option for ஒண்ணு is மொதல், மொதலாம், (modhalaam) மொதலாவது (modhalaavadhu) (Both means 'First').

1) You will use the suffix –ஆம் (aam), when referring to the classroom..

Examples:

a) First Class:

ஒண்ணு (oNNu) (one) + ஆம் (aam) (-st) + வகுப்பு (vaguppu) (class) = ஒண்ணாம் வகுப்பு (oNNaam vaguppu) (First Class)

2) You will use the suffix – ஆவது (aavadhu), when you are referring to a Street, House, shop, person, day etc.

Examples:

a) First Street:

ஒண்ணு (oNNu) (one) + ஆவது (aavadhu) (-st) + தெரு (theru) (street) = ஒண்ணாவது தெரு (oNNaavadhu theru) (First street)

b) Third Shop:

மூணு (muuNu) (three) + ஆவது (aavadhu) (-st) + கடை (kadai) (shop) = மூணாவது கடை (muuNaavadhu kadai) (Third shop)

c) First House:

ஒண்ணு (oNNu) (one) + ஆவது (aavadhu) (-st) + வீடு (viidu) (house) = ஒண்ணாவது வீடு (oNNaavadhu viidu) (First house)

EXERCISES:

A) Write the following numbers in Tamil.

a) 36:_____

b) 78:_____

c) 269:_____

d) 99:_____

e) 966:_____

f) 3689:_____

g) 145:_____

h) 5987:_____

i) 98,758:_____

j) 6,98,750:_____

B) Write the following Ordinal numbers in Tamil.

a) 8th house:_____

b) 7th shop:_____

c) 12th class:_____

d) 16th street:_____

Telling the Time:

Telling the time in Tamil is similar to the way we say in English.

Important Vocabulary for telling time: மணி (maNi) (hour, o'clock); நிமிஷம் (nimisham) (minutes); வினாடி (vinaadi) (seconds)

Example:

a) எட்டு மணி (ettu maNi) (8 o'clock)

b) எட்டு மணி ஆவுது (ettu maNi aavudhu) (It is 8 o'clock)

c) முப்பத்தி ஏழு நிமிஷம் (muppaththi eezhu nimisham) (Thirty Seven minutes)

When you want to indicate 'at' a particular time, then you would use the dative case of மணி (மணிக்கு (manikku) (at time)) proceeded by the appropriate number.

Example:

a) எட்டு மணிக்கு (ettu maNikku) (At 8 o'clock)

b) எட்டு மணிக்கு போவோம் (ettu maNikku poovoom) (Let's go at 8 o'clock)

For every quarter of an hour the below mentioned suffixes are added to the numeral.

- –ஏகால் (eegaal) = 'quarter' (15 minutes)

- -அர (ara) = 'half' (30 minutes)

- –ஏமுக்கா (emukkaa) = 'three quarters' (45 minutes)

Example:

a) மணி என்ன? (Informal) (What is the time?), மணி என்னங்க? (Formal) (What is the time, please?).

b) மணி எட்டேகால்

tl: maNi etteegaal.

lit/t: it's eight fifteen, It's quarter past eight

c) மணி மூணர.

tl: maNi muuNara

lit/t: it's three thirty, It's half past three

d) மணி எட்டேமுக்கா

tl: maNi ctteemukkaa.

lit/t: it's eight forty-five, It's quarter to nine.

e) எட்டேகால் மணிக்கு

tl: etteegaal maNikku.

lit/t: At eight fifteen, at quarter past eight

f) மூணர மணிக்கு

tl: muuNara maNikku.

lit/t: At three thirty, at half past three

g) எட்டேமுக்கா மணிக்கு

tl: etteemukkaa maNikku.

lit/t: At eight forty-five, at quarter to nine.

EXERCISES:

A) Tell the time; let's say that someone is asking you the time every hour from 2 o'clock until 8.

Example: மணி என்ன?

     ரெண்டு மணி ஆவது.

_____

_____

_____

B) Tell the time by every quarter of an hour; let's say that someone is asking you the time every quarter of an hour from 2 o'clock until 4.

Example: மணி என்ன?

     ரெண்டு மணி ஆவது.

     மணி ரெண்டேகால்

_____

_____

_____

C) Translate the time given below in Tamil.

Example: 5.10

Answer: அஞ்சு பத்து

a) 5.25:_____

b) 6.36:_____

c) 11.22:_____

d) 9.27:_____

e) 4.30:_____

Asking for Directions:

When you ask for directions in Tamil, some people will give you directions in Tamil and some will replace some Tamil words with English words while giving you directions especially in the city.

Useful vocabulary while asking for directions:

Tamil	TL	English
பக்கம்	pakkam	Side
இடது	valadhu	Left
வலது	idadhu	Right
நேர்	neer	Straight
பின்னாடி	pinnaadi	Back, Back side
முன்னாடி	munnaadi	Front, Front side
தெரு	theru	Street
போங்க	poongga	Please go
திரும்புங்க	thirumbunga	Please turn

The below table provides you with frequently provided directions:

	Tamil (Village and some places in city)	Tamil (City)	English
⬅	இடது பக்கம் போங்க	Leftல போங்க	Please go Left side
➡	வலது பக்கம் போங்க	Rightல போங்க	Please go Right side
⬆	நேரா போங்க	straightஅ போங்க	Please go straight
⬇	பின்னாடி போங்க	பின்னாடி போங்க	Please go back side

Note:

You can also use "**திரும்புங்க**" instead of "**போங்க**". (e.g. **இடது பக்கம் திரும்புங்க** (plese turn right), **வலது பக்கம்** (please turn left))

Examples:

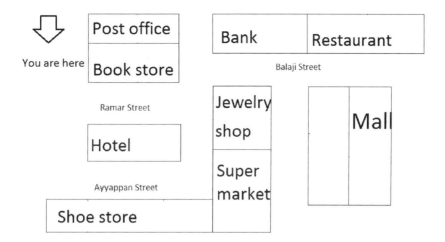

The below example is about asking a person 'how to go to the mall?' and 'he is guiding you', I have split the guide into multiple sentences for easy understanding.

a) Mallக்கு எப்படி போகணு(ம்)?

tl: mallkku eppadi poogaNum

lit: to the mall how should go

t: How to go to the mall?

b) நேர போங்க, இடது பக்கம் திரும்புங்க, அப்புறம் நேர போங்க

tl: <u>n</u>eera poonga idadhu pakkam thirumbungga appuRam <u>n</u>eera poongga

t: Go straight, Turn Left side, After that go straight

c) இடது பக்கம் திரும்புங்க அப்புறம் வலது பக்கம் திரும்புங்க அப்புறம் நேர போங்க

tl: idadhu pakkam thirumbunga appuRam valadhu pakkam thirumbungga appuRam <u>n</u>eera poonga

t: Turn left side, after that turn right side, after that go straight

d) வலது பக்கம் திரும்புங்க அப்புறம் நேர போங்க உங்க வலது பக்கம் Mall இருக்கு(ம்)

tl: valadhu pakkam thirumbungga appuRam <u>n</u>eera poonga unga valadhu pakkam Mall irukku(m)

lit: Turn right side, after that go straight, on your right side Mall will be there.

177

EXERCISES:

A) Look at the below map there is a hotel, a pedestrian who doesn't know where the hotel is comes to you and asks you 'how to go to the hotel?', Give him clear directions.

B) Look at the below map there is a Restaurant, a pedestrian who doesn't know where the Restaurant is comes to you and asks you 'how to go to the Restaurant?', Give him clear directions. ஓட்டல் (oottal) (Hotel, Restaurant).

| Post office |
| Book store |

You are here

| Bank | Restaurant |

Balaji Street

Ramar Street

| Jewelry shop |
| Super market |

| Hotel |

Mall

Ayyappan Street

| Shoe store |

SOLUTIONS

Lesson 10

Exercise A

1) முப்பத்தி ஆறு. 2) எழுவத்தி எட்டு. 3) எரநூத்தி அருவத்தி ஒன்பது. 4) தொன்னூத்தி ஒம்பது. 5) தொள்ளாயிரத்தி அருவத்தி ஆறு. 6) மூணாயிரத்தி அறநூத்தி எண்பத்தி ஒம்பது. 7) நூத்தி நாப்பத்தி அஞ்சு. 8) அஞ்சாயிரத்தி ஒன்பதாயிரத்தி எண்பத்தி ஏழு. 9) தொன்னூத்தி எட்டாயிரத்தி எழுநூத்தி அம்பத்தி எட்டு. 10) ஆறு லட்சத்தி தொன்னூத்தி எட்டாயிரத்தி எழுநூத்தி அம்பது.

TL: 1) muppaththu aaRu. 2) ezhuvaththi ettu. 3) eranuuththi aruvaththi onbadhu. 4) thonnuththi ombadhu. 5) thoLLaayiraththi aruvaththi aaRu. 6) muuNaayiraththi aRanuuththi eNbaththi ombadhu. 7) nuuththu naappaththi anjju. 8) anjaayiraththi onbadhaayiraththi eNbaththi ombadhu. 9) thonnuuththi ettaayiraththi ezhunuuththi ambaththi ettu. 10). aaRu latchaththi thonnuuththi ettaayiraththi ezhunuuththi ambadhu

Exercise B

1) எட்டாவது வீடு. 2) ஏழாவது கடை. 3) பன்னெண்டாவது வகுப்பு. 4) பதினாறாவது தெரு

TL: 1) ettaavadhu viidu. 2) eezhaavadhu kadai. 3) panneNdaavadhu vaguppu 4) padhinaaRaavadhu theru.

Exercise C

1) ரெண்டு மணி ஆவுது, 2) மூணு மணி ஆவுது, 3) நாலு மணி ஆவுது, 4) அஞ்சு மணி ஆவுது, 5) ஆறு மணி ஆவுது, 6) ஏழு மணி ஆவுது, 7) எட்டு மணி ஆவுது.

TL: 1) reNdu maNi aavudhu. 2) muuNu maNi aavudhu. 3) naalu maNi aavudhu. 4) anjju maNi aavudhu. 5) aaRu maNi aavudh. 6) eezhu maNi aavudhu. 7) ettu maNi aavudhu.

Exercise D

1) ரெண்டு மணி ஆவுது. 2) மணி ரெண்டேகால். 3) மணி ரெண்டர. 4) மணி ரெண்டேமுக்கா. 5) மூணு மணி ஆவுது. 6) மணி மூணேகால். 7) மணி மூணர. 8) மணி மூணேமுக்கா. 9) நாலு மணி ஆவுது.

TL: 1) reNdu maNi aavudhu. 2) maNi reNdeegaal. 3) maNi reNdara. 4) maNi reNdeemukkaa. 5) muuNu maNi aavudh. 6) maNi muuNeegaal. 7) maNi muuNara. 8) maNi muuNeemukkaa. 9) naalu maNi aavudhu.

Exercise E

1) அஞ்சு இருவத்தி அஞ்சு. 2) ஆறு முப்பத்தி ஆறு. 3) பதினொன்னு இருவத்தி ரெண்டு. 4) ஒம்பது இருவத்தி ஏழு. 5) நாலு முப்பது.

TL: 1) anjju iruvaththu anjju. 2) aaRu muppaththi aaRu. 3) padhinonnu iruvaththi reNdu. 4) ombadhu iruvaththu eezhu. 5) naalu muppadhu.

Exercise F

1) ஓட்டலுக்கு எப்படி போகணும்(ம்)? நேர போங்க, உங்க வலது பக்கம் ஓட்டல் இருக்கு(ம்)

TL: 1) oottalukku eppadi poogaNum? neera poongga, ungga valadhu pakkam oottal irukku(m).

Exercise G

1) Restaurantக்கு எப்படி போகணும்(ம்)? நேர போங்க, வலது பக்கம் திரும்புங்க, அப்புறம் நேர போங்க, வலது பக்கம் திரும்புங்க, அப்புறம் இடது பக்கம் திரும்புங்க, அப்புறம் நேர போங்க உங்க வலது பக்கம் Restaurant இருக்கு(ம்).

TL: 1) Restaurantkku eppadi poogaNum? neera poonga, valadhu pakkam thirumbungga, appuRam neera poongga, valadhu pakkam thirumbunga, appuRam idadhu pakkam thirumbungga, appuRam neera poonga unga valadhu pakkam Restaurant irukku(m).

CASES

LESSON 11

Content:

LESSON 11: CASES

Earlier, we discussed a little about case endings. Now, we will discuss them in detail.

As discussed earlier, Case endings are added to nouns and pronouns, which will give them the ability to express grammatical relations (e.g. subject, direct object, possession etc.) also the prepositions that we use in English (e.g. 'in', 'to', 'for', 'from', etc.). We usually add these prepositions in English before a noun or the pronoun. E.g. 'In the book', 'with him', 'to the office', 'for her' etc. Whereas in Tamil, we will add these prepositions as a suffix to the word itself (like a word ending) these are called case endings.

In English we use the suffix '-ist' to indicate 'the one who does', e.g. chemist, activist, alchemist, biologist etc. Here, we added the suffix '-ist' to each profession to point out the person who does it.

Important Note:

> You can add only one case suffix to a noun or a pronoun.

There are 8 case endings in Tamil. Kindly find them below.

1) Nominative Case: This is used in the sentence's subject and is a basic form of a noun or a pronoun; you don't have to add any suffix.

Example:

a) அவ(ன்) பாடுறா(ன்) (ava(n) paaduRaa(n)) (He is singing)

b) அவ(ள்) ஓடுறா(ள்) (ava(L) ooduRaa(L)) (She is running)

c) நா(ன்) சாப்பிடுறெ (naa(n) saappiduRe) (I am eating)

d) தமிழ் ரொம்ப அழகா இருக்கு (thamizh romba azhagaa irukku) (Tamil is very beautiful.)

In the above examples, I didn't add any suffix to the subject of the sentence (அவ(ன்), அவ(ள்), நா(ன்), தமிழ்) because it is a Nominative case, the basic form of the noun.

Note:

Since, the Nominative Case is a basic form of the subject you can ignore them, as this is the form we learn in the beginning and we don't have to add any suffix here.

List of Nominative Pronouns:

	Singular Nominative	Plural Nominative
First person	நா(ன்) (naa(n)) (I)	நாம (nama) (we) (listener included) நாங்க(ள்) (naangga(L)) (we) (listener not included)
Second person	நீ (nii) (you) நீங்க(ள்) (niingga(L)) (you) (polite)	நீங்க(ள்) (niingga(L)) (neengga) (you) (polite)
Third person	அவ(ன்) (ava(n)) (he) அவரு (avaru) (he) (1) அவ(ள்) (ava(L)) (she) அவங்க(ள்) (avangga(L)) (she) (polite)	அவங்க(ள்) (avangga(L)) (they-human) (polite)
	அது(adhu) (that) இது(idhu) (this), both the word also means it.	அதுங்க(ள்) (adhungga(L)) (those) இதுங்க(ள்) (idhungga(L)) (these)

Important Note:

From here on, the remaining 7 cases will not use the Nominative case pronoun from the above table. They will use cases from pronouns provided in the respective cases as a table.

2) Accusative Suffix: Accusative case is used in a direct object of the sentence. The suffix used in the Accusative case is அ (a).

What is a Direct Object?

A direct object is a noun or pronoun that receives the action of the verb directly, without any prepositions separating the verb from the receiver. The direct object answers the question "whom?" or "what?" in regards to the verb. A direct object always follows a Transitive verb in English; Transitive verb always follows a direct object in Tamil because, in Tamil, the object of the sentence usually comes next to a verb, whereas in English, it's the opposite.

Direct object follows Transitive Verb: This means Direct object comes or happens after Transitive verb. Subject Verb Object (SVO).

Direct object is followed by Transitive Verb: This means Transitive Verb comes or happens after Direct object. Subject Object Verb (SOV).

The direct object in a sentence is always a noun. It may also be in the form of a noun such as a pronoun, noun clause or noun phrase. However, a direct object will always function as a noun.

What is a Transitive Verb?

Verbs that take a direct object are called Transitive verbs; a noun or pronoun always follows these verbs.

Example in English:

a) Ram is playing Football.

- The above sentence answers the question 'Ram is playing what?'

- What is the direct object in this sentence? The direct object in this sentence is football because the noun 'Football' is the one that answers the question 'what'.

- What is the Transitive verb in this sentence? The Transitive verb in this sentence is 'is playing' because it takes the direct object 'Football' next to it.

Example in Tamil: Vocabulary: கால் (kaal) (Leg); பந்து (pandhu) (Ball); கால்பந்து (kaalpandhu) (Football).

b) ராம் கால்பந்த விளையாடுறா(ன்).

tl: raam kaalpandha viLaiyaaduRaan.

lit: Ram football is playing.

t: Ram is playing football.

In detail: கால்பந்து (kaalpandhu) + அ (a) (Accusative suffix) = கால்பந்த (kaalpandha).

In the above sentence, it answers the question: 'ராம் என்ன விளையாடுறா(ன்)?

tl: raam enna viLaiyaaduRaa(n).

lit: Ram what is playing.

t: What is Ram playing.

- What is the direct object in this sentence? The direct object in this sentence is 'கால்பந்த' (kaalpandha) (Football) because the noun 'கால்பந்த' is the one which answers the question 'என்ன' (enna) (what).

- What is the Transitive verb in this sentence? The Transitive verb in this sentence is 'விளையாடுறா(ன்)' because it takes the direct object 'கால்பந்த' before it.

How to Find the Direct Object in a Sentence in Tamil?

A simple formula below can help you identify a direct object in a sentence.

> ### Formula:
> - Subject + What? or Whom? + Action Verb.
> - What? or Whom? = Direct Object.

Example of Direct Object Sentence Formula:

- கலா (kalaa) (name of a girl) (subject) + புத்தகம (puththagama) (book) (what? or whom?) + எடுத்தா(ள்) (eduththaa(L)) (took) (action verb).
- புத்தகம = direct object.

In detail: புத்தகம் (puththagam) (book) + அ (a) (Accusative suffix) = புத்தகம.

Different Kinds of Direct Objects

Direct objects can be nouns or pronouns. Kindly find the below examples.

Noun as a Direct Object:

a) ராம் கால்பந்த விளையாடுறா(ன்). (Ram is playing football).
- ராம் என்ன விளையாடுறா(ன்) (What is Ram playing?)."கால்பந்த" is the direct object.

b) ரமேஷ் புத்தகம படிக்குறா(ன்) (Ramesh is reading book).
- ரமேஷ் என்ன படிக்குறா(ன்) (What is Ram reading?). "புத்தகம" is the direct object.

Pronoun as a Direct Object:

a) ராம் அத விளையாடுறா(ன்).
tl: raam adha viLaiyaaduRaan.
lit: Ram it is playing.
t: Ram is playing it.

In detail: அது (adhu) (it) + அ (a) (Accusative suffix) = அத (adha) (it).

b) மாலா அவன அடிச்சா(ள்).

tl: maala avana adichchaa(L).

lit: maala him is hitting.

t: maala is hitting him.

In detail: அவ(ன்) (ava(n)) (he) + அ (a) (Accusative suffix) = அவன (avana) (him).

In the above examples, you can see that i added the Accusative suffix to a pronoun அது (it) and அவ(ன்) (him) since they are the direct object of those sentences.

Important Note:

> You cannot add another case suffix to a noun or a pronoun that already contains an Accusative case suffix. The same applies to the entire case suffix. These 8 cases don't like each other so they don't get along in the same noun or a pronoun, but you can add another case suffix to a different noun or a pronoun in a sentence.

Example:

அவனுக்கு பந்த அடிக்கணு(ம்).

tl: avanukku pandha adikkaNu(m).

lit: for him ball wants to him.

t: he wants to hit the ball.

In detail: அவ(ன்) (ava(n)) (he) + உக்கு (ukku) (Dative suffix) = அவனுக்கு (for him).

பந்து (pandhu) (ball) + அ (a) (Accusative suffix) = பந்த (pandha) (ball).

அடிக்க (adikka) (AvP: Hit) + ணு(ம்) (Nu(m)) (want to) = அடிக்கணு(ம்) (want to hit).

In the above example, I used two different case suffixes on two different nouns and pronouns in the same sentence.

Note:

> Accusative case is optional for an unanimated direct object; an unanimated direct object is a thing that is not alive, such as a table, a pen, a book, etc.

Scenarios Where an Accusative Case is Not Applicable Even Though an Object Exists:

1) When the sentence contains a Subject complement instead of a Direct Object:

As I have mentioned earlier, only Transitive verbs can have direct objects. A Transitive verb will only follow a direct object.

In certain scenarios, the Linking verbs often have subject complements instead of a direct object. A linking verb similar to a direct object follows a subject complement but differs because a linking verb instead of an action verb follows it.

Examples of Linking verbs with subject complements:

a) Ram was angry.

- was = linking verb; angry = subject complement.
- ராம் கோபமா இருக்குறா(ன்).
- இருக்குறா(ன்) = linking verb; கோபமா = subject complement.

b) Ramesh is happy.

- is = linking verb; happy = subject complement.
- ரமேஷ் சந்தோஷமா இருக்குறா(ன்).
- இருக்குறா(ன்) = linking verb; சந்தோஷமா = subject complement.

c) Latha is an actor.

- is = linking verb; actor = subject complement.
- லதா ஒரு நடிகை.
- In Tamil, we don't usually use a separate word for 'is' like in English. Here, the linking verb 'is' needs to be understood by you, because there is no need for it to be mentioned in the sentence; நடிகை = subject complement.

In the above examples, even though the subject complement may seem to answer the question "what?" they are not direct objects. Since the words are followed by linking verbs, they are called the subject complements.

Also, direct objects receive the action of the sentence. The direct object of a verb is the thing being acted up, but Linking verbs are not action verbs, so there is no action taking place. Linking verbs connect a subject to its predicate without taking action; they simply re-identify or describe the subject differently.

2) Subject Pronouns are not Direct Objects:

Subject pronouns cannot be direct objects because only object pronouns can be direct objects. Subject pronouns are also known as Nominative Pronouns.

- A subject pronoun should be used only as a subject. A subject pronoun will always complete the action in the sentence.

- An object pronoun should be used only as a direct object. An object pronoun will always receive the action in the sentence.

Examples of Subject and Object Pronoun:

Subject Pronouns (Nominative): நா(ன்) (naa(n)) (I), நீ (nii) (you), நீங்க(ள்) (niingga(L)) (you), நாம (naama) (we), நாங்க(ள்) (naangga(L)) (we).

Object Pronouns (Accusative): எ(ன்) (e(n)) (me, my), உ(ன்) (u(n)) (your), உங்க(ள்) (ungga(L)) (your), நம்ம(ள்) (namma(L)) (our), எங்க(ள்) (engga(L)) (our).

Example:

அவனுக்கு அவள பிடிக்கு(ம்).

tl: avanukku avaLa pidikku(m).

lit: for him her likes.

t: He likes her.

In detail: அவ(ள்) (ava(L)) (she) + அ (a) (Accusative suffix) = அவள (avaLa) (her).

அவ(ன்) (ava(n)) (he) + உக்கு (ukku) (Dative suffix) = அவனுக்கு (for him).

Note:

In the above example, I mentioned 'He likes her' instead of 'He likes she' because this is unacceptable in Tamil grammar, just like in English.

The below table provides the list of Object Pronouns in their respective Accusative case.

Pronoun	Transliteration	English
என்ன	enna	Me
உன்ன	unna	You
உங்கள	unggaLa	You (Formal).
அவன	avana	Him (Informal).
அவர	avara	Him (Formal).
அவள	avaLa	Her (Informal).
அவங்கள	avanggaLa	Them
அத	adha	That (it)
இத	idha	This (it)
நம்ம(ள)	namma(La)	Our (Inclusive)
எங்கள	enggaLa	Our (Exclusive)
அதுங்கள	adhunggaLa	Them
இதுங்கள	idhunggaLa	These
யார	yaara	Whom?

Summary: In short, a direct object is a noun or pronoun that receives the action of the verb.
A direct object will always follow a Transitive verb. A direct object is always a noun or another part of speech functioning as a noun.
Here are some more examples of sentences with direct objects.

a) நாய் புத்தகம கிழிச்சுச்சு.

tl: naay puththagama kizhichchuchchu.

lit: The dog book tore.

t: The dog tore the book.

In detail: புத்தகம் (puththagam) (book) + அ (a) (Accusative suffix) = புத்தகம

b) பைய(ன்) பந்த வீசுறா(ன்).

tl: paiya(n) pandha viisuRaa(n).

lit: The boy ball throws.

t: The boy throws the ball.

In detail: பந்து (pandhu) (ball) + அ (a) (Accusative suffix) = பந்த (pandha) (ball).

c) நீ சாப்பாட சாப்பிட்டெ.

tl: n̲ii saappaada saappitte.

lit: I food ate.

t: You ate food.

EXERCISES:

A) Use the Accusative suffix to translate the following from English to Tamil.

e.g. He called me

Answer: அவ(ன்) என்ன கூப்பிட்டா(ன்) (ava(n) enna kuuppittaa(n))

1) I called him.

_____

2) This boy took the ball.

_____

3) That girl took the book.

_____

4) Ram ate the food.

_____

5) The dog bit him.

_____

6) They read the book.

_____

7) She wrote the letter.

_____

8) I cooked the food.

_____

9) I told the truth.

_____

10) They called us.

_____

3) Dative Case: Dative case suffix refers to the preposition 'To' or 'For'. The Dative case is used in a sentence referring to "giving 'to' someone/something or 'for' someone/something". The suffix to be used in the Dative case is -(உ)க்கு ((u)kku). Here the letter உ is inside the brackets because for some pronouns and words ending with the compound letter containing ஐ (e.g. கை, தை, பை) you would use the Dative suffix -க்கு (kku).

The below table provides the list of pronouns with their respective Dative case.

Pronoun	Transliteration	English
எனக்கு	enakku	To me, For me.
உனக்கு	unakku	To you, For you (Informal).
உங்களுக்கு	unggaLukku	To you, For you (Formal).
அவனுக்கு	avanukku	To him, For him (Informal).
அவருக்கு	avarukku	To him, For him (Formal).
அவளுக்கு	avaLukku	To her, For her (Informal).
அவங்களுக்கு	avanggaLukku	To her, For her (Formal), To Them, For Them.
அதுக்கு	adhukku	To that, For that (it)
இதுக்கு	idhukku	To this, For this (it)
நமக்கு	namakku	To us, For us (Inclusive)
எங்களுக்கு	enggaLukku	To us, For us (Exclusive)
அதுங்களுக்கு	adhunggaLukku	To those, For those
இதுங்களுக்கு	idhunggaLukku	To these, For these
யாருக்கு	yaarukku	To whom, For whom?

Dative case is used in the word on the receiving end. It may also be used in front of some conjugated verbs. Basically, the Dative case is used in Nouns, Pronouns and Verbs.

The Dative case is usually used when referring to 'to' or 'for' the recipient and destination.

Example: A noun with the Dative case is the recipient of the action of verbs like தா (thaa) (give) or the destination of verbs like போ (poo) (go).

Summary: Dative case is similar to 'To' and 'For' in English. The suffix is -(உ)க்கு ((u)kku). This suffix is used when the sentence answers the question 'For whom ...?' or 'Who ...?', with the answer 'For ....' or 'To ....'.

192

Note:

You would notice in the table provided, that for some pronouns I have used the Dative suffix -(உ)க்கு ((u)kku) and for some pronouns I have used the Dative suffix –க்கு (kku). The Pronoun with the Dative suffix provided in the table is fixed; you must memorize them all.

Words Usually Used Next to Dative Case:

1) Suffix: -ணு(ம்) (-Nu(m)), As discussed earlier, this suffix is used to express the 'need' or 'obligation'. When added to the infinitive form of a verb, it can have the sense of 'need' or 'obligation'. Basically -ணு(ம்) is a short form of வேணு(ம்) (veeNu(m)) which means 'want', 'need'. குடுக்க (kudukka) (give) + -ணு(ம்) = குடுக்கணு(ம்) (kudukkaNu(m)) (should give)

The above is a short form of குடுக்க வேணு(ம்) (kudukka veenu(m)) which also means 'should give'.

2) வேண்டா(ம்) (veeNdaa(m)) (do not want, do not need): This word is the complete opposite of வேணு(ம்), It means you don't want to do something or you don't need something.

Example:

a) இந்தியா (indhiyaa) (India) + வ் (v) + உக்கு (ukku) = இந்தியாவுக்கு (indhiyaavukku) (To the India).

b) அமேரிக்கா (ameerikkaa) (America) + வ் (v) + உக்கு (ukku) = அமெரிக்காவுக்கு (ameerikkaavukku) (To the America).

c) ஓட்டல் (oottal) (Hotel) + உக்கு (ukku) = ஓட்டலுக்கு (oottalukku) (To the Hotel).

d) அக்கா (akkaa) (Elder sister) + வ் (v) + உக்கு (ukku) = அக்காவுக்கு (akkaavukku) (For elder sister India).

e) இந்த பேனா அக்காவுக்கு.

tl: indha peenaa akkaavukku.

lit/t: This pen is for elder sister.

Note:

In the above example we are using அக்காவுக்கு (for elder sister) instead of அக்கா (elder sister) because the 'elder sister' is at the receiving end, she is the one who is receiving the pen. Also, this sentence answers the question 'This pen is for whom?'.

f) நா(ன்) இந்தியாவுக்கு போறெ.

tl: <u>n</u>aa(n) i<u>n</u>dhiyaavukku pooRe.

lit: I to the India going.

t: I am going to India.

g) எனக்கு காப்பி வேண்டா(ம்).

tl: enakku kaappi veeNdaa(m).

lit: for me coffee don't want

t: I don't want coffee.

Note:

In the above example we are using எனக்கு (for me) instead of நா(ன்) (I) because I am at the receiving end, I am the one who is receiving the coffee. Also, this sentence answers the question 'This coffee is for whom?

h) அவனுக்கு மருத்துவமனைக்கு போகணு(ம்).

tl: avanukku maruththuvamanaikku poogaNu(m).

lit: for him to the hospital want to go.

t: He wants to go to the Hospital.

In detail: 'மருத்துவமனை' (maruththuvamanai) (hospital) + ய் (y) + உக்கு (ukku) = மருத்துவமனையுக்கு (maruththuvamanaiyukku) (To the hospital).

Note:

In the above example, I am using the Dative case on two different words 'அவ(ன்)' (ava(n)) (him) and 'மருத்துவமனை' (maruththuvamanai) (hospital) because both are at the receiving end. Both 'அவ(ன்)' (him) and 'மருத்துவமனை' (hospital) are the recipients of the verb போ (poo) (To go). You will be able to understand better with the next two examples.

i) அவனுக்கு போகணு(ம்).

tl: avanukku poogaNu(m).

lit: for him must go.

t: He wants to go.

j) மருத்துவமனையுக்கு போகணு(ம்).

tl: maruththuvamanaiyukku poogaNu(m).

lit: to the hospital must go.

t: Must go to the Hospital.

k) கடைக்கு போ.

tl: kadaikku poo.

lit: to the shop go.

t: Go to the shop.

EXERCISES:

B) Use the Dative suffix to translate the following from English to Tamil.

e.g. My elder sister wants coffee

Answer: எ(ன்) அக்காவுக்கு காப்பி வேணு(ம்) (e(n) akkaavukku kaappi veeNu(m))

1) My younger brother wants tea.

_____

2) He does not want to play.

_____

3) I am going to the shop.

_____

4) I do not want to go to America.

_____

5) This book is for elder brother.

_____

6) I want to eat.

_____

7) She wants to cook.

_____

8) I do not want pen.

_____

9) They want a statue.

_____

10) They don't want milk.

_____

195

4) Genititive/Possessive Case:
4) Genititive/Possessive Case: Genitive case suffix refers to the preposition 'of', ''s'. Genitive case is used to indicate possession. The suffix used in Genitive case is -ஓட (ooda).

The Genitive case suffix is optional for both nouns and pronouns, but you should use only the case form pronouns not the Nominative pronouns. The Genitive case suffix is mostly omitted with pronouns rather than with nouns. So, you will find lots of nouns containing this suffix, but rarely will you find a pronoun with this suffix. But you should still learn this to recognize it when required. This suffix is used when the sentence answers the question 'whose', Then the answer would be 'of ....' , '.....'s'.

The table below provides the list of pronouns with their respective Genitive case.

Pronoun with Genitive Suffix	TL	Pronoun without Genitive Suffix	TL	English
என்னோட	ennooda	எ(ன்)	e(n)	My
உன்னோட	unnooda	உ(ன்)	u(n)	Your (Informal).
உங்களோட	unggaLooda	உங்க(ள்)	ungga(L)	Your (Formal).
அவனோட	avanooda	அவ(ன்)	ava(n)	His (Informal).
அவரோட	avarooda	அவரு	avaru	His (Formal).
அவளோட	avaLooda	அவ(ள்)	ava(L)	Her (Informal).
அவங்களோட	avanggaLooda	அவங்க(ள்)	avangga(L)	Her (Formal), Their
அதோட	adhooda	அதோட	adhooda	it's
இதோட	idhooda	இதோட	idhooda	it's
நம்மோட	nammooda	நம்ம(ள்)	namma(L)	Our (Inclusive)
எங்களோட	enggaLooda	எங்க(ள்)	engga(L)	Our (Exclusive)
அதுங்களோட	adhunggaLooda	அதுங்க(ள்)	adhungga(L)	Those
இதுங்களோ	idhunggaLooda	இதுங்க(ள்)	idhungga(L)	These
யாரோட	yaarooda			Whose

196

Example:

எ(ன்) புத்தகம் (e(n) puththagam).

என்னோட புத்தகம் (ennooda puththagam).

lit/t: My Book.

Note:

As mentioned earlier, the Genitive case suffix is optional for both nouns and pronouns; You can use both the sentences mentioned above with or without a suffix, which would still give you the same meaning. Both the above sentences mean 'My book'. Here, I am referring to the 'book belongs to me' and 'I am possessing the book'.

Examples:

a) எங்க(ள்)/எங்களோட புது வண்டி சிவப்பு நிறம்.

tl: engga(L)/enggaLooda pudhu vandi sivappu n̲iRam.

lit/t: Our new vehicle is red.

- எங்க(ள்)/எங்களோட = Pronoun in Genitive Case.
- வண்டி = Noun Receiving Possession.

b) இது உ(ன்)/உன்னோட பூனை.

tl: idhu u(n)/unnooda puunai.

lit/t: This is your cat.

- உன்/உன்னோட = Pronoun in Genitive Case.
- பூனை = Noun Receiving Possession.

c) இது இந்தியாவோட கொடி.

tl: idhu in̲dhiyaavooda kodi.

lit/t: This is India's flag.

- இந்தியாவோட = Pronoun in Genitive Case.
- கொடி = Noun Receiving Possession.

d) இது அந்த கைபேசியோட simcard.

tl: idhu an̲dha kaipeesiyooda simcard.

lit/t: This is that phones simcard.

e) எது அவ(ள்)/அவளோட புத்தகம்.

tl: edhu ava(L)/avaLooda puththagam.

lit/t: Which is her book?.

EXERCISES:

C) Use the Genitive suffix to translate the following from English to Tamil.

E.g. This is your Dog

Answer: இது உன்னோட நாய் (idhu unnooda <u>n</u>aay)

1) Is this your dog?

_____

2) Whose cat is this?

_____

3) This is your food.

_____

4) This is vehicles flag.

_____

5) Is this her book?

_____

6) Whose vehicle is that?

_____

7) This is America's Flag.

_____

8) She is his wife (Hint: With respect)

_____

9) She is my wife.

_____

10) He is my husband.

_____

5) Instrumental Case: Instrumental case suffix refers to the preposition ' because of ', 'by'. Instrumental case is used to indicate with which or by whom the action was performed. The suffix to be used in Instrumental case is –ஆல (aala).

The Genitive case suffix is used in both nouns and pronouns. We may also use the Genitive case in front of some conjugated verbs. This suffix is used when the sentence answers the question 'because of whom' 'by which/using which'.

The table below provides the list of pronouns with their respective Instrumental case.

Pronoun	Transliteration	English
என்னால	ennaala	By me, Because of me.
உன்னால	unnaala	By you, Because of you.
உங்களால	unggaLaala	By you, Because of you (Formal).
அவனால	avanaala	By him, Because of him (Informal).
அவரால	avaraala	By him, Because of him (Formal).
அவளால	avalaala	By her, Because of her (Informal).
அவங்களால	avanggaLaala	By Them, Because of Them.
அதால	adhaala	By that, Because of that (it)
இதால	idhaala	By this, Because of this (it)
நம்மால	nammaala	By us, Because of us(Inclusive)
எங்களால	enggaLaala	By us, Because of us (Exclusive)
அதுங்களால	adhunggaLaala	By them, Because of them
இதுங்களால	idhunggaLaala	By these, Because of these
யாரால	yaaraala	By whom, Because of whom

When you are referring to 'by ...' using the Instrumental case suffix then the word 'முடியும்' (mudiyum) (could) and 'முடியாது' (mudiyaadhu) (could not) usually comes next to it. When these words are used independently:

முடியும் – I can do.

முடியல – I could not do.

Examples:

a) அவனால பேச முடியல.

tl: avanaala peesa mudiyala.

lit: by him talk could not.

t: he could not talk.

- அவனால = Pronoun in Instrumental Case.
- பேச = Infinitive being performed using the instrument.

b) அவனால நா(ன்) கீழ விழுந்தெ.

tl: avanaala naa(n) kiizha vizhundhe.

lit: because of him I fell down.

t: I fell down because of him.

- அவனால = Pronoun in Instrumental Case.
- விழுந்தெ = Conjugated verb being performed using the instrument.

c) இந்த நாயால அவ(ள்) அழுறா(ள்).

tl: indha naayaala ava(L) azhuRaa(L).

lit: this because of the dog she is crying.

t: She is crying because of this dog.

d) அவரால ஓட முடியு(ம்).

tl: avaraala ooda mudiyu(m).

lit: by him run could.

t: he could run.

e) அதால சாப்பிட முடியல.

tl: adhaala saappida mudiyala.

lit: by it eat could not.

t: it could not eat.

EXERCISES:

D) Use the Instrumental suffix to translate the following from English to Tamil.

E.g. He could not run

Answer: அவனால ஓட முடியல (avanaala ooda mudiyala)

1) She could not sleep.

_____

2) They could not walk.

_____

3) Because of him I couldn't go to the hotel.

_____

4) Because of my wife I couldn't go to the shop.

_____

5) Can you eat?

_____

6) Yes, I can eat.

_____

7) No, I could not eat.

_____

8) I could not eat because of him

_____

9) I could not play this game

_____

10) I can play this game.

_____

6) Sociative Case: Sociative case suffix refers to the preposition 'along with'. Sociative case is used to indicate the person, animal or an object along with 'whom/that' the action was performed. It is used when you are socializing and is not restricted to just a person. It also includes animals and objects, for e.g. you along with your friend or family, a spoon along with the fork, Simcard along with a phone etc. The suffix to be used in the Instrumental case is -ஓட or –கூட (ooda or kuuda). You can use both -ஓட or –கூட suffix for Sociative case, both give you the same meaning, but some exceptions are there. Kindly find them below.

1) –ஓட (ooda) - This Sociative suffix can be used for both living (person, animals) and non-living things (Object).

2) -கூட (kuuda) This Sociative suffix can be used only for living things (person, animals).

The suffix for the Sociative case is the same as the suffix for the Genitive case but don't worry, since we are using the same suffix for both you can use them without thinking much about it.

Since the suffix for Sociative and Genitive is the same, you can refer to the list of pronoun table given under the Genitive case.

Examples:

a) அவனோட நா(ன்) partyக்கு போனெ.

tl: avanooda naa(n) partykku poone.

lit: along with him I to the party went.

t: I went to the party along with him.

- அவனோட = Pronoun in Sociative Case.
- நா(ன்) = Pronoun Receiving social aspect.

Note:

In the above example, you can see that I have used both Sociative and Dative case in the same sentence. Multiple cases can co-exist in the same sentence but they cannot co-exist in the same word.

b) நா(ன்) அவளோட விளையாடுனெ.

tl: naa(n) avaLooda viLaiyaadune.

lit: I along with her was playing.

t: I was playing along with her.

c) புத்தகமோட பேனா இருந்தது.

tl: puththagamooda peenaa iru<u>n</u>dhadhu.

lit: along with the book, pen was there.

t: The pen was along with the book (Alternate: The pen was next to the book).

- புத்தகமோட = Pronoun in Sociative Case.
- பேனா = Noun which indicates it was next to another object.

d) Simcardஓட கைபேசி இருந்தது.

tl: simcardooda kaipeesi iru<u>n</u>dhadhu.

lit: along with the simcard phone was there.

t: The phone was there along with the simcard.

e) நா(ன்) எ(ன்) அம்மாவோட இருந்தெ.

tl: <u>n</u>aa(n) e(n) ammaavooda iru<u>n</u>dhe.

lit: I along with my mother was there.

t: I was there with my mom.

- அம்மாவோட = Pronoun in Sociative Case.
- நா(ன்) = Pronoun Receiving social aspect.

f) அவ(ள்) என் தங்கையோட படிச்சா(ள்).

tl: ava(L) en thanggaiyooda padichchaa(L).

lit: she my along with younger sister studied.

t: She studied along with my younger sister.

g) இது அவங்களோட வந்துது.

tl: idhu avanggaLooda va<u>n</u>dhudhu.

lit: it along with them came.

t: It came along with them.

- அவங்களோட = Pronoun in Sociative Case.
- இது = Pronoun Receiving social aspect.

EXERCISES:

E) Use the Sociative suffix to translate the following from English to Tamil.

e.g. I will come to your home tomorrow with ram

Answer: நா(ன்) ராமோட நாளைக்கு உன் வீட்டுக்கு வறெ

tl: naa(n) raamooda naaLaikku un viittukku vaRe

lit: I along with ram tomorrow your house will come.

t: I will come to your house along with Ram

1) I ate my breakfast with my wife.

_____

2) I went shopping along with my husband.

_____

3) I was with my friends yesterday.

_____

4) The book was along with the pencil.

_____

5) I will sit with my friend, Maala.

_____

7) Locative Case: Locative case suffix refers to the preposition 'on' 'In' 'at'. It indicates the location of things (objects, place, etc.) and living things (people, animals). It is used when referring to a noun located with a person or in a thing, E.g. you are on the bus, you are in a park, a pen with him etc.

The suffix to be used in the Locative case is –ல (la) for things (Object place etc.), -(கி)ட்ட ((ki)tta) for living things (person and animals).

The table below provides the list of pronouns with their respective Locative case.

Locative Suffix for Living things	Transliteration	English
என்கிட்ட	engitta	With me
உன்கிட்ட	ungitta	With you (Informal).
உங்ககிட்ட	unggagitta	With you (Formal).
அவன்கிட்ட	avangitta	With him (Informal).
அவருகிட்ட	avarugitta	With him (Formal).
அவள்கிட்ட	avaLgitta	With Her (Informal).
அவங்ககிட்ட	avanggagitta	With Her (Formal), With Their
அதுகிட்ட	adhugitta	With that (it)
இதுகிட்ட	idhugitta	With this (it)
நம்மகிட்ட	nammagitta	With us (Inclusive)
எங்ககிட்ட	enggagitta	With us (Exclusive)
அதுங்ககிட்ட	adhunggagitta	With them
இதுங்ககிட்ட	idhunggagitta	With these

Locative Suffix for Things	Transliteration	English
Busல	busla	in the bus
carல	carla	in the car
ஓட்டல்ல	oottalla	in hotel
வீட்டுல	viittula	in the house
கடைல	kadaila	in the shop
கைபேசில	kaipeesila	in the mobile

Examples:

a) அவங்க(ள்) கடைல இருக்குறாங்க.

tl: avangga(L) kadaila irukkuRaangga.

lit: they in the shop are.

t: They are in the shop.

- கடைல = Noun in Locative Case.
- அவங்க(ள்) = Pronoun which is in the location.

b) கைபேசில Simcard இருக்கு.

tl: kaipeesila Simcard irukku.

lit: in the cell phone Simcard is.

t: Sim card is in the cell phone.

c) எ(ன்) வீடு அமெரிக்கால இருக்கு.

tl: e(n) viidu amerikkaala irukku.

lit: my house in America is.

t: My house is in America.

- அமெரிக்கால = Place in Locative Case.
- எ(ன்) வீடு = This indicates what is being located.

206

d) நா(ன்) வேலைல இருக்குறெ.

tl: naa(n) veelaila irukkuRe.

lit: I at work am.

t: I am at work.

e) என்கிட்ட பேனா இருக்கு.

tl: engitta peenaa irukku.

lit: with me pen have.

t: I have pen with me.

- என்கிட்ட = Pronoun in Locative Case.
- பேனா = Noun which is being located.

f) உங்ககிட்ட ஒரு புத்தகம் இருக்கா?

tl: unggagitta oru puththagam irukkaa.

lit: with you a book do you have?

t: Do you have a book with you?

g) அவன்கிட்ட வீடு இருக்கு.

tl: avangitta viidu irukku.

lit: with him house have.

t: He has a house with him.

h) கேமரால Battery இருக்கா?

tl: keemaraala Battery irukkaa.

lit: in the camera battery is there?

t: Is there a battery in the camera?

i) சாப்பாட்டுல உப்பு இருக்கா?

tl: saappaattula uppu irukkaa.

lit: in the food salt is there?

t: Is there salt in the food?

EXERCISES:

F) Try Asking Maala if she has the below mentioned politely 'using Locative suffix'.

Example:

Book.

Answer: உங்ககிட்ட புத்தகம் இருக்கா? (unggagitta puththagam irukkaa?)

1) Pen.

_____

2) Phone

_____

3) Dog

_____

4) Cat

_____

5) House

_____

G) Try Responding to question 'Where are you' for the below mentioned 'using Locative suffix'.

Example:

Bus.

Answer: நா(ன்) Busல இருக்கெ (naa(n) busla irukke) (I am in the Bus)

1) Hotel.

_____

2) Beach

_____

3) Park

_____

4) Shop

_____

5) House

_____

H) Use Locative suffix to translate the following from English to Tamil.

E.g. He is in the Bus

Answer: அவ(ன்) Busல இருக்கா(ன்) (ava(n) Busla irukkaa(n))

1) My house is in America.

_____

2) Is your house in Chennai?

_____

3) Does she have a pen?

_____

4) I am at Taj Mahal.

_____

5) I am at the Mall

_____

8) Ablative Case: Ablative case suffix refers to the preposition 'from'. Ablative case indicates where or from whom you got something, E.g. I got the pen from him, the bulb got electricity from the generator etc. It is used to indicate both people and things.

The suffix to be used in the Ablative case is -லருந்து (larundhu) for things (Object place etc.), -(கி)ட்டருந்து ((ki)ttarundhu) for living things (person and animals). This suffix answers the question "from where".

The table below provides the list of pronouns with their respective Ablative case.

Ablative Suffix for Living things	Transliteration	English
என்கிட்டருந்து	engittarundhu	From me
உன்கிட்டருந்து	ungittarundhu	From you (Informal).
உங்ககிட்டருந்து	unggagittarundhu	From you (Formal).
அவன்கிட்டருந்து	avangittarundhu	From him (Informal).
அவருகிட்டருந்து	avarugittarundhu	From him (Formal).
அவள்கிட்டருந்து	avaLgittarundhu	From Her (Informal).
அவங்ககிட்டருந்து	avanggagittarundhu	From Her (Formal), With Their
அதுகிட்டருந்து	adhugittarundhu	From that (it)
இதுகிட்டருந்து	idhugittarundhu	From this (it)
நம்மகிட்டருந்து	nammagittarundhu	From us (Inclusive)
எங்ககிட்டருந்து	enggagittarundhu	From us (Exclusive)
அதுங்ககிட்டருந்து	adhunggagittarundhu	From them
இதுங்ககிட்டருந்து	idhunggagittarundhu	From these

Ablative Suffix for Things	Transliteration	English
Busலருந்து	buslarundhu	From bus
carலருந்து	carlarundhu	From car
ஓட்டல்லருந்து	oottallarundhu	From hotel
வீட்டுலருந்து	viittularundhu	From house
கடைலருந்து	kadailarundhu	From shop
கைபேசிலருந்து	kaipeesilarundhu	From mobile

Examples:

a) அவங்க(ள்) கடைலருந்து வர்றாங்க.

tl: avangga(L) kadailarundhu varRaangga.

lit: they from the shop are coming.

t: They are coming from the shop.

- கடைலருந்து = Noun in Ablative Case.
- அவங்க(ள்) = Pronoun which is from the location.

b) நா(ன்) அவ(ன்) கைபேசிலருந்து கூப்பிட்டெ.

tl: naa(n) ava(n) kaipeesilarundhu kuuppitte.

lit: I from his mobile phone called.

t: I called from his mobile phone.

- கைபேசிலருந்து = Noun in Ablative Case.
- அவ(ன்) = Pronoun from where the object is from.

c) நா(ன்) அமெரிக்கலருந்து வர்றென்.

tl: naa(n) amerikkalarundhu varRen.

lit: I from America am coming.

t: I am coming from America.

- அமெரிக்கலருந்து = Place in Ablative Case.
- நா(ன்) = Pronoun which is from the location.

d) அவ(ன்) அவள்கிட்டேருந்து பேனா வாங்குனா(ன்).

tl: ava(n) avaLkitteerundhu peenaa vaanggunaa(n).

lit: He from her pen took.

t: He took pen from her.

- அவள்கிட்டேருந்து = Pronoun in AblativeCase.
- அவ(ன்) = Pronoun which received.

e) நீ யாருகிட்டேருந்து இந்த car வாங்குனெ?.

tl: nii yaarukitteerundhu indha car vaanggune.

lit: you from whom this car bought.

t: From whom did you bought this car?.

- யாருகிட்டேருந்து = Question word in Ablative Case.
- Car= Noun which is being received.

Note:

You can use Ablative case even with question words, like given in the above example.

f) நா(ன்) அவன்கிட்டேருந்து இந்த car வாங்குனெ.

tl:naa(n) avankitteerundhu indha car vaanggune.

lit: I from him this car bought.

t: I bought this car from him.

g) நா(ன்) அவன்கிட்டேருந்து எடுத்தெ.

tl: naa(n) avankitteerundhu eduththe.

lit: I from him took.

t: I took from him.

h) அவ(ன்) வங்கிலருந்து பணம் எடுத்தா(ன்).

tl: ava(n) vanggilarundhu paNam eduththaa(n).

lit: he from the bank money took.

t: He took the money from the bank.

EXERCISES:

I) Try Responding to question 'From where do you come?' for the below mentioned 'using Ablative suffix'.

Example:

I; India.

Answer: நா(ன்) இந்தியாலருந்து வர்றென். (I am coming from India)

1) I; Bus.

_____

2) I; Car.

_____

3) I; Hotel.

_____

4) I; House.

_____

5) I; Shop.

_____

J) Try Responding to question 'from whom did you get this ….?' for the below mentioned 'using Ablative suffix'.

Example:

Her; Money.

Answer: நா(ன்) அவள்கிட்டருந்து பணம் வாங்கினெ (naa(n) avaLkittarundhu

paNam vaanggine) (I got the money from her)

1) Him; Jewels;

_____

2) Them; Vehicle;

_____

3) You (Formal); Book;

_____

4) You (Informal Formal); Pencil;

_____

5) Her; House.

_____

K) Use Ablative suffix to translate the following from English to Tamil.

E.g. He is in the bus (change it)

Answer: அவ(ன்) Busல இருக்கா(ன்) (ava(n) Busla irukkaa(n))

1) I am speaking from the cell phone.

_____

2) They bought from him.

_____

3) He took water from her.

_____

4) I am coming from London

_____

5) From whom did you bought this book?

_____

List of Pronouns for Different Cases

The below table provides the list of cases form pronoun for all 7 cases except nominative.

Case form pronoun	Accusative	Dative	Genitive/ Sociative
-----	-அ	-உக்கு	-ஓட
என்	என்ன	எனக்கு	என்னோட
உன்	உன்ன	உனக்கு	உன்னோட
உங்க(ள்)	உங்கள	உங்களுக்கு	உங்களோட
அவ(ன்)	அவன	அவனுக்கு	அவனோட
அவரு	அவர	அவருக்கு	அவரோட
அவ(ள்)	அவள	அவளுக்கு	அவளோட
அவங்க(ள்)	அவங்கள	அவங்களுக்கு	அவங்களோட
அது	அத	அதுக்கு	அதோட
இது	இத	இதுக்கு	இதோட
நம்ம	நம்ம	நமக்கு	நம்மோட
எங்க(ள்)	எங்கள	எங்களுக்கு	எங்களோட
அதுங்க(ள்)	அதுங்கள	அதுங்களுக்கு	அதுங்களோட
இதுங்க(ள்)	இதுங்கள	இதுங்களுக்கு	இதுங்களோட
யார்	யார	யாருக்கு	யாரோட

Instrumental	Locative	Ablative
-ஆல	-(கி)ட்ட	-(கி)ட்டேருந்து
என்னால	என்கிட்ட	என்கிட்டருந்து
உன்னால	உன்கிட்ட	உன்கிட்டருந்து
உங்களால	உங்ககிட்ட	உங்ககிட்டருந்து
அவனால	அவன்கிட்ட	அவன்கிட்டருந்து
அவரால	அவருகிட்ட	அவருகிட்டருந்து
அவளால	அவள்கிட்ட	அவள்கிட்டருந்து
அவங்களால	அவங்ககிட்ட	அவங்ககிட்டருந்து
அதால	அதுகிட்ட	அதுகிட்டருந்து
அதால	இதுகிட்ட	இதுகிட்டருந்து
நம்மால	நம்மகிட்ட	நம்மகிட்டருந்து
எங்களால	எங்ககிட்ட	எங்ககிட்டருந்து
அதுங்களால	அதுங்ககிட்ட	அதுங்ககிட்டருந்து
இதுங்களால	இதுங்ககிட்ட	இதுங்ககிட்டருந்து
யாரால	யார்கிட்ட	யார்கிட்டருந்து

Note:

Case form pronoun is the base pronoun from which you add the case suffix endings; you should not confuse this with nominative pronouns (e.g. நா(ன்)))

FYI: In Tamil, we use many suffixes, but these 7 case suffixes (Accusative, Dative, Genitive, Instrumental, Sociative, Locative, Ablative) are the most important and the most frequently used ones. You will find this suffix in most of the sentences. You can even form many sentences with just this suffix and verb conjugation.

Short Summary of Cases:

Case	Summary
Accusative:	The suffix is '-அ'. This suffix is used when the sentence answers the question of 'what' and 'whom', the answer would be 'is ...'.
Dative:	Same as the preposition 'to' in English. The suffix is '-உக்கு'. This suffix is used when the sentence answers the question 'for whom', the answer would be 'to ...'.
Genitive:	Same as the preposition 'of' ''s' in English. The suffix is '-ஐL'. This suffix is used when the sentence answers the question 'whose' and the answer would be 'of ....' , '....'s'.
Instrumental:	Same as the preposition 'By' 'Because of' in English. The suffix is '-ஆல'. This suffix is used when the sentence answers the question "because of whom" "by which/using which".
Sociative:	Same as the preposition 'along with' in English. The suffix is '-ஐL'. This suffix is used when the sentence answers the question 'whom did you go with'.
Locative:	Same as the preposition 'on' 'In' 'at' in English. This suffix indicates location. For things it is '-ல' and the suffix for a person is '-(கி)ட்L' this suffix is used when the sentence answers the question of "where are you" for things, "with whom are you" for a person,
Ablative:	Same as the preposition "from" in English. The suffix is –லருந்து for things and -(கி)ட்டேருந்து for a person. This suffix answers the question "from where".

217

Example: புத்தகம் (puththagam) (book)

Case	With case ending	Transliteration	English
Nominative	புத்தகம்	puththagam	Book
Accusative	புத்தகம	puththagama	The Book
Dative	புத்தக(முக்கு	puththagamukku	To the book, for the book
Genitive	புத்தகமோட	puththagamooda	Book's
Instrumental	புத்தகமால	puththagamaala	By the book, because of the book
Sociative	புத்தகமோட	puththagamooda	Along with the book
Locative	புத்தகம்ல	puththagamla	In the book
Ablative	புத்தகம்லருந்து	puththagamlarundhu	From the book

Example: அவன் (avan) (He)

Case	With case ending	Transliteration	English
Nominative	அவ(ன்)	ava(n)	He
Accusative	அவன	avana	Him
Dative	அவனுக்கு	avanukku	To him, for him
Genitive	அவனோட	avanooda	His
Instrumental	அவனால	avanaala	By him, because of him
Sociative	அவனோட	avanooda	Along with the him
Locative	அவன்கிட்ட	avankitta	With him
Ablative	அவன்கிட்டேருந்து	avankitteerundhu	From him

EXERCISES:

L) Match the following Case in the first column with the appropriate case suffix in the second column.

1.	Nominative	a.	-ஆல
2.	Accusative	b.	-(கி)ட்ட
3.	Dative	c.	None
4.	Genitive	d.	-ஓட
5.	Instrumental	e.	-அ
6.	Sociative	f.	-உக்கு
7.	Locative	g.	-லருந்து
8.	Ablative	h.	-ஓட

M) Choose the correct pronoun and object with case endings and nominative.

e.g. _____ chocolate வேணு(ம்) (I want Chocolate)

a. நா(ன்)   b. எனக்கு   c. என்னோட

Right Answer: எனக்கு

1. _____ தண்ணி வருது (Water is coming from that)

a. அது   b. அதோட   c. அதுலருந்து

2. நா _____ பூனைய வாங்குனெ (I took the cat from him)

a. அவன்கிட்டேருந்து   b. அவனுக்கு   c. அவ(ன்)

3. _____ ஒரு யோசனை இருக்கு (He has an idea)

a. அவன   b. அவ(ன்)   c. அவன்கிட்ட

4. _____ நாய வாங்குனெ (I bought the dog)

a. நா   b. என்கிட்டருந்து   c. எனக்கு

5. அவங்க(ள்) _____ இருக்காங்க(ள்) (They are in the vehicle)

a. வண்டிகிட்டருந்து   b. வண்டில   c. வண்டி

219

6. அவ(ள்) _____ சாப்பாடு சாப்பிட்டா(ள்) (She ate lunch with him)

a. அவனால   b. அவன்கிட்ட   c. அவனோட

7. நா(ன்) _____ பள்ளிக்கு போனே (I went to school with him)

a. அவன   b. அவ(ன்)   c. அவன்கூட

8. _____ நா(ன்) அந்த கடைக்கு போனே (I went to that shop because of them)

a. அவங்களால   b. அவங்ககிட்ட   c. அவங்களோட

9. _____ அந்த கடைக்கு போனாங்க(ள்) (They went to that shop)

a. அவங்க(ள்)   b. அவங்களுக்கு   c. அவங்களோட

10. _____ நா(ன்) அந்த கடைக்கு போனே (I went to that shop with them)

a. அவங்ககூட   b. அவங்களோட   c. அவங்க(ள்)

11. _____ இந்த மாசம் வேலைக்கு போனே (I went to work this month)

a. என்ன   b. நா(ன்)   c. என்னால

12. நா(ன்) எ(ன்) _____ சாப்பாடு வாங்கி கொடுத்தெ (I bought food for my wife)

a. மனைவிக்கு   b. மனைவியோட   c. மனைவிகிட்ட

13. _____ கதவ மூடினாங்க(ள்) (They closed the door)

a. அவங்ககூட   b. அவங்களோட   c. அவங்க(ள்)

14. அவங்க(ள்) _____ படிச்சாங்க(ள்) (They read the letter)

a. கடிதம   b. கடிதமாலா   c. கடிதமோட

15. நா(ன்) அவங்க(ள்) _____ வாங்குனே (I bought from their shop)

a. கடைலருந்து   b. கடைல   c. கடை

16. _____ தண்ணி இருக்கு (He has water)

a. அவன்   b. அவன்கிட்ட   o. அவ(ன்)

17. நா(ன்) _____ வாங்குனே (I bought from them)

a. அவங்ககிட்ட   b. அவங்களோட   c. அவங்ககிட்டருந்து

18. அவங்க(ள்) _____ அம்மா (She is my mother)

a. என்னோட   b. என்கிட்ட   c. என்கிட்டருந்து

19. _____ நிறைய வேணு(ம்) (I want a lot)

a. என்   b. எனக்கு   c. நா(ன்)

20. _____ இங்க வரணு(ம்) (You must come here)

a. நீ   b. என்னால   c. என்னோட

N) Translate the following using the appropriate pronoun and object with case endings and nominative.

Example: She is eating

அவ(ள்) சாப்பிடுறா(ள்)

1) I could not sleep because of him

_____

2) She could not drink milk

_____

3) She wants to go to work.

_____

4) She likes them.

_____

5) I have a thing

_____

6) She is at work

_____

7) I went to sleep with my wife.

_____

8) We are running.

_____

9) He wants to go to school.

_____

10) I took the water from your room

_____

11) The boy was with the girl.

_____

12) That is your bag.

_____

13) Ramesh is eating the food.

_____

14) They are sleeping.

_____

15) That cat can run

_____

16) From whom did you buy this pencil?

_____

17) They are playing with him.

_____

18) I don't want jewelry.

_____

19) Ram is reading a letter.

_____

20) Our new house is white color.

_____

21) She is coming from the school.

_____

22) Honey is in the bag

_____

23) That is their Team's name.

_____

SOLUTIONS

Lesson 11

Exercise A

1) நா(ன்) அவன கூப்பிட்டெ.

naa(n) avana kuuppitte

2) இந்த பைய(ன்) பந்த எடுத்தா(ன்)

indha paiyan pandha eduththaa(n)

3) அந்த பொண்ணு புத்தகம எடுத்தா(ள்)

andha poNNu puththagama eduththaa(L)

4) ராம் சாப்பாட சாப்பிட்டா(ன்)

raam saappaada saappittaa(n)

5) நாய் அவன கடிச்சுச்சு

nay avana kadichchuchchu

6) அவங்க(ள்) புத்தகம படிச்சாங்க

avangga(L) puththagama padichchaangga

7) அவ(ள்) கடிதம் எழுதினா(ள்)

ava(L) kadidham ezhudhinaa(L)

8) நா(ன்) சாப்பாடு சமைச்செ

naa(n) saappaadu samaichche

9) நா(ன்) உண்மைய சொன்னெ

naa(n) uNmaiya sonne

10) அவங்க(ள்) எங்கள கூப்பிட்டாங்க(ள்)

avangga(L) enggaLa kuuppittaangga(L)

Exercise B

1) எ(ன்) தம்பிக்கு டீ வேணு(ம்)

e(n) thambikku tii veeNu(m)

2) அவனுக்கு விளையாட வேண்டா(ம்)

224

avanukku viLAiyaada veeNdaa(m)

3) நா(ன்) கடைக்கு போறெ

naa(n) kadaikku pooRe

4) எனக்கு அமெரிக்காவுக்கு போக வேண்டா(ம்)

enakku amerikkaavukku pooga veeNdaa(m)

5) இந்த புத்தகம் என் அண்ணாவுக்கு

indha puththagam en aNNaavukku

6) எனக்கு சாப்பிடணு(ம்)

enakku sappidaNu(m)

7) அவளுக்கு சமைக்கணு(ம்)

avaLukku samaikkaNu(m)

8) எனக்கு இந்த பேனா வேண்டா(ம்)

enakku indha peenaa veeNdaa(m)

9) அவங்களுக்கு சிலை வேணு(ம்)

avanggaLukku silai veeNu(m)

10) அவங்களுக்கு பால் வேண்டா(ம்)

avanggaLukku paal veeNdaa(m)

Exercise C

1) இது உன்னோட நாயா?

idhu unnooda naayaa?

2) யாரோட பூனை இது?

yaarooda puunai idhu?

3) இது உன்னோட சாப்பாடு

idhu unnooda sappaadu

4) இது வண்டியோட கொடி

idhu vaNdiyooda kodi

5) இது அவளோட புத்தகமா?

idhu avaLooda puththagamaa?

6) யாரோட வண்டி அது?

yaarooda vaNdi idhu?

7) இது அமெரிக்காவோட கொடி

idhu amerikkaavooda kodi

8) அவங்க(ள்) அவரோட மனைவி

avangga(L) avarooda manaivi

9) அவ(ள்) என்னோட மனைவி

ava(L) ennooda manaivi

10) அவரு என்னோட புருஷன்

avaru ennooda purushan

Exercise D

1) அவளால தூங்க முடியல

avaLaala thuungga mudiyala

2) அவங்களால நடக்க முடியல

avanggaLaala nadakka mudiyala

3) அவனால நா(ன்) ஓட்டலுக்கு போக முடியல

avanaala naa(n) oottalukku pooga mudiyala

4) எ(ன்) மனைவியால நா(ன்) கடைக்கு போக முடியல

en manaiviyaala naa(n) kadaikku pooga mudiyala

5) உன்னால சாப்பிட முடியுமா?

unnaala sappida mudiyumaa?

6) ஆம், என்னால சாப்பிட முடியு(ம்)

aam, ennaala saappida mudiyu(m)

7) இல்ல, என்னால சாப்பிட முடியல

illa, ennaala saappida mudiyum

8) அவனால நா(ன்) சாப்பிட முடியல

avanaala naa(n) sappida mudiyala

9) என்னால இந்த விளையாட்ட விளையாட முடியல

ennaala indha viLaiyaatta viLaiyaada mudiyala

10) என்னால இந்த விளையாட்ட விளையாட முடியு(ம்)

ennaala indha viLaiyaatta viLaiyaada mudiyu(m)

Exercise E

1) நா(ன்) எ(ன்) மனைவியோட டிபன் சப்பிட்டெ

naa(n) e(n) manaiviyooda tipan saappitte

2) நா(ன்) எ(ன்) புருஷனோட கடைக்கு போனெ

naa(n) e(n) purushanooda kadaikku poone

3) நா(ன்) நேத்து என் நண்பர்களோட இருந்தெ

naa(n) neeththu en naNbargaLooda irundhe

4) புத்தகம் பென்சிலோட இருந்தது

puththagam pensilooda irundhadhu

5) நா(ன்) எ(ன்) தோழி மாலாவோட உக்காருவெ

naa(n) e(n) thoozhi maalaavooda ukkaaruve

Exercise F

1) உங்ககிட்ட பேனா இருக்கா?

unggagitta peenaa irukkaa?

2) உங்ககிட்ட கைபேசி இருக்கா?

unggagitta kaipeesi irukkaa?

3) உங்ககிட்ட நாய் இருக்கா?

unggagitta naay irukkaa?

4) உங்ககிட்ட பூனை இருக்கா?

unggagitta puunai irukkaa?

5) உங்ககிட்ட வீடு இருக்கா?

unggagitta viidu irukkaa?

Exercise G

1) நா(ன்) ஓட்டல்ல இருக்கெ

naa(n) oottalal irukke

2) நா(ன்) பீச்ல இருக்கெ

naa(n) biichla irukke

3) நா(ன்) பார்க்ல இருக்கெ

naa(n) paarkla irukke

4) நா(ன்) கடைல இருக்கெ

naa(n) kadaila irukke

5) நா(ன்) வீட்டுல இருக்கெ

naa(n) viittula irukke

Exercise H

1) எ(ன்) வீடு அமெரிக்கால இருக்கு

e(n) viidu amerikkaala irukku

2) உ(ன்) வீடு சென்னைல இருக்கா?

u(n) viidu chennaila irukkaa?

3) அவள்கிட்ட பேனா இருக்கா?

avaLkitta peenaa irukkaa?

4) நா(ன்) Taj mahalல இருக்கெ

naa(n) Taj mahalla irukke

5) நா(ன்) Mallல இருக்கெ

naa(n) mallla irukke

Exercise I

1) நா(ன்) Busலருந்து வர்றென்.

naa(n) buslarundhu varRen

2) நா(ன்) Carலருந்து வர்றென்.

naa(n) carlarundhu varRen

228

3) நா(ன்) ஓட்டல்லருந்து வர்றென்.

naa(n) oottallarundhu varRen

4) நா(ன்) வீட்டுலருந்து வர்றென்.

naa(n) viittularundhu varRen

5) நா(ன்) கடைலருந்து வர்றென்.

naa(n) kadailarundhu varRen

Exercise J

1) நா(ன்) அவன்கிட்டருந்து நகைகள் வாங்குனெ

naa(n) avankittarundhu nagaigaL vaanggune

2) நா(ன்) அவங்ககிட்டருந்து வண்டி வாங்குனெ

naa(n) avanggakittarundhu vaNdi vaanggune

3) நா(ன்) உங்ககிட்டருந்து புத்தகம் வாங்குனெ

naa(n) unggakittarundhu puththagam vaanggune

4) நா(ன்) உன்கிட்டருந்து பென்சில் வாங்குனெ

naa(n) unkittarundhu pensil vaanggune

5) நா(ன்) அவள்கிட்டருந்து வீடு வாங்குனெ

naa(n) avankittarundhu viidu vaanggune

Exercise K

1) நா(ன்) கைபேசிலருந்து பேசுறெ

naa(n) kaipeesilarundhu peesuRe

2) அவங்க(ள்) அவன்கிட்டருந்து வாங்குனாங்க(ள்)

avangga(L) avankittarundhu vaanggunaangga(L)

3) அவ(ன்) அவள்கிட்டருந்து தண்ணி எடுத்தா(ன்)

avan avaLkittarundhu thaNNi eduththaa(n)

4) நா(ன்) லண்டன்லருந்து வறெ

naa(n) laNdanlarundhu vaRe

5) யார்கிட்டருந்து புத்தகம் வாங்குனெ?

229

yaarkittaru<u>n</u>dhu puththagam vaanggune?

Exercise L

1) c ; 2) e; 3) f; 4) d; 5) a; 6) h; 7) b; 8) g.

Exercise M

1) c; 2) a; 3) c; 4) a; 5) b; 6) c; 7) c; 8) a; 9) a; 10) b; 11) b; 12) a; 13) c ; 14) a ; 15) a ; 16) b ; 17) c ; 18) a ; 19) b ; 20) a.

Exercise N

1) அவனால நா(ன்) தூங்க முடியல

avanaala <u>n</u>aa(n) thuungga mudiyala

2) அவளால பால் குடிக்க முடியல

avaLaala paal kudikka mudiyala

3) அவளுக்கு வேலைக்கு போகணு(ம்)

avaLukku veelaikku poogaNu(m)

4) அவளுக்கு அவங்கள பிடிக்கு(ம்)

avaLukku avanggaLa pidikku(m)

5) என்கிட்ட ஒரு பொருள் இருக்கு

enkitta oru poruL irukku

6) அவ(ள்) வேலைல இருக்கா

ava(L) veelaila irukkaa

7) நா(ன்) எ(ன்) மனைவியோட தூங்குனெ

<u>n</u>aa(n) e(n) manaiviyooda thuunggune

8) நாங்க(ள்) ஓடுறோ(ம்)

<u>n</u>aangga(L) ooduRoo(m)

9) அவனுக்கு பள்ளிக்கு போகணு(ம்)

avanukku paLLikku poogaNu(m)

10) நா(ன்) உ(ன்) அறைலருந்து தண்ணி எடுத்தெ

<u>n</u>aa(n) u(n) aRailarundhu thaNNi eduththe

230

11) பைய(ன்) பொண்ணோட இருந்தா(ன்)

paiya(n) poNNooda irundhaa(n)

12) இது உன்னோட பை

idhu unnooda pai

13) ரமேஷ் சாப்பாட சாப்பிடுறா(ன்)

rameesh saappaada saappiduRaa(n)

14) அவங்க(ள்) தூங்குறாங்க(ள்)

avangga(L) thuungguRaangga

15) அந்த பூனையால ஓட முடியு(ம்)

andha puunaiyaala ooda mudiyu(m)

16) யார்கிட்டருந்து இந்த பென்சில வாங்குனெ

yaarkittarundhu indha pensila vaanggune

17) அவங்க(ள்) அவனோட விளையாடுறாங்க(ள்)

avangga(L) avanooda viLaiyaaduRaangga(L)

18) எனக்கு நகை வேண்டா(ம்)

enakku nagai veeNdaa(m)

19) ராம் ஒரு கடிதம படிக்குறா(ன்)

raam oru kadithama padikkuRaa(n)

20) எங்களோட புது வீடு வெள்ளை நிறம்

enggaLooda pudhu viidu veLLai niRam

21) அவ(ள்) பள்ளிலருந்து வர்றா(ள்)

ava(L) paLLilarundhu varRaa(L)

22) பைல தேன் இருக்கு

paila theen irukku

23) அது அவங்க(ள்) அணியோட பெரு

adhu avangga(L) aNiyooda peru

ADJECTIVES AND ADVERBS

LESSON 12

Content:

- Adjectives
- Adverbs
- Exercises

LESSON 12: ADJECTIVES AND ADVERBS

Adjective:

An adjective is a word that describes or modifies a noun in a sentence. An Adjective is used with a noun to describe or to point out the person, animal, place or thing's color, shape, size, demonstrative, quality, number or quantity. An adjective is a word that is used along with a noun to add more to its meaning.

An adjective can be formed in Tamil by adding suffixes to nouns or verbs. The most commonly used suffixes to make an adjective are –ஆன (aana) and –அ (a). The suffix –ஆன is used to make an adjective out of a noun and the suffix –அ is used to make an adjective out of a verb.

Adjectives Made from Noun Using the Suffix –ஆன:

1) Inherent or simple adjectives: Tamil has only a few Inherent adjectives. These words have adjectival functions but are not derived from any other word. They are not derived from another word so it is best to memorize them, because there are only a few, but they are frequently used while making sentences.

Some Frequently used Inherent Adjectives are given below:

Inherent Adjective	Transliteration	Meaning
நல்ல	nalla	Good
கெட்ட	ketta	Bad
பெரிய	periya	Big
சின்ன	sinna	Small
கொஞ்சம்	konjam	Little, some
புது	pudhu	New
பழைய	azhaiya	Old
சாதா/சாதாரணம்	saadha/saadhaaraNam	Ordinary

234

2) Derived adjectives: These adjectives are created by taking a noun or a verb and adding an adverbial suffix to it, thus making it an adjective. Most of the adjectives in Tamil belong to this category.

Category Wise Derived Adjectives are Given Below:

2a) Sizes:

Noun	Meaning	Adjective Suffix	Adjective	Transliteration	Meaning
வட்டம்	Circle	+ ஆன =	வட்டமான	vattamaana	Circular
ஆழம்	Depth	+ ஆன =	ஆழமான	aazhamaana	Deep
நீளம்	Length	+ ஆன =	நீளமான	niiLamaana	Long
குறுகள்	Narrow	+ ஆன =	குறுகலான	kuRugalaana	Narrow
குட்டை	Short	+ ஆன =	குட்டையான	kuttaiyaana	Short
சதுரம்	Quare	+ ஆன =	சதுரமான	sadhuramaana	Square
நேர்	Straight	+ ஆன =	நேரான	neeraana	Straight
உயரம்	Height	+ ஆன =	உயரமான	uyaramaana	Tall
தடி	Stick	+ ஆன =	தடியான	thadiyaana	Thick
ஒல்லி	Skinny	+ ஆன =	ஒல்லியான	olliyaana	Thin
அகலம்	Width	+ ஆன =	அகலமான	agalamaana	Wide

2b) Taste:

Noun	Meaning	Adjective Suffix	Adjective	Transliteration	Meaning
சுவை	Taste	+ ஆன =	சுவையான	suvaiyaana	Tasty
கசப்பு	Bitter	+ ஆன =	கசப்பான	kasappaana	Bitter
புளிப்பு	Sour	+ ஆன =	புளிப்பான	puLippaana	Sour
காரம்	Spicy	+ ஆன =	காரமான	kaaramaana	Spicy
இனிப்பு	Sweet	+ ஆன =	இனிப்பான	inippaana	Sweet

2c) Qualities:

Noun	Meaning	Adjective Suffix	Adjective	Transliteration	Meaning
மோசம்	Dishonest	+ ஆன =	மோசமான	moosamaana	Worse
அழகு	Beauty	+ ஆன =	அழகான	azhagaana	Beautiful
சுத்தம்	Clean	+ ஆன =	சுத்தமான	suththamaana	Clean
சரி	Okay	+ ஆன =	சரியான	sariyaana	Correct
இருட்டு	Dark	+ ஆன =	இருட்டான	iruttaana	Dark
கஷ்டம்	Difficult	+ ஆன =	கஷ்டமான	kashtamaana	Difficult
அழுக்கு	Dirt	+ ஆன =	அழுக்கான	azhukkaana	Dirty
எளிது	Easy	+ ஆன =	எளிதான	eLidhaana	Easy
காலி	Empty	+ ஆன =	காலியான	kaaliyaana	Empty
விலை அதிகம்	Expensive	+ ஆன =	விலை அதிகமான	vilai adhigamaana	Expensive
வேகம்	Speed	+ ஆன =	வேகமான	veegamaana	Fast
கனம்	Heavy	+ ஆன =	கனமான	kanamaana	Heavy
விலை கம்மி	Less expensive	+ ஆன =	விலை கம்மியான	vilai kammiyaana	Less expensive
லேசா	Light	+ ஆன =	லேசான	leesaana	Light
சத்தம்	Noise	+ ஆன =	சத்தமான	saththamaana	Noisy
அமைதி	Silence	+ ஆன =	அமைதியான	amaidhiyaana	Quiet
மெது	Slow	+ ஆன =	மெதுவான	medhuvaana	Slow
மிருது	Soft	+ ஆன =	மிருதுவான	mirudhuvaana	Soft
அசிங்கம்	Ugly	+ ஆன =	அசிங்கமான	asingamaana	Ugly
பலவீனம்	Weak	+ ஆன =	பலவீனமான	palaviinamaana	Weak
ஈரம்	Wet	+ ஆன =	ஈரமான	iiramaana	Wet
தவறு	Wrong	+ ஆன =	தவறான	thavaRaana	Wrong
இளமை	Young	+ ஆன =	இளமையான	iLamaiyaana	Young

2d) Quantitative:

Noun	Meaning	Adjective Suffix	Adjective	Transliteration	Meaning
குறைவு	Lack	+ ஆன =	குறைவான	kuRaivaana	Less
ஏராளம்	Lot	+ ஆன =	ஏராளமான	eeraaLamaana	Many
அதிகம்	More	+ ஆன =	அதிகமான	adhigamaana	Lot
முழுமை	Entirely	+ ஆன =	முழுமையான	muzhumaiyaana	Whole

2e) Numeral:

Example: ஒரு புத்தகம் (oru puphthgam) (a book), ரெண்டு வண்டி (reNdu vaNdi) (two vehicles).

Here, the numbers that come before the noun describe the same quantity. The numbers are adjectives in this scenario.

2f) Color:

Example:

a) சிவப்பு புத்தகம் (sivappu puththagam) (red book).

b) மஞ்சள் வண்டி (manjjaL vaNdi) (yellow vehicle).

Here the color that comes before the noun describes the same quantity. The colors are adjectives in this scenario.

Note:

> The adjective form of colors can also be represented differently when you use the suffix -ஆன next to it.

Example:

a) சிவப்பு + ஆன = சிவப்பான புத்தகம் (The book which is red)

b) மஞ்சள் + ஆன = மஞ்சளான வண்டி (The vehicle which is yellow)

c) அந்த சிவப்பான புத்தகம எடு

tl: andha sivappaana puththagama edu

lit: that the book which is in red color take

t: Take the book which is red color

In the above example, you are pointing out a bunch of books and asking the other person to take only the book, which is red.

d) அந்த சிவப்பு புத்தகம எடு

tl: andha sivappu puththagama edu

lit: that red book take

t: Take that red book.

Based on the example above, you can only point to a particular red book and ask the other person to take it. You cannot point to a green book and ask the other person to take a red book.

2f) Demonstrative Adjective:

Earlier, we have discussed the demonstrative pronouns; there, you would find two pronouns (இந்த (indha) (this - adjective), அந்த (andha) (that - adjective) which refers to an adjective. Since we have already discussed this topic I will not discuss it again. If you have any doubts, please refer to the sub heading "Difference between இந்த (indha) (this - adjective), அந்த (andha) (that - adjective), எந்த? (endha) (which? - adjective) and இது (idhu) (this - noun) அது (adhu) (that - noun) எது? (edhu) (which? - noun)" in Lesson 4: Pronoun.

More Examples on Sentences with Adjective:

a) இது ஒரு அழகான உலகம்

tl: idhu oru azhagaana ulagam

lit/t: This is a beautiful world

b) அது பழைய இடம்

tl: adhu pazhaiya idam

lit/t: That is an old place

c) கொஞ்சம் காப்பி குடுங்க

tl: konjjam kaappi kudungga

lit: some coffee please give me

t: Please give me some coffee

d) அது ஒரு நீளமான பாதை

tl: adhu oru niiLamaana padhai

lit/t: That is a long path

e) இது காரமான சாப்பாடு

tl: idhu kaaramaana saappaadu

lit/t: This is spicy food

f) அது ஒரு சுத்தமான தண்ணி

tl: adhu oru suththamaana thaNNi

lit/t: that is a clean water

g) அவ(ன்) ஒரு பலவீனமான பைய(ன்)

tl: ava(n) oru palaviinamaana paiyan

lit/t: He is a weak boy

h) அங்க அதிகமான நாய்கள் இருக்கு

tl: angga adhigamaana naaygaL irukku

lit/t: There are lots of dogs there

i) எனக்கு அஞ்சு நண்பர்கள் இருக்காங்க

tl: enakku anjju naNbargal irukkaangga

t: I have five friends

EXERCISES:

A) Choose the correct adjective as per the English translation.

E.g. அவ(ள்) ஒரு _____ பொண்ணு (She is a short girl)

a. குட்டையான   b. உயரமான   c. அகலமான

Right Answer: குட்டையான

1. அவ(ன்) ஒரு _____ பைய(ன்) (He is a Tall boy)

a. குட்டையான   b. உயரமான   c. அகலமான

2. அது ஒரு _____ பாதை (That is a wide path)

a. அகலமான   b. நீளமான   c. ஆழமான

3. அது ஒரு _____ பழம் (It is a sour fruit)

a. புளிப்பான   b. கசப்பான   c. இனிப்பான

4. அது _____ சாப்பாடு (It is sweet food)

a. கசப்பான   b. புளிப்பான   c. இனிப்பான

5. இது _____ நகை (This is expensive jewelry)

a. மோசமான   b. விலை கம்மியான   c. விலை அதிகமான

6. இது ஒரு _____ கேள்வியா? (Is this a difficult question?)

a. கஷ்டமான   b. கனமான   c. சரியான

7. இங்க _____ வீடுக(ள்) இருக்கு (There are lots of house's here)

a. குறைவான   b. முழுமையான   c. அதிகமான

8. அது ஒரு _____ நாய் (That is a fast dog)

a. கனமான   b. வேகமான   c. பலவீனமான

9. அது ரொம்ப _____ அறை (That is a dark room)

a. ஈரமான   b. இருட்டான   c. மிருதுவான

10. அது ஒரு _____ நாய் (That is a white dog)

a. வெள்ளை   b. கருப்பு   c. சாம்பல்

B) Translate the following using the appropriate Adjectives.

Example: She is a beautiful girl (Polite)

அவங்க(ள்) ஒரு அழகான பொண்ணு

1) He is a thin boy.

2) It is a red phone.

3) Take the phone which is red.

4) This is a tasty fruit.

5) This is a heavy bag.

6) That is a soft skin.

7) It is a wet floor.

8) I have seven brothers.

9) It is a circular jewelry

10) It is an ordinary coffee.

Adverbs:

An adverb is a word that describes or changes a verb, an adjective, clause, sentence or another adverb. Adverbs in Tamil are used more extensively than in English. A noun can be made as an adverb by adding the suffix –ஆ (aa).

Examples: Similar to the examples you saw in the adjectives, to change a noun into an adverb, just add the suffix -ஆ instead of -ஆன.

Taste:

Noun	Meaning	Adjective Suffix	Adverb	Transliteration	Meaning
சுவை	Taste	+ ஆ =	சுவையா	suvaiyaa	Tasty
கசப்பு	Bitter	+ ஆ =	கசப்பா	kasappaa	Bitter
புளிப்பு	Sour	+ ஆ =	புளிப்பா	puLippaa	Sour
காரம்	Spicy	+ ஆ =	காரமா	kaaramaa	Spicy
இனிப்பு	Sweet	+ ஆ =	இனிப்பா	inippaa	Sweet

You may also use an adverb in a sentence when the below rule is satisfied:

1) When there is a conjugated verb in a sentence (e.g. இருக்குறாங்க(ள்)).

2) It is a noun-noun sentence (Sentence containing 2 nouns, usually subject and object) and one of the nouns is stating something about the other noun, then it must be converted into an adverb.

For Example:

a) நா(ன்) ஆசிரியரா இருக்கெ.
tl: naa(n) aasiriyaraa irukke
lit: I teacher am
t: I am a teacher

Detail: ஆசிரியர் (aasiriyar) (teacher) + ஆ (aa) = ஆசிரியரா (aasiriyaraa) (Adverb) (being a teacher)

நா(ன்) (naa(n)) (I) – This is a Pronoun (another form of noun).

ஆசிரியர் (aasiriyar) (Tecaher) - This is also a noun, which says something about the other noun நா, this noun tells us that the other noun is a teacher.

இருக்கெ (irukke) (am) – This is the conjugated verb of இரு.

As you see above, this sentence satisfies the entire rule that I mentioned earlier. It contains a conjugated verb, two nouns in which the one says that the other is a teacher. Hence we change the noun which says about the other noun into an adverb.

Thus, ஆசிரியர் (Teacher) (Noun) became ஆசிரியரா (teacher) (Adverb).

b) நீ அழகா இருக்கெ
tl: nii azhagaa irukke
lit: You beauty are
t: You are beauty (To be more precise: You are being beauty)

Detail: அழகு (azhagu) (beauty) + ஆ (Adverb suffix) = அழகா (being beauty) (Adverb)

Now you would ask if both mean beauty, both give the same meaning then why should I add the suffix ஆ unnecessarily and change it into an adverb?. Well, this may make sense in English, but in Tamil, it wouldn't, the reason being:

When you say நீ அழகு இருக்கெ to a girl in Tamil, she will be confused because you told her two sets of sentences without any connection between them. You told her 'You are' and then 'beauty'. She is confused when you say it because you pointed out to her by saying 'நீ இருக்கெ' 'you are', then all of sudden you said 'அழகு' 'beauty', she is confused because in her mind she thinks 'are you calling her beautiful or some other girl beautiful or some other thing as beautiful'. She would never know the correct message you are passing because you didn't say it properly.

But when you say 'நீ அழகா இருக்கெ' to a girl in Tamil, she will be happy. She is not confused now because you told her clearly that 'she is a beauty', Now there is a connection between 'நீ இருக்கெ' 'you are' and 'அழகா' 'beauty', so now it is easy for her to understand that you are praising her not some other person or something else.

c) அவ(ன்) சந்தோஷமா சாப்பிடுறா(ன்)
tl: ava(n) sandhooshamaa saappiduRaa(n)
lit: He happily is eating
t: He is eating happily

Details: சந்தோஷம் (sandhoosham) (happy) + ஆ (Adverb suffix) = சந்தோஷமா (sandhooshamaa) (happily) (Adverb)

d) அவ(ள்) நிம்மதியா தூங்குனா(ள்)

tl: ava(L) <u>n</u>immadhiyaa thuunggunaa(L)

lit: She peacefully slept

t: He slept peacefully

Details: நிம்மதி (<u>n</u>immadhi) (happy) + ஆ (Adverb suffix) = நிம்மதியா (<u>n</u>immadhiyaa) (peacefully) (Adverb)

e) உங்க(ள்) வண்டி ரொம்ப சுத்தமா இருக்கு

tl: ungga(L) vaNdi romba suththamaa irukku

lit: your vehicle very clean is

t: Your vehicle is very clean.

Important Note:

Adverbs in Tamil are used much broader than in English. In Tamil, adverbs are used for directions, manners etc. Studying everything will be much more complicated as you will hardly use them. The rules and examples I have given above are frequently used, so you must understand and use them while forming a sentence.

EXERCISES:

C) Choose the correct Adverb as per the English translation.

E.g. அவ(ள்) _____ பேசுறா(ள்) (She is speaking beautifully)

a. அழகா   b. அழகு   c. அழஅழகாக

Right Answer: அழகா

1. அவ(ன்) _____ இருக்கா(ன்) (He is Tall)

a. குட்டையான   b. குட்டையா   c. குட்டை

2. அந்த பாதை ரொம்ப _____ இருக்கு (That path is very wide)

a. அகலமான   b. அகலமா   c. அகலம்

3. இந்த பழம் _____ இருக்கு (This fruit is bitter)

a. கசப்பு   b. கசப்பான   c. கசப்பா

4. இந்த சாப்பாடு _____ இருக்கு (This food is sweet)

a. இனிப்பா   b. இனிப்பு   c. இனிப்பான

5. அந்த நகை _____ இருக்கு (That jewelry is expensive)

a. விலை அதிகமான   b. விலை அதிகம்   c. விலை அதிகமா

6. அந்த நாய் _____ இருந்துச்சு (That dog was grey color)

a. சாம்பலாக   b. சாம்பலா   c. சாம்பல்

7. இங்க வீடுக(ள்) _____ இருந்துது (There were less house here)

a. குறைவா   b. குறைவான   c. குறைவு

8. அந்த நாய் _____ ஓடுச்சு (That dog ran fast)

a. வேகமா   b. வேகமான   c. வேகம்

9. அந்த அரை ரொம்ப _____ இருந்துச்சு (That room was very dark)

a. இருட்டு   b. இருட்டான   c. இருட்டா

10. அந்த நாய் ரொம்ப _____ இருந்துச்சு (That dog was very black)

a. கருப்பா   b. கருப்பு   c. கருப்பாக

D) Translate the following using the appropriate Adverb.

Example: She was very beautiful (Polite)

அவங்க ரொம்ப அழகா இருந்தாங்க

1) That boy was thin.

2) I can run very fast.

3) I could not eat fast.

4) This fruit is very tasty.

5) This bag is heavy.

6) That skin was very soft.

7) That floor was wet.

8) I can sing very beautifully.

9) That jewelry is circular.

10) This coffee is ordinary.

SOLUTIONS

Lesson 12

Exercise A

1) b; 2) a; 3) a; 4) c; 5) c; 6) a; 7) c; 8) b; 9) b; 10) a.

Exercise B

1) அவரு ஒரு ஒல்லியான பைய(ன்)

avaru oru olliyaana paiya(n)

2) அது ஒரு சிவப்பு கைபேசி

adhu oru sivappu kaipeesi

3) சிவப்பான கைபேசிய எடு

sivappaana kaipeesiya edu

4) இது ஒரு சுவையான பழம்

idhu oru suvaiyaana pazham

5) இது ஒரு கனமான பை

idhu oru kanamaana pai

6) அது ஒரு மிருதுவான தோல்

adhu oru murudhuvaana thool

7) இது ஒரு ஈரமான தரை

idhu oru iiramaana tharai

8) எனக்கு ஏழு அண்ணன்கள் இருக்காங்க(ள்)

enakku eezhu aNNangaL irukkaangga(L)

9) அது ஒரு வட்டமான நகை

adhu oru vattamaana na̱gai

10) அது ஒரு சாதாரணமான காப்பி

adhu oru saadhaaraNamaana kappi

Exercise C

1) b; 2) b; 3) c; 4) a; 5) c; 6) b; 7) a; 8) a; 9) c; 10) a.

Exercise D

1) அந்த பைய(ன்) ஒல்லியா இருந்தா(ன்)

andha paiya(n) olliyaa irundhaa(n)

2) என்னால ரொம்ப வேகமா ஓட முடியு(ம்)

ennaala romba veegamaa ooda mudiyu(m)

3) என்னால வேகமா சாப்பிட முடியல

ennaala veegamaa saappida mudiyala

4) இந்த பழம் ரொம்ப சுவையா இருக்கு

indha pazham romba suvaiyaa irukku

5) இந்த பை கனமா இருக்கு

indha pai kanamaa irukku

6) அந்த தோல் ரொம்ப மிருதுவா இருந்துது

andha thool romba mirudhuvaa irundhudhu

7) அந்த தரை ஈரமா இருந்துச்சு

andha tharai iiramaa irundhuchchu

8) என்னால ரொம்ப அழகா பாட முடியு(ம்)

ennaala romba azhagaa paada mudiyu(m)

9) அந்த நகை வட்டமா இருக்கு

andha nagai vattamaa irukku

10) இந்த காப்பி சாதாரணமா இருக்கு

indha kaappi saadhaaraNamaa irukku

NEGATION

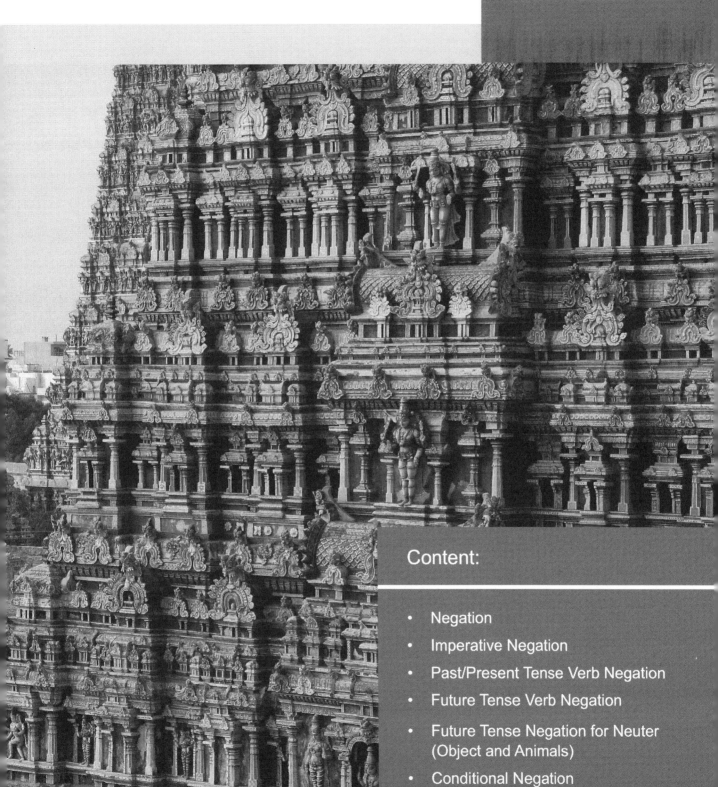

LESSON 13

Content:

LESSON 13: NEGATION

In Tamil, we use different forms of negation, which will be discussed one by one.

1) வேண்டா(ம்) (veeNdaa(m)) (do not want, do not need): This word is the complete opposite of வேணு(ம்), It means you don't want to do something, you don't need something. We have already discussed and practiced this in Lesson 10: Cases.

2) In Tamil, we have separate words for saying 'you are able to do it', 'you are unable to do it' and 'you will not do it'. We briefly discussed it in Lesson 10: Cases, under the heading 'Instrumental case'. Now we will see more examples:

- முடியு(ம்) (mudiyu(m)) - Can do or will be able to do (Future/near present)

- முடியுது (mudiyudhu) - Can do or am able to do (Present Tense)

- முடிஞ்சுது (mudinjjudhu) - was able to do (Past Tense)

- முடியல (mudiyala) – Could not do.

- முடியாது (mudiyaadhu) – Cannot / Will not do.

Examples:

a) அவனால ஓட முடியல.

tl: avanaala ooda mudiyala.

lit: by him run could not.

t: he could not run.

b) அவனால ஓட முடியாது.

tl: avanaala ooda mudiyaadhu.

lit: by him run will not.

t: he will not run.

c) அவனால ஓட முடியு(ம்).

tl: avanaala ooda mudiyu(m).

t: he can run.

d) அவனால ஓட முடிஞ்சுது.

tl: avanaala ooda mudinjjudhu.

lit: by him run was able to.

t: he was able to run.

e) அவரால சமைக்க முடியல.

tl: avaraala samaikka mudiyala.

lit: by him cook could not.

t: he could not cook.

More Examples:

Case	Infinitive	Capability	Tamil	English
அவனால	பாட	முடியு(ம்)	அவனால பாட முடியு(ம்)	He can sing
அவனால	பாட	முடியுது	அவனால பாட முடியுது	He is able to sing
அவனால	பாட	முடிஞ்சுது	அவனால பாட முடிஞ்சுது	He was able to sing
அவனால	பாட	முடியல	அவனால பாட முடியல	He could not sing
அவனால	பாட	முடியாது	அவனால பாட முடியாது	He will not sing
என்னால	ஆட	முடியு(ம்)	அவனால ஆட முடியு(ம்)	I can dance
என்னால	ஆட	முடியுது	அவனால ஆட முடியுது	I am able to dance
என்னால	ஆட	முடிஞ்சுது	அவனால ஆட முடிஞ்சுது	I was able to dance
என்னால	ஆட	முடியல	அவனால ஆட முடியல	I could not dance
என்னால	ஆட	முடியாது	அவனால ஆட முடியாது	I will not dance

3) We have separate words for saying that, 'Like', 'don't like'.

- பிடிக்கு(ம்) (pidikku(m)) - Like

- பிடிக்காது - (pidikkaadhu) – Do not like

- பிடிக்கல - (pidikkala) – Did not like

The difference between பிடிக்காது and பிடிக்கல is, when you say பிடிக்காது – 'It means you will never like it and you haven't tried it'. When you say பிடிக்கல, It means you have tried it but you didn't like it'. You should use the Dative case for the subject like before.

Examples:

a) எனக்கு chocolate பிடிக்கு(ம்).

tl: enakku chocolate pidikku(m).

lit: for me chocolate like.

t: I like chocolate.

b) எனக்கு chocolate பிடிக்காது.

tl: enakku chocolate pidikkaadhu.

lit: for me chocolate don't like.

t: I don't like chocolate.

c) எனக்கு அவன பிடிக்காது

tl: enakku avana pidikkaadhu.

lit: for me him don't like

t: I don't like him.

d) எனக்கு அந்த கடைய பிடிக்காது.

tl: enakku andha kadaiya pidikkaadhu.

lit: for me that shop don't like

t: I don't like that shop.

e) எனக்கு உங்க(ள்) சமையல பிடிக்கல.

tl: enakku unga(L) samaiyala pidikkala.

lit: for me your cooking didn't like

t: I didn't like your cooking.

4) We have separate words for saying that, 'know', 'don't know'.

- தெரியு(ம்) (theriyu(m)) - Know

- தெரியாது (theriyaadhu) – Do not know

You should use the Dative case for the subject, while using the above words.

Examples:

a) எனக்கு சமைக்க தெரியு(ம்).

tl: enakku samaikka theriyu(m).

lit: for me to cook know

t: I know how to cook.

b) எனக்கு அவங்கள தெரியு(ம்).

tl: enakku avanggaLa theriyu(m)

lit: for me them know.

t: I know them

c) எனக்கு அவன தெரியாது

tl: enakku avana theriyaadhu.

lit: for me him don't know

t: I don't know him.

d) எனக்கு அந்த இடம தெரியாது.

tl: enakku andha idama theriyaadhu.

lit: for me that place don't know

t: I don't know that place.

e) எனக்கு சமைக்க தெரியாது.

tl: enakku samaikka theriyaadhu.

lit: for me to cook don't know

t: I don't know how to cook.

f) எனக்கு பறக்க தெரியாது.

tl: enakku paRakka theriyaadhu.

lit/t: I don't know how to fly.

5) We have separate words for saying, 'understand', 'don't understand'.

- புரியுது (puriyudhu) – Understand
- புரியாது (puriyaadhu) – Do not understand
- புரியல (puriyala) – Did not understand

You should use the Dative case for the subject while you use the above words.

Examples:

a) எனக்கு புரியுது

tl: enakku puriyudhu

lit: for me understand

t: I understand

b) எனக்கு புரியல

tl: enakku puriyala

lit: for me done understand

t: I don't understand.

c) எனக்கு நீ பேசுறது புரியல

tl: enakku nii peesuRadhu puriyala

lit: for me you speaking don't understand

t: I don't understand what you are speaking.

Note:

The suffix '-றது' when added to a verb, then it means 'the process of verbs action', For Example: பேசுறது, this is derived from the root verb பேசு, it means 'the process of speaking'

d) அவனுக்கு நா(ன்) சொல்றது புரியல

tl: avanukku naa(n) solRadhu puriyala

lit: for him I saying don't undertsnad

t: He doesn't understand what I am saying.

e) அவங்களுக்கு புரியுது.

tl: avangalukku puriyudhu

lit:/t: They undertsand.

6) We have separate words for saying, 'there is', 'there is not'.

- இருக்கு (irukku) – Is there

- இல்ல (illa) – There is not

Examples:

a) நாளைக்கு கடை இருக்கா?

tl: naaLaikku kadai irukkaa?

lit: Tomorrow shop is there?

t: Is there shop tomorrow.

b) நாளைக்கு கடை இருக்கு

tl: naaLaikku kadai irukku

lit: Tomorrow shop there is

t: There is shop tomorrow

c) என்கிட்ட பேனா இல்ல

tl: enkitta peenaa illa

lit: with me pen is not there

t: I don't have a pen with me

d) என்கிட்ட chocolate இருக்கு

tl: enkitta chocolate irukku

lit: with me chocolate is there

t: I have chocolate with me

e) என்கிட்ட chocolate இல்ல

tl: enkitta chocolate illa

lit: with me chocolate is not there

t: I don't have chocolate with me.

f) எனக்கு உன் மேல கோபம் இல்ல

tl: enakku un meela koobam illa

lit: for me you on anger is not there

t: I don't have anger on you

7) We have separate words for saying, 'enough', 'not enough'.

- போது(ம்) (poodhu(m)) – Enough, sufficient

- போதாது (poodhaadhu) – Not enough, not sufficient

Examples:

a) எனக்கு போது(ம்)

tl: enakku podhu(m)

lit: for me enough

t: Enough for me

b) எனக்கு போதாது

tl: enakku podhaadhu

lit: for me not enough

t: Not enough for me

c) எனக்கு இந்த Ice cream போதாது

tl: enakku indha Ice cream poodhaadhu

lit: for me this Ice cream is not enough

t: This Ice cream is not enough for me

d) எனக்கு இந்த சாப்பாடு போது(ம்)

tl: enakku indha saappaadu poodhu(m)

lit: for me this food is enough

t: This food is enough for me

e) அவனுக்கு இவ்வளவு பணம் போது(ம்)

tl: avanukku ivLavu paNam poodhu(m)

t: This much money is enough for him

f) அவளுக்கு அந்த பழம் போதாது

tl: avaLukku andha pazham poodhaadhu

lit: for her that fruit is not enough

t: That fruit is not enough for her.

8) Imperative Negation:

The Imperative negation is made by adding either of the suffixes -ஆத (aadha) (informal) or -ஆதீங்க (aadhiingga) (formal) to the infinitive form of the verb. It's used to command or request someone or something not to do it.

Examples:

Infinitive	Informal Imperative negation	TL	Formal Imperative negation	TL	English
எடுக்க	எடுக்காத	edukkaadha	எடுக்காதீங்க	edukkaadhiinga	Please don't take
குடிக்க	குடிக்காத	kudikkaadha	குடிக்காதீங்க	kudikkaadhiinga	Please don't drink
படிக்க	படிக்காத	padikkaadha	படிக்காதீங்க	padikkaadhiinga	Please don't study
வர்	வராத	varaadha	வராதீங்க	varaadhiinga	Please don't come
ஆட	ஆடாத	aadaadha	ஆடாதீங்க	aadaadhiinga	Please don't dance
ஊத்த	ஊத்தாத	uuththaadha	ஊத்தாதீங்க	uuththaadhiinga	Please don't pour
எழுத	எழுதாத	ezhudhaadha	எழுதாதீங்க	ezhudhaadhiinga	Please don't write
ஓட	ஓடாத	oodaadha	ஓடாதீங்க	oodaadhiinga	Please don't run

a) என்னோட புத்தகம எடுக்காதீங்க

tl: ennooda puththagama edukkaadhiingga

lit: my book please don't take

t: Please don't take my book.

b) இங்க வராத

tl: ingga varaadha

lit: here don't come

t: Don't come here.

c) அங்க எழுதாத

tl: angga ezhudhaadha

t: Don't write there.

9) Past/Present Tense Verb Negation:

The verb can be negated in both past and present tense for humans and using the suffix –ல being added to the infinitive of the verb.

Examples:

Pronoun	Infinitive	Tense negation suffix	Negated verb in Past and Present Tense	English
நா(ன்)	எடுக்க	-ல	எடுக்கல	I didn't take
நீ	குடிக்க	-ல	குடிக்கல	You didn't drink
அவ(ன்)	படிக்க	-ல	படிக்கல	He didn't study
அவரு	வர	-ல	வரல	He didn't come
அவ(ள்)	ஆட	-ல	ஆடல	She didn't dance
அவங்க(ள்)	ஊத்த	-ல	ஊத்தல	They didn't pour
நாங்க(ள்)	எழுத	-ல	எழுதல	We didn't write
நாம	ஓட	-ல	ஓடல	We didn't run

a) என்னோட புத்தகம நீ எடுக்கல

tl: ennooda puththagama n̲ii edukkala

lit: my book you didn't take

t: You didn't take my book

b) நா(ன்) தண்ணீர் ஊத்தல

tl: naa(n) thaNNiir uuththala

lit: I water didn't pour

t: I did'nt pour the water

c) நா(ன்) பார்ட்டிக்கு வரல

tl: naa(n) paarttikku varala

lit: I to the party not coming

t: I am not coming to the party

10) Future Tense Verb Negation:

Future tense negation for a person:

When the subject of the sentence is a human, then the verb is negated for the future tense using the suffix –மாட்ட் being added to the infinitive of the verb and then you add the verb suffix (PNG).

Examples:

Pronoun	Infinitive	Future tense negation suffix	Verb suffix (PNG)	Negated verb in future tense	English
நா(ன்)	எடுக்க	-மாட்ட்-	-எ	எடுக்கமாட்டெ	I will not take
நீ	குடிக்க	-மாட்ட்-	-எ	குடிக்கமாட்டெ	You will not drink
அவ(ன்)	படிக்க	-மாட்ட்-	-ஆ(ன்)	படிக்கமாட்டா(ன்)	He will not study
அவரு	வர	-மாட்ட்-	-ஆரு	வரமாட்டாரு	He will not come
அவ(ள்)	ஆட	-மாட்ட்-	-ஆ(ள்)	ஆடமாட்டா(ள்)	She will not dance
அவங்க(ள்)	ஊத்த	-மாட்ட்-	-ஆங்க	ஊத்தமாட்டாங்க(ள்)	They will not pour
நாங்க(ள்)	எழுத	-மாட்ட்-	-ஒ(ம்)	எழுதமாட்டோ(ம்)	We will not write
நாம	ஒட	-மாட்ட்-	-ஒ(ம்)	ஒடமாட்டோ(ம்)	We will not run

a) நா(ன்) அவனோட வரமாட்டெ

tl: naa(n) avanooda varamaatte

lit: I along with him will not come

t: I will not come along with him

b) அவ(ள்) அவங்களோட ஆடமாட்டா(ள்)

tl: ava(L) avanggaLooda aadamaattaa(L)

lit: she along with them will not dance

t: She will not dance along with them.

259

Future Tense Negation for Neuter (Object and Animals):

When the subject of the sentence is a neuter noun, then the verb is negated for the future tense using a suffix.

1) Weak Verbs: For weak verbs the suffix –ஆது should be added directly to the root of the verb.

2) Strong Verbs: For strong verbs the suffix –ஆது should be added to the infinitive of the verb.

Examples for the Strong Verb:

Pronoun	Infinitive	Future tense negation suffix	Negated verb in future tense	English
அது	எடுக்க	-ஆது	எடுக்காது	It will not take
அது	குடிக்க	-ஆது	குடிக்காது	It will not drink
அது	படிக்க	-ஆது	பிடிக்காது	It will not study

Examples of the Weak Verbs:

Pronoun	Verb root	Future tense negation suffix	Negated verb in future tense	English
அது	ஆடு	-ஆது	ஆடாது	It will not dance
அது	ஊத்து	-ஆது	ஊத்தாது	It will not pour
அது	எழுது	-ஆது	எழுதாது	It will not write
அது	ஓடு	-ஆது	ஓடாது	It will not run

Note:

However, there are some exceptions where you will use the infinitive form of the verb even though it is a weak verb.

Examples for the weak verb for which we would use the infinitive form:

Pronoun	Infinitive	Future tense negation suffix	Negated verb in future tense	English
அது	வர	-ஆது	வராது	It will not come
அது	போக	-ஆது	போகாது	It will not go
அது	நிக்க	-ஆது	நிக்காது	It will not stand
அது	கேட்க	-ஆது	கேட்காது	It will not listen

260

11) Conditional Negation:

This kind of negation is rarely used in a conversation and requires many suffixes, so please don't spend much time on this topic. Conditional negation is used as an equivalent of using 'If' in English.

a) One way of introducing the 'If clause' in a sentence is by adding the suffix –ஆட்டா to the infinitive (Infinitive + ஆட்டா).

Example:

நீ சமைக்காட்டா என்னால சாப்பிட முடியாது.

tl: ṉii samaikkaattaa ennaala saappida mudiyaadhu

lit: you if you don't cook I eat will not be.

t: If you don't cook, I will not be able to eat.

b) Alternatively, you can also introduce the 'If clause' in a sentence by adding the suffix – லண்ணா to the infinitive (Infinitive + லண்ணா).

Example:

நீ சமைக்கலண்ணா என்னால சாப்பிட முடியாது.

tl: ṉii samaikklaNNaa ennaala saappida mudiyaadhu

lit: you if you don't cook I eat will not be.

t: If you don't cook, I will not be able to eat.

நீ Ticket வாங்கலன்னா என்னால படத்துக்கு போக முடியாது.

tl: ṉii Ticket vaanggalannaa ennaala padaththukku pooga mudiyaadhu

lit: you if you don't buy ticket I to the movie go cannot

t: If you don't buy the ticket, I cannot go to the movie

EXERCISES:

A) Match the following Tamil word in the first column with the appropriate English translation form in the second column.

1.	முடியு(ம்)	a.	Don't Know
2.	போது(ம்)	b.	Like
3.	போதாது	c.	Know
4.	முடியல	d.	Understand
5.	முடியாது	e.	Imperative negation (Command or a request)
6.	வேணு(ம்)	f.	Don't like
7.	வேண்டாம்	g.	Can do or will be able to do
8.	பிடிக்கு(ம்)	h.	Future Tense negation for human
9.	பிடிக்காது	i.	Could not do
10.	தெரியு(ம்)	j.	Future Tense negation for neuter (Object, Animals)
11.	தெரியாது	k.	Didn't like
12.	புரியுது	l.	There is not
13.	புரியல	m.	Conditional negation (If)
14.	இருக்கு	n.	Not enough, Insufficient
15.	இல்ல	o.	Want
16.	-ஆத /அதீங்க	p.	Is there
17.	-மாட்ட்	q.	Will not do
18.	-ஆது	r.	Don't understand
19.	-ல	s.	Do not want
20.	பிடிக்கல	t.	Enough, sufficient
21.	-ஆட்டா/லண்ணா	u.	Past / Present Tense negation

B) Fill in the blanks with the right word or suffix.

Example: என்னால இந்த வண்டிய ஓட்ட _____ (I can drive this vehicle)

Answer: முடியு(ம்)

1. என்னால இந்த வண்டிய ஓட்ட _____ (I was able to drive this vehicle)

2. உனக்கு இந்த கேள்விக்கு பதில் _____? (Do you know the answer for this question?)

3. அவன்கிட்ட _____ (Please don't give to him)

4. அந்த நாய் _____ (That dog won't bite)

5. என்னால இந்த வண்டிய ஓட்ட _____ (I am able to drive this vehicle)

6. எனக்கு இந்த கடிதம் _____ (I understand this letter)

7. எனக்கு நாளைக்கு வேலை _____ (I have work tomorrow)

8. எனக்கு இந்த விளையாட்டு _____ (I don't like this game)

9. எனக்கு நாளைக்கு வேலை _____ (I don't have work tomorrow)

10. எனக்கு இந்த கேள்விக்கு பதில் _____ (I don't know the answer for this question)

11. அவ(ன்) தண்ணி _____ (He will not drink water)

12. என்னால இந்த வண்டிய ஓட்ட _____ (I could not drive this vehicle)

13. இந்த கடைல காப்பி _____ (Don't drink coffee in this shop)

14. எனக்கு இந்த கடிதம் _____ (I don't understand this letter)

15. எனக்கு இந்த விளையாட்டு _____ (I like this game)

C) Translate the following.

Example: I can read this book
Answer: என்னால இந்த புத்தகம படிக்க முடியு(ம்)

1. Please don't eat food in this shop

_____

2. Do you know the house on that street?

_____

3. He will not drink at work

_____

4. That dog won't run

_____

5. I could not speak with him

_____

6. I understand this game

_____

7. I have a bag

_____

8. I don't like this food

_____

9. I like that girl

_____

10. I don't know him

_____

11. Please don't take this phone

_____

264

12. I am able to speak to the boy

_____

13. I was able to speak to the girl

_____

14. I don't understand this game

_____

15. I don't have a bag

_____

16. This coffee is enough for me

_____

17. I don't like him.

_____

18. I didn't scream.

_____

19. That tea is not enough for me.

_____

SOLUTIONS

Lesson 13

Exercise A

1) g; 2) t; 3) n; 4) i; 5) q; 6) o; 7) s; 8) b; 9) f; 10) c; 11) a; 12) d; 13) r ; 14) p ; 15) l ; 16) e ; 17) h ; 18) j ; 19) g ; 20) k ; 21) m.

Exercise B

1) முடிஞ்சுது. 2) தெரியுமா. 3) குடுக்காதீங்க. 4) கடிக்காது. 5) முடியு(ம்). 6) புரியுது. 7) இருக்கு. 8) பிடிக்காது. 9) இல்ல. 10) தெரியாது. 11) குடிக்கமாட்டா(ன்). 12) முடியல. 13) குடிக்காத. 14) புரியல. 15) பிடிக்கு(ம்).

TL: 1) mudinjjushu. 2) theriyumaa. 3) kudukkaadhiingga. 4) kadikkaadhu. 5) mudiyu(m). 6) puriyudhu. 7) irukku. 8) pidikkaadhu. 9) illa. 10) theriyaadhu. 11) kudikkamaattaa(n). 12) mudiyala. 13) kudikkaadha. 14) puriyala. 15) pidikku(m)

Exercise C

1) இந்த கடைல சாப்பாடு சாப்பிடாதீங்க

indha kadaila saappaadu saappidaadhiingga

2) அந்த தெருல இருக்குற வீடு தெரியுமா?

andha therula irukkuRa viidu theriyumaa

3) அவ(ன்) வேலைல குடிக்கமாட்டா(ன்)

ava(n) veelaila kudikkamaattaa(n)

4) அந்த நாய் ஓடாது

andha nay oodaadhu

5) என்னால அவன்கிட்ட பேச முடியல

ennaala avankitta peesa mudiyala

6) எனக்கு இந்த விளையாட்டு புரியுது

enakku indha viLaiyaattu puriyudhu

7) என்கிட்ட பை இருக்கு

enkitta pai irukku

8) எனக்கு இந்த சாப்பாடு பிடிக்கல

enakku indha saappaadu pidikkala

9) எனக்கு அந்த பொண்ண பிடிக்கு(ம்)

enakku andha poNNa pidikku(m)

10) எனக்கு அவன தெரியாது

enakku avana theriyaadhu

11) இந்த கைபேசிய எடுக்காதீங்க

indha kaipeesiya edukkaadhiingga

12) என்னால அந்த பையன்கிட்ட பேச முடியு(ம்)

ennaala andha paiyankitta peesa mudiyu(m)

13) என்னால அந்த பொண்ணுகிட்ட பேச முடிஞ்சுது

ennaala andha poNNukitta peesa mudinjjudhu

14) எனக்கு இந்த விளையாட்டு புரியல

enakku indha viLaiyaattu puriyala

15) என்கிட்ட பை இல்ல

enkitta pai illa

16) இந்த காப்பி எனக்கு போதாது

indha kaappi enakku poodhaadhu

17) எனக்கு அவன பிடிக்கல

enakku avana pidikkala

18) நா கத்தல

naa kaththala

19) அந்த டீ எனக்கு போதாது

andha tii enakku poodhaadhu

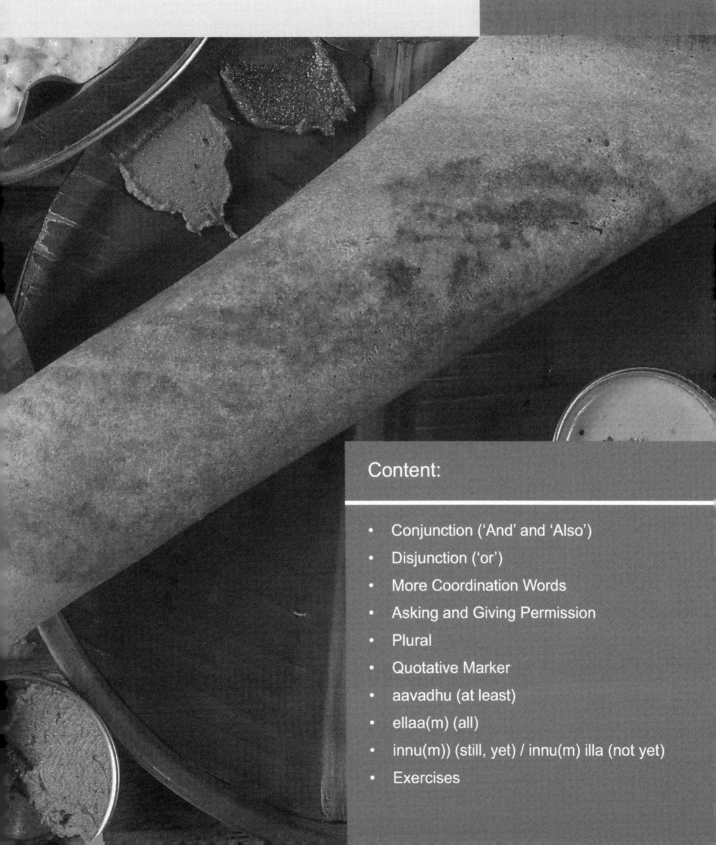

LESSON 14

Content:

LESSON 14: IMPORTANT SUFFIXES

1) Conjunction ('And' and 'Also')

When you add the suffix -உ(ம்) to a noun or an adverb, it will give you the meaning of 'also' in English. If you add it to a succession of two or more words, then it will coordinate and join them together in a sentence equivalent to the English word 'and'.

Note:

> In English, when a group of nouns is conjoined together, we add 'and' at the end. E.g. 'Mary, Peter, Kathy and Ronald went to church', In this example I added 'and' at the end of the conjunction, but in Tamil you have to add the suffix –உ(ம்) to each and every noun. E.g. மேரியு(ம்), பீட்டரு(ம்), கேத்தியு(ம்), ரொனால்டு(ம்), churchக்கு போனாங்க(ள்).

In the above example, I added the suffix –உ(ம்) to every noun.

Example:

a) எனக்கு டியு(ம்) குடுங்க

tl: enakku tiiyu(m) kudunga

lit: to me also tea please give

t: Please give me tea also

Vocabulary: தோசை, இட்லி, சாம்பார் are a type of food in Tamil Nadu

b) எனக்கு டியு(ம்) காப்பியு(ம்) தோசையு(ம்) இட்லியு(ம்) சாம்பாரு(ம்) குடுங்க

tl: enakku tiiyu(m), kaappiyu(m), thoosaiyu(m), idliyu(m), saambaaru(m) kudunga.

lit: to me tea and coffee and dosa and Idly and sambar please give

t: Please give me tea, coffee, dosa, Idly and sambar.

Note:

> Using the suffix –உ(ம்) for referring 'and' is optional, you can even make a sentence without using the suffix –உ(ம்) and it still means the same.

c) எனக்கு ஒரு டி காப்பி தோசை இட்லி சாம்பார் குடுங்க

tl: enakku tii, kaappi, thoosai, idli, saambaar kudunga.

lit: to me tea and coffee and dosa and Idly and sambar please give

t: Please give me tea, coffee, dosa, Idly and sambar.

2) Disjunction ('or')

There are different ways of adding 'or' in a Tamil sentence, so please don't stress too much about it, you can use any one of the method I have given below and the other person will understand you well. Everything I have mentioned below are frequently used and it all depends on the person and their dialect.

a) When there is more than one interrogative noun, then you will add the interrogative suffix –ஆ (aa) to both of them to mention 'or' in between them.

Example:

உங்களுக்கு டியா காப்பியா?

tl: unggaLukku tiiyaa kaappiyaa

lit: for you tea or coffee

t: Would you prefer tea or coffee.

b) Alternatively, you can also use the words அல்லது (alladhu) (or) or இல்லனா (illanaa) (or else, otherwise).

Example:

உங்களுக்கு டியா அல்லது காப்பியா?

tl: unggaLukku tiiyaa alladhu kaappiyaa

lit: for you tea or coffee

t: Would you prefer tea or coffee.

Note:

The word அல்லது / இல்லனா is used in many other ways; it can also be used to conjoin two sentences. The word இல்லனா is very frequently used in spoken than அல்லது.

Example:

அவ(ன்) ஆடுவா(ன்) இல்லனா நா(ன்) ஆடுவெ

tl: ava(n) aaduvaa(n) illanaa <u>naa</u>(n) aaduve

lit/t: He will dance or else I will dance

அவ(ன்) பாடுவா(ன்) அல்லது நா(ன்) பாடுவெ

tl: ava(n) paaduvaa(n) alladhu <u>naa</u>(n) paaduve

lit/t: He will sing or I will sing

3) More Coordination Words:

a) ஆனா (aanaa) (But):

Examples:

அவன எனக்கு பிடிக்கு(ம்) ஆனா அவன்கிட்ட நா(ன்) பேசமாட்ட

tl: avana enakku pidikku(m) aanaa avankitaa <u>naa</u>(n) peesamatta

lit: him for me like but with him I don't speak

t: I like him but I don't speak to him

அவரு சமைக்குறாரு ஆனா நல்ல இல்ல

tl: avaru samaikkuRaaru aana <u>nalla illa</u>

lit: He is cooking but good not

t: His cooking but it is not good

b) அதனால (adhanaala) (So, because of that):

Examples:

நேத்து நா(ன்) சாப்பிடல அதனால எனக்கு இப்ப ரொம்ப பசிக்குது

tl: <u>neeththu naa</u>(n) saappidala adhanaala enakku ippa romba pasikkudhu

lit: yesterday I didn't eat so for me now very feeling hungry

t: Yesterday I didn't eat so I am feeling very hungry now.

நேத்து அவகிட்ட நா(ன்) சண்ட பொட்டெ அதனால இப்ப அவ(ள்) என்கிட்ட பேசமாட்டா(ள்)

tl: _neeththu avakitta _naa(n) saNda potte adhanaala ippa ava(L) enkitta peesamaattaa(L)

lit: yesterday with her I fought because of that now she with me will not speak

t: Yesterday I fought with her because of that she will not speak to me.

c) ஏண்ணா (eeNNaa) (because):

Examples:

எனக்கு இப்ப ரொம்ப பசிக்குது ஏண்ணா நேத்து நா(ன்) சாப்பிடல

tl: enakku ippa romba pasikkudhu eeNNaa _neeththu _naa(n) saappidala

lit: for me now very feeling hungry because yesterday I didn't eat.

t: I am feeling very hungry now because I didn't eat yesterday.

அவ(ள்) என்கிட்ட பேசமாட்ட ஏண்ணா நேத்து அவகிட்ட நா(ன்) சண்ட பொட்டெ

tl: ava(L) enkitta peesamaatta eeNNaa neththu avakitta naa(n) saNda potte

lit: she with me will not speak because yesterday with her I fought.

t: She will not speak to me because yesterday I fought with her.

d) அப்புறம் (appuRam) (after that):

Examples:

நா(ன்) கடைக்கு போனெ அப்புறம் காப்பி வாங்குனெ

tl: _naa(n) kadaikku poone appuRam kaappi vaanggune

lit: I to the shop went after that I bought coffee.

t: I went to the shop after that I bought coffee

நா(ன்) புத்தகம படிச்செ அப்புறம் படம் பார்த்தெ

tl: _naa(n) puththagama padichche appuRam padam paarththe

lit: I book read after that I the film saw

t: I read the book after that I saw the film

4) Asking and Giving Permission:

The suffix –அட்டு(ம்) (attu(m)) or –லா(ம்) (laam) is added to an infinitive verb to give permission. The suffix –லா(ம்) (laam) is the most frequently used one though.

Examples:

a) நாம கடைக்கு போகலாமா?

tl: naama kadaikku poogalaamaa

lit: we to the shop shall we go

t: Shall we go to the shop?

b) நா(ன்) புத்தகம வாங்கலாமா?

tl: naa(n) puththagama vaanggalaamaa

lit: I book shall I buy

t: Shall I buy the book?

c) நா(ன்) உங்க(ள்) வீட்டுக்கு வரட்டுமா?

tl: naa(n) ungga(L) viittukku varattumaa

lit: I your house shall I come

t: Shall I come to your house?

d) நா(ன்) உங்க(ள்) வீட்டுக்கு வரலாமா?

tl: naa(n) ungga(L) viittukku varalaamaa

lit: I your house shall I come

t: Shall I come to your house?

274

5) Plural

You can make most of the noun plural by adding the suffix –கள் (gaL) to it.

Note:

If the word ends with the last letter ம், remove the last letter and then add the suffix –ங்கள் (ngga(L)) (e.g புத்தகம் = புத்தக + ங்க(ள்) = புத்தகங்க(ள்)).

Examples:

Singular form	Plural Suffix	Plural form	TL	English
ஆண்	-கள்	ஆண்கள்	aaNgal	Men
பெண்	-கள்	பெண்கள்	peNgal	Women
குழந்தை	-கள்	குழந்தைகள்	kuzhandhaigal	Childrens
பள்ளி	-கள்	பள்ளிகள்	paLLigal	Schools
மாணவர்	-கள்	மாணவர்கள்	maaNavargal	Students
நிறுவனம்	-ங்கள்	நிறுவனங்கள்	niruvananggal	Companies
கேள்வி	-கள்	கேள்விகள்	keeLvigal	Questions
வேலை	-கள்	வேலைகள்	veelaigal	Jobs

6) Quotative Marker

Quotative markers are used to indicate, what follows next is a quote (e.g. "No way!"). The suffix –னு is a quotative marker like 'that' in English.

Examples:

a) ராம்கிட்ட நாளைக்கு வீட்டுக்கு வர போறெனு சொன்னெ

tl: raamkitta na̲aLaikku viittukku vara pooRenu sonne

lit: to ram tomorrow to the house come going to told

t: Told ram that I am going to come to the house

b) அப்பாவ கேட்டெனு சொல்லு

tl: appaava keettenu sollu

lit: father I asked tell

t: Tell your father that I asked about him

7) -ஆவது (aavadhu) (at least)

This suffix usually comes after a noun.

Examples:

a) அவ(ன்) (avan) (he) + ஆவது (aavadhu) (atleast) = அவனாவது (avanaavadhu) (at least him).

b) அவனாவது படிக்கட்டும்

tl: avanaavadhu padikkattum

lit: at least him let read

t: At least let him read

c) ஒரு நாளைக்கு ஒரு மணி நேரமாவது சாப்பாடு சாப்பிடுவா(ன்)

tl: oru naaLaikku oru maNi neeramaavadhu saappaadu saappiduvaa(n)

lit: a for tomorrow one at least hours food he eats

t: For a day he eats food for at least one hour.

8) எல்லா(ம்) (ellaa(m)) (all):

This word/suffix usually comes after the noun, this can be used as a suffix and as a word.

Examples:

நாம (naama) (we) + எல்லா(ம்) (ellaa(m)) (all) = நாமெல்லாம் (naamellaam) (We all).

நாங்க (naangga) (we) + எல்லா(ம்) = நாங்கெல்லாம் (naanggellaam) (We all).

நீங்க(ள்) (niingga(L)) (you) + எல்லா(ம்) = நீங்களெல்லாம் niinggaLellaam (You all).

அவங்க(ள்) (avangga(L)) (They) + எல்லா(ம்) = அவங்களெல்லாம் avanggaLellaam (They all).

9) இன்னு(ம்) (innu(m)) (still, yet),
இன்னு(ம்) இல்ல (innu(m) illa) (not yet).

Examples:

a) Scenario: Let's take a scenario of a father and son in train:

Son: வந்துட்டோமா? (vandhuttoomaa) (Have we reached yet?)

Father: இன்னு(ம்) கொஞ்ச(ம்) நேரம் (innu(m) konjja(m) neeram) (Still a little more time).

Son: வந்துட்டோமா? (vandhuttoomaa) (Have we reached yet?)

Father: இன்னு(ம்) இல்ல (innu(m) (illa) (Not yet)

b) முடிச்சிட்டியா? இன்னு(ம்) இல்ல.
tl: mudichchittiyaa (innu(m) (illa)
lit/t: Have you finished? Not yet.

EXERCISES:

A) Match the following Tamil word and suffix in the first column with the appropriate English translation form in the second column.

1.	அல்லது, இல்லனா	a.	But
2.	-உ(ம்)	b.	Because
3.	ஆனா	c.	Asking and giving permission
4.	அதனால	d.	Quotative Marker (that)
5.	ஏண்ணா	e.	At least
6.	அப்புறம்	f.	Plural
7.	இன்னு(ம்)	g.	So, Because of that
8.	-கள்	h.	All
9.	-னு	i.	Conjunction ('And' and 'Also')
10.	-ஆவது	j.	Still, yet
11.	எல்லா(ம்)	k.	Disjunction ('or')
12.	-அட்டு(ம்), -லா(ம்)	l.	After that

B) Fill in the blanks with the right word or suffix.

Example: _____ எனக்கு பசிக்குது (Because I am feeling hungry)

Answer: ஏண்ணா

1. நா(ன்) வருவெ _____ நா(ன்) அவன்கிட்ட பேசமாட்ட (I will come but I will not speak to him)

2. நேத்து நா(ன்) ஓடல _____ நா(ன்) இப்ப ஓடுறெ (Yesterday I didn't ran because of that I am running now)

3. அவங்க(ள்) இப்ப சாப்பிடுறாங்க(ள்) _____ அவங்களுக்கு பசிக்குது (They are eating now because they are hungry)

4. _____ beachக்கு _____? (Shall we all go to the beach?)

5. _____ போறெ (At least I will go)

6. அவங்க(ள்) ஆடுனாங்க(ள்) _____ பாடுனாங்க(ள்) (They danced after that they sang)

278

7. _____ சாப்பாடு வேணு(ம்) (I also want food)

8. அவ(ன்) நல்ல சாப்பிடுவா(ன்) _____ சமைக்க தெரியாது (He eats well but he doesn't know to cook)

9. அவ(ன்) உங்க்ளோட _____ (He shall play with you)

10. எனக்கு _____ _____ வேணு(ம்) (I want book and pen)

11. அந்த புத்தகம் எனக்கு பிடிக்கல _____ நா(ன்) அத வாங்கல (I didn't like that book because of that I didn't buy it)

12. நா(ன்) உங்ககிட்ட _____? (Shall I speak with you?)

13. அவ(ள்) தண்ணி குடிச்சா(ள்) _____ விளையாடுனா(ள்) (She drank water after that she played)

14. _____ சாப்பிடுறெ (At least I will eat)

15. நா(ன்) தூங்கல _____ எனக்கு தூக்கம் வரல (I did not sleep because I am not getting sleep)

C) Translate the following.

Example: At least he will eat

Answer: அவனாவது சாப்பிடுவா(ன்)

1. Yesterday I didn't walk because of that I am walking now

_____

2. They laughed after that they sang

_____

3. He shall walk with you

_____

4. I will come but I will not drink with him

_____

5. At least they will find

_____

6. I also want to study

_____

7. She drank water after that she laughed

_____

8. I didn't like that coffee because of that I didn't buy it

_____

9. Shall we all go to the mall?

_____

10. They are drinking now because they are thirsty

_____

11. At least she will sing

_____

12. He talks well but he doesn't know to sing.

_____

13. I want cat and dog

_____

14. Shall I speak to you?

_____

15. I did not wipe because I did not spill the water.

_____

SOLUTIONS

Lesson 14

Exercise A

1) k; 2) i; 3) a; 4) g; 5) b; 6) l; 7) j; 8) f; 9) d; 10) e; 11) h; 12) c.

Exercise B

1) ஆனா. 2) அதனால. 3) ஏண்ணா. 4) நாமெல்லா(ம்) போகலாமா. 5) நானாவது 6) அப்புறம். 7) எனக்கும். 8) ஆனா. 9) விளையாடலா(ம்). 10) புத்தகமு(ம்) பேனாவு(ம்). 11) அதனால. 12) பேசலாமா. 13) அப்புறம். 14) நானாவது. 15) ஏண்ணா.

TL: 1) aanaa. 2) adhanaala. 3) eeNNaa. 4) naamellaa(m) poogalaamaa. 5). naanaavadhu 6) appuRam. 7) enakkum. 8) aanaa. 9) viLaiyaadalaa(m). 10) puththagamu(m) peenaavu(m). 11) adhanaala. 12) peesalaamaa. 13) appuRam. 14) naanaavadhu. 15) eeNNaa.

Exercise C

1) நேத்து நா(ன்) நடக்கல அதனால இப்ப நா(ன்) நடக்குறெ

neeththu(n) naa nadakkala adhanaala ippa naa(n) nadakkuRe

2) அவங்க(ள்) சிரிச்சாங்க(ள்) அப்புறம் அவங்க(ள்) பாடுனாங்க(ள்)

avangga(L) sirichchaangga(L) appuRam avangga(L) paadunaangga(L)

3) அவ(ன்) உன்னோட நடக்கலாம்

ava(n) unnooda nadakkalaam

4) நா(ன்) வருவெ ஆனா நா(ன்) அவனோட குடிக்கமாட்டெ

naa(n) varuve aanaa naa(n) avanooda kudikkamatte

5) அவங்களாவது கண்டுபிடிப்பாங்க

avanggaLaavadhu kaNdupidippaangga

6) எனக்கும் படிக்கணு(ம்)

enakkum padikkaNu(m)

7) அவ(ள்) தண்ணி குடிச்சா(ள்) அப்புறம் சிரிச்சா(ள்)

ava(L) thaNNi kudichchaa(L) appuRam sirichchaa(L)

8) எனக்கு அந்த காப்பி பிடிக்கல அதனால நா(ன்) அத வாங்கல

enakku andha kaappi pidikkala adhanaala naa(n) adha vaanggala

9) நாம Mallக்கு போகலாமா?

naama mallkku poogalaamaa

10) அவங்க(ள்) இப்ப தண்ணி குடிக்குறாங்க(ள்) ஏண்ணா அவங்களுக்கு தாகமா இருக்கு

avangga(L) ippa thaNNi kudikkuRaangga(L) eeNNaa avanggaLukku thaagamaa irukku

11) அவளாவது பாடுவா(ள்)

avaLaavadhu paaduvaa(L)

12) அவ(ன்) நல்ல பேசுவா(ன்) ஆனா அவனுக்கு பாட தெரியாது

ava(n) nalla peesuvaa(n) aanaa avanukku paada theriyaadhu

13) எனக்கு பூனையும் நாயும் வேணு(ம்)

enakku puunaiyum naayum veeNu(m)

14) நா(ன்) உங்ககிட்ட பேசலாமா?

naa(n) unggakitta peesalaamaa

15) நா(ன்) துடைக்கல ஏண்ணா நா(ன்) தண்ணி ஊத்தல

naa(n) thudaikkala eeNNaa naa(n) thaNNi uuththala

Content:

- Vocabulary

LESSON 4A:
VOCABULARY

Vocabulary

Kindly find below the table with the useful Tamil vocabulary used in this book. I recommend memorizing these vocabularies in your free time either by using the "my little word land" website or the traditional method of reading and memorizing from the book. But don't spend too much time on it, 15 minutes daily will be good.

These are the advantages of memorizing vocabulary.

1) You will recollect the vocabulary while reading the book.

2) You will make multiple sentences apart from the examples I have given you because you have lots of vocabularies in your arsenal right now

3) Much easier to do the exercise from the book.

4) Helps you to practice reading and recognizing the Tamil script.

5) Helps you to practice pronunciation and many more.

Vocabulary	Transliteration	Meaning
வேணு(ம்)	veeNu(m)	Want, need
புத்தகம்	puththagam	Book
முடியல	mudiyala	Could not
என்ன	enna	What?
ஏன்	een	Why?
ஏது	eedhu	How did you get?
யாரு	yaaru	Who?

Vocabulary	Transliteration	Meaning
எங்க	engga	Where?
எப்ப	eppa	When?
எது	edhu	Which (noun)?
எந்த	e_ndha	Which (adjective)?
எப்படி	eppadi	How?
எத்தன	eththana	How many?
எவ்வளவு	evLavu	How much?
குடை	kudai	Umbrella
புகை	pugai	Smoke
பசி	pasi	Hungry
தம்பி	thambi	Younger brother
தொப்பி	thoppi	Hat
அம்மா	ammaa	Mother
மாமா	maamaa	Uncle
தெரு	theru	Street
கொசு	kosu	Mosquito
குரங்கு	kuranggu	Monkey
பூ	puu	Flower
கண்	kaN	Eye
இடம்	Idam	Place
கல்	kal	Stone
புல்	pul	Grass
பல்	pal	Tooth
கால்	kaal	Leg
பால்	paal	Milk
கதை	kadhai	Story
தேன்	theen	Honey

Vocabulary	Transliteration	Meaning
தோல்	thool	Skin
நிறுவனம்	niRuvanam	Company
கேள்வி	keeLvi	Question
வேலை	veelai	Work
தண்ணி	thaNNi	Water
பணம், காசு	paNam, kaasu	Money
உண்மை	uNmai	Truth
அறை	aRai	Room
நிறைய	niRaiya	A lot
புண்	puN	Sore
பெண்	peN	Lady, women, female
வால்	vaal	Tail
நாள்	naaL	Day
நா(ன்)	naa(n)	I
நீ	nii	You (informal)
நீங்க(ள்)	niingga(L)	You (formal)
அவ(ன்)	ava(n)	He, his (informal)
அவரு	avaru	He, his (formal)
அவ(ள்)	ava(L)	She, her (informal)
அவங்க(ள்)	avangga(L)	She, her (formal), they
அது	adhu	That
இது	idhu	This
எ(ன்)	e(n)	My
உ(ன்)	u(n)	Your
உங்க(ள்)	ungga(L)	Your (formal)
நாம	naama	We (listener included)
நாங்க(ள்)	naangga(L)	We (listener not included)

286

Vocabulary	Transliteration	Meaning
நம்ம	namma	Our (listener included)
எங்க(ள்)	engga(L)	Our (listener not included)
அதுங்க(ள்)	adhungga(L)	Those
இதுங்க(ள்)	idhungga(L)	These
கடை	kadai	Shop
இங்க	ingga	Here
இப்ப	ippa	This time, now
இவ்ளவு	ivLavu	This much
இத்தன	iththana	This many
இப்படி	ippadi	Like this, this way/manner
இன்னிக்கு	innikku,	This day or today
அங்க	angga	There
அப்ப	appa	That time, then
அவ்ளவு	avLavu	That much
அத்தன	aththana	That many
அப்படி	appadi	Like that, that way/manner
அன்னிக்கு	annikku,	That's day
எந்நிக்கு	ennikku,	Which day?
அண்ணா, அண்ணன்	aNNaa, aNNan	Elder brother
அக்கா	akkaa	Elder sister
அய்யா	ayyaa	Elderly person
பேனா	peenaa	Pen
தக்காளி	thakkaaLi	Tomato
பெரு	peru	Name
ரூபாய்	ruubaay	Rupees
தல	thala	Head
வியாபாரம்	viyaabaaram	Business

Vocabulary	Transliteration	Meaning
பையன்	paiyan	Boy
வண்டி	vaNdi	Vehicle
வீடு	viidu	House
சாப்பாடு	saappaadu	Food
பேராசிரியர்	peeraasiriyar	Professor
காபி	kaapi	Coffee
நேத்து	neeththu	Yesterday
நாளைக்கு	naaLaikku	Tomorrow
வகுப்பு	vaguppu	Class
மணி	maNi	Hour, o'clock, time
நிமிஷம்	nimisham	Minutes
வினாடி	vinaadi	Seconds
பக்கம்	pakkam	Side
வலது	valadhu	Right
இடது	idadhu	Left
நேர்	neer	Straight
பின்னாடி	pinnaadi	Back, Back side
முன்னாடி	munnaadi	Front, Front side
அப்புறம்	appuRam	After that
ரொம்ப	romba	Very
பந்து	pandhu	Ball
நடிகை	nadigai	Actress
ஓட்டல்	oottal	Hotel
மருத்துவமனை	maruththuvamanai	Hospital
பூனை	puunai	Cat
கொடி	kodi	Flag
கைபேசி	kaipeesi	Mobile phone

Vocabulary	Transliteration	Meaning
உப்பு	uppu	Salt
வங்கி	vanggi	Bank
யோசனை	yoosanai	Idea
பள்ளி	paLLi	School
மாசம்	maasam	Month
வருஷம்	varusham	Year
கதவு	kadhavu	Door
பாதை	paadhai	Path
நகை	nagai	Jewelry
நாய்	naay	Dog
சமையல்	samaiyal	Cooking
பழம்	pazham	Fruit
காய்கறி	kaaygari	Vegetables
கறி	kaRi	Meat
டீ	tii	Tea
சண்டை	saNdai	Fight
ஆண்	aaN	Men
குழந்தை	kuzhandhai	Kid, children
மாணவர்	maaNavar	Student
திங்ககிழம	thinggakizhama	Monday
செவ்வாய்கிழம	sevvaaykizhama	Tuesday
புதன்கிழம	pudhankizhama	Wednesday
வியாழகிழம	viyaazhakizhama	Thursday
வெள்ளிகிழம	veLLikizhama	Friday
சனிகிழம	sanikizhama	Sarurday
ஞாயிற்றுகிழம	njaayiRRukizhama	Sunday
கிழம	kizhama	Week

Vocabulary	Transliteration	Meaning
மனைவி	manaivi	Wife
புருஷன்	purushan	Husband
நண்பர்	naNbar	Male friend (polite)
நண்பன்	naNban	Male friend (informal)
பென்சில்	pensil	Pensil
தோழி	thoozhi	Female friend
பொருள்	poruL	Thing, object
அணி	aNi	Team
கடிதம்	kadidham	Letter
பை	pai	Bag
தரை	tharai	Floor
பொண்ணு	poNNu	Girl

TAMIL SENTENCES FOR CONVERSATION

LESSON 4B

Content:

- Greetings
- Self-Introduction
- Family
- Travel
- Asking for Directions
- Shopping
- Restaurant
- Learning Tamil
- Eating / Drinking
- Day to day Tamil sentences
- Weather
- and more...

LESSON 4B:
TAMIL SENTENCES FOR CONVERSATION

<u>Attention!</u>

As mentioned in the beginning of lesson 1. I have created a video tutorial in YouTube explaining how to use the book and the content of the book in video format.

Kindly go to the below link to access the YouTube playlist of me pronuncing each and every sentences multiple times in video format.

www.tinyurl.com/tamilvideos1

Note:

It is advisable for the learners not to concentrate on learning sentences or role-play scenarios before learning other lessons in this book because Tamil grammar is different from English grammar. If you look at Tamil sentences before learning Tamil grammar, you will be confused and find it difficult to understand the Tamil sentences. When you learn Tamil grammar and then look at these sentences, you will be able to understand and learn the sentences well.

The above statement is simply a suggestion, as it is the best way to learn Tamil. However, there are some exceptions as well.

1. Learning these Tamil sentences and role-play scenarios can be done simultaneously with other lessons (Tamil grammar). This would help you understand Tamil grammar better and improve your vocabulary.

2. Some of you might be interested in learning a few sentences in Tamil to practice with native Tamil speakers, and you might not be interested in Tamil grammar at all. Then, these Tamil sentences and role-play scenarios are for you.

The sentences in the below table will be provided in the form below.

Example:

How are you doing?

எப்டி இருக்கீங்க?

tl: yepdi irukkiingga?

In Detail: yepdi - how, irukkiingga - doing (present tense)

Transliteration (tl) - This is the transliteration of the Tamil script; in simple words, this is how a Tamil pronunciation would be if it's written in Tamil.

Disclaimer Alert!

In the Tamil sentences for conversation and role-play scenarios given in this book, I have used Chennai, or in other words, a city-based Tamil. I would have used some English words instead of Tamil words in some sentences and the Tamil words will be so modern that they will even be slightly different from the grammar lessons provided in the book. I did this because this is how most of the Tamil people in Tamil Nadu speak in daily conversations, and you can use these sentences right away.

It is possible that when you ask a Tamil speaker to speak to you slowly, he will start speaking to you in old Tamil (sentamil). When this happens, please ask them: Is this how they would speak on a daily basis with other Tamil speakers? Request that they speak with you in modern Tamil and not old Tamil (sentamil). The same would also happen when you ask them to teach you some Tamil sentences or words and once again ask them to teach you only modern Tamil and whether these words or sentences they would use on a daily basis. This is a common issue that many of my students face, but it can be easily alleviated when you tell them that you are learning modern Tamil for conversation.

As mentioned in the beginning of the book, the Tamil language spoken in Tamil Nadu and Sri Lanka is somewhat different. The Tamil spoken in Sri Lanka is more pure and they use old Tamil (sentamil), while the Tamil spoken in Tamil Nadu is modern Tamil. The difference is not that big, we understand ourselves very well, it's just a different accent, that's all. It's comparable to the difference between American English and Australian English.

Since I have used the Tamil Nadu Tamil (Modern Tamil), when you use these Tamil sentences or words with the Srilankan Tamil speakers, you will find that the Tamil they speak is a bit different. But regardless, you can easily switch to Srilankan Tamil, because only the ending and a few words will be different and everything else will stay the same. You may ask them to explain the difference and they will do it easily for you, so don't worry.

Conversation with Tamil people

In many places in the western world, if someone wants to start a conversation with strangers they met on a train or a friend of your friend etc. They would start the conversation by talking about the weather, sports, something they did, or some current event in their country. Later, after a few days they would start asking more personal questions about what they do for a living, if they are married or if they have kids etc. Although it may not be fixed, this changes from country to country, but in my experience, this is what I have observed so far. I may not be entirely correct. If this is the case, forgive me.

In Tamil nadu, when a person initiates a conversation with a stranger or a friend of a friend, etc. It is completely natural and socially acceptable to ask the questions below.

a) What is your name? b) Where are you from? c) Which is your hometown? d) Where are you working? e) What is your job designation? f) Do you have brothers and sisters? g) If you have, then where are they? And What do they do for a living? h) Where are your parents? And What do they do? i) Are you married? j) What does your wife do?, does she work somewhere? k) Do you have kids? l) If so, What is their name?, How old are they? And Where are they studying? etc.

The whole point of asking such questions is to try to have a conversation with others, with these questions you can find some common ground and end up having more conversations.

The whole point of asking such questions is to try to have a conversation with others, with these questions you can find some common ground and end up having more conversations.

Due to the tropical climate in most of India, we seldom talk about the weather, and most conversations about it will be limited to a single sentence. In order to initiate a conversation with the Tamil people, it's recommended to ask questions and share more about yourself.

People in India are more interested in cricket and movies, so that would be good for conversations as well.

Note:

In this 'Tamil sentences for conversation' lesson, you are going to get trained for having such conversations with Tamil people.

Greetings

	English	Tamil	Literal Translation
1	Hello	வணக்கம்	vaNakkam

Note:

The word "hello" is scarcely used in spoken Tamil. Maybe in some Tamil Nadu villages, a few people might use them when giving a speech or being very polite. Besides that, they are rarely used in spoken Tamil.

2	How are you?	எப்டி இருக்கீங்க?	epdi irukkiingga?

Note:

In the western world, people use the sentence 'How are you?'in greeting or at the beginning of the conversation. But in Tamil, we say 'How are you?' only when you are aware that the person is or was sick, the person's mood is bad or something is wrong and you are asking the person 'How are you?' to show an actual concern for the person. Or let's say you are meeting a person again after a few days or weeks, when you start the conversation, you can start by saying 'How are you?' because in the meantime their circumstances might have changed and you are asking 'How are you?' as a genuinely concerned person.

Let's say you meet a stranger in Tamil nadu and you start the conversation by saying 'எப்டி இருக்கீங்க' (How are you?) As a way of greeting and being polite. Then the stranger would start wondering 'Do I know this person?' 'Have we met before?' 'Why is he concerned about my wellbeing' and they will be confused. So, it's better to use the sentence 'எப்டி இருக்கீங்க' (How are you?) Only when the situation is as stated above.

3	I am doing good	நா நல்லா இருக்கெ	naa nallaa irukke
4	Good morning	காலை வணக்கம்	kaalai vaNakkam

People rarely say 'Good morning' in Tamil, so it's better not to learn or use it.

Goodbye!: There are multiple ways of saying 'goodbye!' in Tamil. We shall look at them below.

5	Let's see each other later	பாப்போ	paappo

Note:

> This is used when you are in a video call or when you are speaking to a person and you want to say 'goodbye!'

6	Let's speak on an another day	இன்னொரு நாள் பேசுவோ	innoru naaL peesuvo

Note:

> This is used when you are in a voice call or just speaking to someone and you want to say 'goodbye!'

7	See you next time	போயிட்டு வறே	pooyittu vaRe

Note:

> When you visit someone's house or place as a guest, you'll say this before departing. For example, you will not use this sentence in a police station or hospital, because we do not want to come back to this place again. This sentence doesn't necessarily mean that you will definitely come back to their house again. It's just a gesture, that's all. Despite the fact that you may never meet them or come back to their house again, you will still say this as a sweet gesture before leaving.

Cultural point: In Tamil nadu, people will often invite you to their house and during conversations they might say that they will visit you one day. When they do, just say 'yes' or 'of course', but please don't take these things very seriously and start making plans, all of this is a sweet gesture to show their hospitality. Before coming to your house, they will give you a call so that you can make plans, you can go to their house as and when you want but of course you will have to inform them in advance. Inviting someone to their house is a common affair in India. It shows our hospitality, but there is no pressure on you.

8	Thank you	நன்றி	<u>n</u>andri

Note:

When someone in Tamil nadu says 'Thank you', then they really mean it. It's not just a matter of courtesy or politeness. Personally, I like to use 'Thank you' often and I would recommend you do the same but don't expect others to use it often, they would use it only when it is absolutely necessary.

9	You are welcome	பரவாயில்ல	paravaayilla
10	Sorry	மன்னிச்சிடுங்க	mannichchidungga

Note:

The word 'sorry' is used rarely in Tamil because the word 'sorry' holds a lot of value and meaning for us. So the Tamils will only say "sorry" when they think they are, and not simply to be polite.

11	Please	தயவுசெஞ்சு	dhayavusenjju

Note:

This word is not commonly used in Tamil. In my life, I've only used this word four times, and it was to make my mom buy me ice cream. When you use this word, it is like you are literally begging others for a favor, which is why people will refrain from using it. This word is used in situations like when you want to borrow some money or ask for a huge favor.

Cultural point: Since words like 'Sorry', 'Thank you' and 'Please' hold a lot of value in Tamil, when Tamil people speak in English, they will not use these words until or unless they really mean it. But in the western world and in many other places, 'Sorry', 'Thank you', and 'Please' are used as a means of being polite, but they really don't mean it. Tamil people may be considered rude due to this, but that's not the case. It is just a difference in the language and the culture.

12	Have you finished eating?	சாப்டாச்சா?	saaptaachchaa?
13	I have finished eating	சாப்டாச்சு	saaptaachchu
14	Did you eat?	சாப்டிங்களா?	saaptiinggaLaa?
15	I ate	சாப்ட்டெ	saaptte

Cultural point: It is customary in Tamil nadu to ask a person whom you know very well, 'during lunch time, around 1pm-2pm, and during dinner time, around 8pm-10pm, 'have you finished eating?' or 'did you eat'. Sometimes when you are speaking to them over the phone, you can ask them these questions. This is a friendly gesture that shows that you care about that person. In addition, let's say you ask them this question when you meet them and if they have not eaten yet, then you may even invite them to eat along with you or you can tell them that you should eat soon as it's lunch time now and ask why they haven't eaten yet. (Note: This is purely optional, please don't feel pressured to do any of this. It's only a friendly gesture, that's all.)

Cultural point (Calling by their First name): In Tamil Nadu, most people have their father's name as their last name. Everyone prefers that you address them by their first name, calling them by their last name will be awkward because you address that person by his father's name. If you know a person even a little bit, like an acquaintance, you can start addressing them by their first name, unlike in other cultures where you can only address a person by their first name if they consider you their friend.

Self-Introduction

	English	Tamil	Literal Translation
16	What is your name?	உங்க பேரு என்ன?	ungga peeru yenna?
17	My name is Rachel	எ பேரு Rachel	ye peeru rachel
18	I am a Canadian	நா Canadian	naa Canadian
19	Where were you born and grow up?	நீங்க பிறந்து வளந்தது எங்க?	niingga piRandhu vaLandhadhu yengga?
20	I was born in and grew up in Canada	நா பிறந்து வளந்தது Canadaல	naa piRandhu vaLandhadhu Canadala
21	Where are you coming from?	நீங்க எங்கருந்து வர்றீங்க?	niingga yenggarundhu varRiingga?
22	I'm coming from Canada	நா Canadaலருந்து வர்றெ	naa Canadalarundhu varRe
23	Where are you living in Canada?	Canadaல எங்க இருக்கீங்க?	Canadala yengga irukkiingga?
24	I am living in Toronto	நா Torontoல இருக்கெ	naa Torontola irukke
25	In which city do you live now? / Where do you live now?	நீங்க இப்ப எந்த ஊர்ல இருக்கீங்க / நீங்க இப்ப எங்க இருக்கீங்க?	niingga ippa yendha uurla irukkiingga / niingga ippa yengga irukkiingga?
26	I live in New York now	நா இப்ப New yorkல இருக்கெ	naa ippa New yorkla irukke
27	What are you studying?	என்ன படிக்குறீங்க?	yenna padikkuRiingga?
28	I am studying Economics	நா Economics படிக்குறெ	naa Economics padikkuRe

29	Where are you studying?	எங்க படிக்குறீங்க?	yengga padikkuRiingga?
30	I am studying in Oxford university	நா Oxford universityல படிக்குறெ	naa Oxford universityla padikkuRe
31	What / where do you work?	என்ன / எங்க வேல செய்றீங்க / பாக்குறீங்க?	yenna / yengga veela seiRiingga / paakkuRiingga?
32	I work in New York in Dell company as a computer programmer	நா New yorkல Dell companyல computer programmerஆ வேல செய்றெ / பாக்குறெ	naa New yorkla Dell companyla computer programmeraa veela seiRe / paakkuRe
33	Where did you study?	எங்க படிச்சீங்க?	yengga padichchiingga?
34	I studied in Canada	நா Canadaல படிச்செ	naa Canadala padichche
35	What have you studied?	என்ன படிச்சிருக்கீங்க?	yenna padichchirukkiingga?
36	I did my undergrad at the University of Toronto and my masters at Oxford	நா University of Torontoல undergrad படிச்செ, Oxfordல masters படிச்செ	naa University of Torontola undergrad padichche, Oxfordla masters padichche
37	I have studied Computer science engineering in university of Toronto	நா University of Torontoல Computer science Engineering படிச்சிருக்கெ	naa University of Torontola computer science engineering padichchirukke

Note:

When Tamil people ask you about your job or where you work or what your job designation is. Then, instead of giving them the exact answer, it would be better to tell them in which city or country you work and the name of the company and your designation there, like in the example I have given above. If you don't tell them these details, then that's what they are going to ask you next, so it's better for you to give an answer in the format that I have provided. Same goes for studies, tell them both your college name and your course name.

EXERCISES:

Fill in the blanks with your personal info below for practising.

1) ye peeru _____ (my name is)

2) naa _____ (I am (nationality))

3) naa piRandhu vaLandhadhu _____ la (I am born and brought up in)

4) naa _____ larundhu varRe (I am coming from_____)

5) naa _____ la irukke (I am living in)

6) naa ippoo _____ la irukke (I am in _____ now)

7) If you are a student, then fill the below info's:

8) naa _____ padikkuRe (I am studying)

9) naa _____ la padikkuRe (I am studying in Oxford university)

10) If you are working, then fill the below info's

11) naa _____ la _____ la _____ aa veela seiRe / paakkuRe (I am working in (city) in (company name) as (designation)

12) naa _____ la padichche (I studied in (city)

13) naa _____ la undergrad padichche, _____ la masters padichche (I studied undergrad in (university name) masters in (university name)

14) naa _____ la _____ padichchirukke (I studied in (college name) (course name))

Family

	English	Tamil	Literal Translation
38	Husband	கணவர் (formal) (written) / புருஷன் (informal) (spoken)	kaNavar / purushan
39	Wife	மனைவி (formal) (written) / பொண்டாட்டி (informal) (spoken)	manalvi / puNdaatti
40	Mother	அம்மா	ammaa
41	Father	அப்பா	appaa
42	Grandfather	தாத்தா	thaaththaa
43	Grandmother	பாட்டி	paatti
44	Elder brother	அண்ணா	aNNaa
45	Elder sister	அக்கா	akkaa
46	Younger brother	தம்பி	thambi
47	Younger sister	தங்கச்சி	thanggachchi

At the beginning of the conversation, when they inquire about your family. They will usually ask these three questions: a) How are they doing? b) Where are they located now? c) Where are they working?. It's a way of showing interest and concern for your family members.

48	How many siblings do you have?	உங்களுக்கு கூட பொறந்தவங்க இருக்காங்களா?	unggaLukku kuuda poRandhavangga irukkaanggaLaa?
49	Do you have brothers and sisters?	உங்களுக்கு அண்ணா அக்கா இருக்காங்களா?	unggaLukku aNNaa akkaa irukkaanggaLaa?
50	I have one elder brother and one younger sister	எனக்கு ஒரு அண்ணா ஒரு அக்கா இருக்காங்க	yenakku oru aNNaa oru akkaa irukkaangga
51	I have no siblings	எனக்கு கூட பொறந்தவங்க யாரும் இல்ல	yenakku kuuda poRandhavangga yaarum illa
52	Marriage	கல்யாணம்	kalyaaNam
53	Are you married?	உங்களுக்கு கல்யாணம் ஆயிடுச்சா?	unggaLukku kalyaaNam aayiduchchaa?
54	I am married	எனக்கு கல்யாணம் ஆயிடுச்சு	yenakku kalyaaNam aayiduchchu
55	I am not married	எனக்கு கல்யாணம் ஆகல	yenakku kalyaaNam aagal
56	I have a boyfriend	எனக்கு ஒரு boyfriend இருக்காரு	yenakku oru boyfriend irukkaaru
57	I have a girlfriend	எனக்கு ஒரு girlfriend இருக்காங்க	yenakku oru girlfriend irukkaangga

Male Family members

If the family member is a male person. e.g. husband, father, grandfather, elder brother, younger brother. Then, in the below questions and sentences, all you have to do is just replace the name of one family member with another. Since they are all male, the verb conjugation will still be the same. The verb conjugation for Male (formal) always ends with the suffix –ஆரு (-aaru) irrespective of the tense.

Father:

58	How is your father?	உங்க அப்பா எப்டி இருக்காரு?	ungga appaa yepdi irukkaaru?
59	My father is doing well	எ அப்பா நல்லா இருக்காரு?	ye appaa nallaa irukkaaru?
60	Where is your father?	உங்க அப்பா எங்க இருக்காரு?	ungga appaa yengga irukkaaru?
61	My father is in America	அப்பா Americaல இருக்காரு	appaa americala irukkaaru
62	What does your father do?	உங்க அப்பா என்ன பண்றாரு?	ungga appaa yenna paNdRaaru?
63	Where does your father work?	உங்க அப்பா எங்க வேல செய்றாரு / பண்றாரு / பாக்குறாரு?	ungga appaa yengga veela seyRaaru / paNdRaaru/ paakkuRaaru?
64	Father is working in Microsoft as a Manager	அப்பா Microsoftல Managerஆ வேல செய்றாரு / பண்றாரு / பாக்குறாரு	appaa Microsoftla Manageraa veela seyRaaru / paNdRaaru / paakkuRaaru
65	My father is a houseman (In Tamil: He is taking care of the house)	அப்பா வீட்ட பாத்துக்குறாரு	ammaa viitta paaththukkuRaaru

In Tamil, there are three verb conjugations to indicate the verb 'to work'. வேல செய் (to do work), வேல பண்ணு (to do work), வேல பார் (to see work). All three of these verbs indicate 'to work' in Tamil and all three are commonly used in spoken Tamil. Because of this, you have to memorize all these three verb forms and, during conversation, look out for them. As much as the person who asks you the question has the choice of choosing one out of the three, you have the same choice as well. e.g. when someone asks you 'உங்க அப்பா எங்க வேல செய்றாரு?

(ungga appaa yengga vela seiRaaru?) (where is your father working?)' you can respond by saying 'அப்பா Microsoftல Managerஆ வேல பாக்குறாரு' (appaa Microsoftla Manageraa vela paakkuRaaru) (Father is working in Microsoft as a Manager). As you can see in this sentence, I used a different conjugation for the answer than what is used in the question. I would suggest you memorize all three verb conjugations of the verb 'to work' so that you recognize it when someone uses it, but you always use just one verb conjugation while responding.

Husband:

66	How is your husband?	உங்க புருஷன் எப்டி இருக்காரு?	ungga purushan yepdi irukkaaru?
67	My husband is doing good	எ புருஷன் நல்லா இருக்காரு	ye purushan nallaa irukkaaru
68	Where is your husband?	உங்க புருஷன் எங்க இருக்காரு?	ungga purushan yengga irukkaaru?
69	My husband is in America	எ புருஷன் America-லல் இருக்காரு	ye purushan americala irukkaaru
70	What does your husband do?	உங்க புருஷன் என்ன பண்றாரு?	ungga purushan yenna paNdRaaru?
71	Where does your husband work?	உங்க புருஷன் எங்க வேல செய்றாரு / பண்றாரு / பாக்குறாரு?	ungga purushan yengga veela seyRaaru / paNdRaaru/ paakkuRaaru?
72	Husband is working in Microsoft as a Manager	எ புருஷன் Microsoftல Managerஆ வேல செய்றாரு / பண்றாரு / பாக்குறாரு	ye purushan Microsoftla Manageraa veela seyRaaru / paNdRaaru / paakkuRaaru

Elder brother / younger brother:

73	How is your elder brother / younger brother?	உங்க அண்ணா / தம்பி எப்டி இருக்காரு?	ungga aNNaa / thambi yepdi irukkaaru?
74	My elder brother / younger brother is doing good	எ அண்ணா / தம்பி நல்லா இருக்காரு	ye aNNaa / thambi nallaa irukkaaru
75	Where is your elder brother / younger brother?	உங்க அண்ணா / தம்பி எங்க இருக்காரு?	ungga aNNaa / thambi yengga irukkaaru?
76	My elder brother / younger brother is in America	எ அண்ணா / தம்பி Americaல இருக்காரு	ye aNNaa / thambi americala irukkaaru
77	What does your elder brother / younger brother do?	உங்க அண்ணா / தம்பி என்ன பண்றாரு?	ungga aNNaa / thambi yenna paNdRaaru?
78	Where does your elder brother / younger brother work?	உங்க அண்ணா / தம்பி எங்க வேல செய்றாரு / பண்றாரு / பாக்குறாரு?	ungga aNNaa / thambi yengga veela seyRaaru / paNdRaaru / paakkuRaaru?
79	Elder brother / younger brother is working in Microsoft as a Manager	எ அண்ணா / தம்பி Microsoftல Managerஆ வேல செய்றாரு / பண்றாரு / பாக்குறாரு	ye aNNaa / thambi Microsoftla Manageraa veela seyRaaru / paNdRaaru / paakkuRaaru
80	What does your elder brother / younger brother study?	உங்க அண்ணா / தம்பி எங்க / என்ன படிக்குறாரு?	ungga aNNaa / thambi yengga / yenna padikkuRaaru?
81	My elder brother / younger brother study's commerce in California university	எ அண்ணா / தம்பி California universityல Commerce படிக்குறாரு	ye aNNaa / thambi California universityla Commerce padikkuRaaru

306

Female Family members

If the family member is a female person. e.g. wife, mother, grandmother, elder sister, younger sister. Then, in the below questions and sentences, all you have to do is just replace the name of one family member with another. Since they are all female, the verb conjugation will still be the same. The verb conjugation for Female (formal) always ends with the suffix –ஆங்க (-aangga) irrespective of the tense.

Mother:

82	How is your mother?	உங்க அம்மா எப்டி இருக்காங்க?	ungga ammaa yepdi irukkaangga?
83	My mother is doing good	எ அம்மா நல்லா இருக்காங்க	ye ammaa <u>nallaa</u> irukkaangga
84	Where is your mother?	உங்க அம்மா எங்க இருக்காங்க?	ungga ammaa yengga irukkaangga?
85	My mother is in America	அம்மா Americaல இருக்காங்க	ammaa americala irukkaangga
86	What does your mother do?	உங்க அம்மா என்ன பண்றாங்க?	ungga ammaa yenna paNdRaangga?
87	Where does your mother work?	உங்க அம்மா எங்க வேல செய்றாங்க / பண்றாங்க / பாக்குறாங்க?	ungga ammaa yengga veela seyRaangga / paNdRaangga/ paakkuRaangga?
88	Mother is working in Microsoft as a Manager	அம்மா Microsoftல Managerஆ வேல செய்றாங்க / பண்றாங்க / பாக்குறாங்க	ammaa Microsoftla Manageraa veela seyRaangga/paNdRaangga / paakkuRaangga
89	My mom is a house wife (In Tamil: She is taking care of the house)	அம்மா வீட்ட பாத்துக்குறாங்க	ammaa viitta paaththukkuRaangga

Wife:

90	How is your wife?	உங்க பொண்டாட்டி எப்டி இருக்காங்க?	ungga poNdaatti yepdi irukkaangga?
91	My wife is doing good	எ பொண்டாட்டி நல்லா இருக்காங்க	ye poNdaatti nallaa irukkaangga
92	Where is your wife?	உங்க பொண்டாட்டி எங்க இருக்காங்க?	ungga poNdaatti yengga irukkaangga?
93	My wife is in America	எ பொண்டாட்டி Americaல இருக்காங்க	ye poNdaatti americala irukkaangga
94	What does your wife do?	உங்க பொண்டாட்டி என்ன பண்றாங்க?	ungga poNdaatti yenna paNdRaangga?
95	Where does your wife work?	உங்க பொண்டாட்டி எங்க வேல செய்றாங்க / பண்றாங்க / பாக்குறாங்க?	ungga poNdaatti yengga veela seyRaangga / paNdRaangga/ paakkuRaangga?
96	Wife is working in Microsoft as a Manager	எ பொண்டாட்டி Microsoftல Managerஆ வேல செய்றாங்க / பண்றாங்க / பாக்குறாங்க	ye poNdaatti Microsoftla Manageraa vela seyRaangga / paNdRaangga / paakkuRaangga

Elder sister / younger sister:

97	How is your elder sister / younger sister?	உங்க அக்கா / தங்கச்சி எப்டி இருக்காங்க?	ungga akkaa / thanggachchi yepdi irukkaangga?
98	My elder sister / younger sister is doing good	எ அக்கா / தங்கச்சி நல்லா இருக்காங்க	ye akkaa / thanggachchi nallaa irukkaangga
99	Where is your elder sister / younger sister?	உங்க அக்கா / தங்கச்சி எங்க இருக்காங்க?	ungga akkaa / thanggachchi yengga irukkaangga?
100	My elder sister / younger sister is in America	எ அக்கா / தங்கச்சி Americaல இருக்காங்க	ye akkaa / thanggachchi americala irukkaangga
101	What does your elder sister / younger sister do?	உங்க அக்கா / தங்கச்சி என்ன பண்றாங்க?	ungga akkaa / thanggachchi yenna paNdRaangga?
102	Where does your elder sister / younger sister work?	உங்க அக்கா / தங்கச்சி எங்க வேல செய்றாங்க / பண்றாங்க / பாக்குறாங்க/	ungga akkaa / thanggachchi yengga veela seyRaangga / paNdRaangga/ paakkuRaangga?
103	Elder sister / younger sister is working in Microsoft as a Manager	எ அக்கா / தங்கச்சி Microsoftல Managerஆ வேல செய்றாங்க / பண்றாங்க / பாக்குறாங்க	ye akkaa / thanggachchi Microsoftla Manageraa veela seyRaangga / paNdRaangga / paakkuRaangga
104	Where does your elder sister / younger sister study?	உங்க அக்கா / தங்கச்சி எங்க / என்ன படிக்குறாங்க?	ungga akkaa / thanggachchi yengga / yenna padikkuRaangga?
105	My elder sister / younger sister study's commerce in California university	எ அக்கா / தங்கச்சி California universityல Commerce படிக்குறாங்க	ye akkaa / thanggachchi California universityla Commerce padikkuRaangga

309

If you are married and you have kids, then the below are applicable for you and you can use it during conversations otherwise you can skip this table.

106	Do you have kids?	உங்களுக்கு பசங்க இருக்காங்களா?	unggaLukku pasangga irukkaanggaLaa?
107	Do you have a baby?	உங்களுக்கு குழந்த இருக்கா?	unggaLukku kuzhandha irukkaa?
108	I don't have kids / baby	எனக்கு பசங்க / குழந்த இல்ல	yenakku pasangga / kuzhandha illa
109	I have a son	எனக்கு ஒரு பையன் இருக்கான்	yenakku oru paiyan irukkaan
110	What does your son do?	உங்க பையன் என்ன பண்றாரு?	ungga paiyan yenna paNdRaaru?
111	What does your son study?	உங்க பையன் என்ன படிக்குறாரு?	ungga paiyan yenna padikkuRaaru?
112	My son is studying _____ in America	எ பையன் Americaல _____ படிக்குறான்	ye paiyan americala _____ padikkuRaan
113	My son is working in Microsoft as a Manager	எ பையன் Microsoftல Managerஆ வேல செய்றான் / பண்றான் / பாக்குறான்	ye paiyan Microsoftla manageraa veela seyRaan / paNdRaan / paakkuRaan
114	I have a daughter	எனக்கு ஒரு பொண்ணு இருக்காள்	yenakku oru poNNu irukkaaL
115	What does your daughter do?	உங்க பொண்ணு என்ன பண்றாங்க?	ungga poNNu yenna paNdRaangga?
116	What does your daughter study?	உங்க பொண்ணு என்ன படிக்குறாங்க?	ungga poNNu yenna padikkuRaangga?
117	My daughter is studying _____ in America	எ பொண்ணு Americaல _____ படிக்குறாள்	ye poNNu americala _____ padikkuRaaL
118	My daughter is working in Microsoft as a Manager	எ பொண்ணு Microsoftல Managerஆ வேல செய்றாள் / பண்றாள் / பாக்குறாள்	ye poNNu microsoftla manageraa veela seyRaaL / paNdRaaL / paakkuRaaL

310

If one of your parents has passed away, then you can use the below sentence when they inquire about your parents.

119	My Father is dead	எ(ன்) அப்பா இறந்துட்டாரு	yen appaa iRandhuttaaru
120	My Mom is dead	எ(ன்) அம்மா இறந்துட்டாங்க	yen ammaa iRandhuttaangga

When introducing someone:

121	He (formal)	அவரு	avaru
122	She (formal)	அவங்க	avangga
123	He (informal)	அவன்	avan
124	She (informal)	அவள்	avaL
125	He is my father / husband / elder brother / younger brother	அவரு எ அப்பா / புருஷன் / அண்ணா / தம்பி	avaru ye appaa / purushan / aNNaa / thambi
126	She is my mom / wife / elder sister / younger sister	அவங்க எ அம்மா / பொண்டாட்டி / அக்கா / தங்கச்சி	avangga ye ammaa / poNdaatti / akkaa / thanggachchi
127	He is my son	அவன் எ பையன்	avan ye paiyan
128	She is my daughter	அவள் எ பொண்ணு	avaL ye poNNu

Travel

	English	Tamil	Literal Translation
129	I don't know Tamil	எனக்கு தமிழ் தெரியாது	yenakku thamizh theriyaadhu
130	I know Tamil	எனக்கு தமிழ் தெரியும்	yenakku thamizh theriyum
131	I know little Tamil	எனக்கு தமிழ் கொஞ்சம் தெரியும்	yenakku thamizh konjjam theriyum
132	Do you know English?	உங்களுக்கு English தெரியுமா?	unggaLukku English theriyumaa?
133	When did you arrive in Chennai?	நீங்க எப்ப chennaiக்கு வந்தீங்க?	niingga yeppa chennaikku vandhiingga ?
134	I came to Chennai 2 days ago	நா Chennaiக்கு ரெண்டு நாளைக்கு முன்னாடி வந்தெ	naa Chennaikku reNdu naaLaikku munnaadi vandhe
135	It has been 2 days since I came to Chennai	நா Chennaiக்கு வந்து ரெண்டு நாள் ஆகுது	naa Chennaikku vandhu reNdu naaL aagudhu
136	How long are you in Chennai?	Chennaiல எவ்ளோ நாளா இருக்கீங்க?	Chennaila yevLoo naaLaa irukkiingga?
137	I am in Chennai for 2 weeks	நா Chennaiல ரெண்டு வாரமா இருக்கெ	naa Chennaila reNdu vaaramaa irukke
138	How long will you be in Chennai?	எவ்ளோ நாள் Chennaiல இருப்பீங்க?	yevLoo naaL Chennaila iruppiingga?
139	I am staying in Chennai for 3 weeks	நா மூணு வாரத்துக்கு Chennaiல இருப்பெ	naa muuNu vaaraththukku Chennaila iruppe
140	Where and all did you go in Chennai?	Chennaiல எங்கெல்லா போனீங்க?	Chennaila yenggellaa pooniingga?

141	What and all, did you tour in Chennai	Chennaiல என்னெல்லா சுத்தி பாத்தீங்க	Chennaila yennellaa suththi paatthiingga
142	I toured the Marina beach, Mahaballipuram, Valluvar kottam, Mylapore Temple, Dakshin Chitra Heritage museum in Chennai	நா Chennaiல Marina beach, Mahaballipuram, Valluvar kottam, Mylapore Temple, Dakshin Chitra Heritage museum சுத்தி பாத்தெ	naa Chennaila Marina beach, Mahaballipuram, Valluvar kottam, Mylapore Temple, Dakshin Chitra Heritage museum suththi paaththe
143	I did shopping in Pothys	நா Pothysல shopping பண்ணெ	naa Pothysla shopping paNNe
144	Which other places are you going to?	வேற எங்கெல்லாம் போறீங்க?	veeRa yenggellaam pooRiingga?
145	Will you tour any other city / town?	மத்த ஊருக்கு சுத்தி பாக்க போவீங்களா?	maththa uurukku suththi paakka pooviinggaLaa?
146	No, I will only be in Chennai	இல்ல, Chennai மட்டும் தான்	illaa, Chennai mattum dhaan
147	I am going to tour Madurai for 4 days and Thanjavur for 2 days.	நா நாலு நாள் madurai, ரெண்டு நாள் Thanjavur சுத்தி பாக்க போறெ	naa naalu naaL madurai, reNdu naaL Thanjavur suththi paakka pooRe
148	What and all, are you going to tour in Madurai?	Maduraiல என்னெல்லா சுத்தி பாக்க போறீங்க?	Maduraila yennellaa suththi paakka pooRiingga?
149	I am going to tour the Meenakshi amman temple, Keezhadi museum, Naicker palace etc.	நா Maduraiல meenakshi amman temple, Keezhadi museum, naicker palace சுத்தி பாக்க போறெ	naa Maduraila meenakshi amman temple, Keezhadi museum, naicker palace suththi paakka pooRe

Asking for Directions:

	English	Tamil	Literal Translation
150	Where is the hospital?	Hospital எங்க இருக்கு?	Hospital yengga irukku?
151	How to go to the Railway station?	Railway stationக்கு எப்டி போகணும்?	Railway stationkku yepdi poogaNum?
152	Please go	போங்க	poongga
153	Please turn	திரும்புங்க	thirumbungga
154	There	அங்க	angga
155	Here	இங்க	ingga
156	It's on the left	Leftல இருக்கு	Leftla irukku
157	It's on the right	Rightல இருக்கு	Rightla irukku
158	It's on the backside	பின்னாடி இருக்கு	pinnaadi irukku
159	It's on the front side	முன்னாடி இருக்கு	munnaadi irukku
160	Go left, go right, go backside, go straight	Leftல போங்க, Rightல போங்க, பின்னாடி போங்க, straightஆ போங்க	Leftla poongga, Rightla poongga, pinnaadi poongga, straightaa poongga
161	When will the train come?	Train எப்ப வரும்?	Train yeppa varum?
162	In which platform does the train come?	எந்த Platformல train வரும்?	yendha Platformla train varum?
163	Where will the bus come?	Bus எங்க வரும்?	Bus yengga varum?

314

Shopping:

	English	Tamil	Literal Translation
164	Where can I get an apple?	apple எங்க கிடைக்கும்?	apple yengga kidaikkum?
165	Where is the Vegetable shop?	காய்கறி கட எங்க இருக்கு?	kaaygaRi kada yengga irukku?
166	How much is apple?	apple எவ்ளோ?	apple yevᴸoo?
167	Apple _____ rupees	apple _____ ரூபா	apple _____ ruubaa
168	What is this?	இது என்ன?	idhu yenna?
169	What is that?	அது என்ன?	adhu yenna?
170	How much is this / that?	இது / அது எவ்ளோ?	idhu / adhu yevLoo?
171	What is the price of this / that?	இது / அது என்ன வில?	idhu / adhu yenna vila?
172	Give me this	இது குடுங்க	idhu kudungga
173	Give me that	அது குடுங்க	adhu kudungga
174	Pack this / that	இது / அது Pack பண்ணுங்க	idhu / adhu Pack paNNungga
175	How much in total?	எவ்ளோ ஆச்சு?	yevLoo aachchu?
176	Do you have change for 500 rupees?	500 rupeesக்கு change இருக்கா?	500 rupeeskku change irukkaa?
177	Yes, I have	இருக்கு	irukku
178	No, I don't have	இல்ல	illa
179	Give me two apples, three oranges	ரெண்டு Apple மூணு Orange குடுங்க	reNdu Apple muuNu Orange kudungga

315

Restaurant:

	English	Tamil	Literal Translation
180	What do you want to eat?	உங்களுக்கு சாப்பிட என்ன வேணும்?	unggaLukku saappida yenna veeNum?
181	What is there to eat (If there is no menu card available)?	சாப்பிடுறதுக்கு என்ன இருக்கு?	saappiduRadhukku yenna irukku?
182	Please give me a menu card	ஒரு Menu card குடுங்க	oru Menu card kudungga
183	Please give me one plate idly, two dosas, one apple juice	ஒரு plate இட்லி, ரெண்டு தோசை, ஒரு apple juice	oru plate idli, reNdu dhoosai, oru apple juice
184	Do you have hot water?	சுடு தண்ணி இருக்கா?	sudu thaNNi irukkaa?
185	Do you have Ice water?	Ice water இருக்கா?	Ice water irukkaa?
186	Yes available	இருக்கு	irukku
187	Please give me two tumblers of hot water	சுடு தண்ணி ரெண்டு Tumbler குடுங்க	sudu thaNNi reNdu Tumbler kudungga
188	Please give me two tumblers of Ice water	Ice water ரெண்டு Tumbler குடுங்க	Ice water reNdu Tumbler kudungga
189	Do you have a teaspoon, fork and knife?	teaspoon, fork, knife இருக்கா?	teaspoon, fork, knife irukkaa?
190	Please give me a teaspoon, fork and knife	teaspoon, fork, knife குடுங்க	teaspoon, fork, knife kudungga
191	Please give me a teaspoon, two forks and three knives	ஒரு teaspoon, ரெண்டு fork, மூணு கத்தி குடுங்க	oru teaspoon, reNdu fork, muuNu kaththi kudungga
192	Do you want anything else?	வேற ஏதாவது வேணுமா / வேறேதாவது வேணுமா?	veeRa yeedhaavadhu veeNumaa / veeReedhaavadhu veeNumaa?

193	That's it	அவ்ளோதான்	avLoodhaan
194	Please give me the bill	Bill குடுங்க	Bill kudungga
195	Without spiciness	காரம் இல்லாம	kaaram illaama
196	Please give me one fried rice	ஒரு Fried rice குடுங்க	oru Fried rice kudungga
197	Please give me a fried rice without spiciness	காரம் இல்லாம ஒரு Fried rice குடுங்க	kaaram illaama oru Fried rice kudungga
198	Please give me very less spicy fried rice	காரம் கம்மியா ஒரு Fried rice குடுங்க	kaaram kammiyaa oru Fried rice kudungga
199	Please don't put chili powder/ green chili	காரம் போடாதீங்க	kaaram poodaadhiingga
200	Without salt / don't put salt	உப்பு இல்லாம / உப்பு போடாதீங்க	uppu illaama / uppu poodaadhiingga
201	Without sugar / don't put sugar	சக்கர இல்லாம / சக்கர போடாதீங்க	sakkara illaama / sakkara poodaadhiingga
202	Please give me a tea without sugar	சக்கர இல்லாம ஒரு டி குடுங்க	sakkara illaama oru tii kudungga
203	Please give me a tea, please don't put any sugar in it.	ஒரு டி குடுங்க, சக்கர போடாதீங்க	oru di kudungga, sakkara poodaadhiingga
204	This is tasting good	இது நல்லா இல்ல	idhu nallaa illa
205	This is tasting good	இது நல்லா இருக்கு	idhu nallaa irukku
206	This idly is tasting good	இந்த இட்லி நல்லா இல்ல	indha idli nallaa illaa
207	This idly is not tasting good	இந்த இட்லி நல்லா இருக்கு	indha idli nallaa irukku
208	I want this	எனக்கு இது வேணும்	yenakku idhu veeNum
209	I don't want this	எனக்கு இது வேண்டாம்	yenakku idhu veeNdaam

Learning Tamil

	English	Tamil	Literal Translation
210	I am learning Tamil	நா தமிழ் கத்துகிட்டு இருக்க	naa thamizh kaththukittu irukke
211	I don't know Tamil	எனக்கு தமிழ் தெரியாது	yenakku thamizh theriyaadhu
212	I know Tamil	எனக்கு தமிழ் தெரியும்	yenakku thamizh theriyum
213	I know little Tamil	எனக்கு தமிழ் கொஞ்சம் தெரியும்	yenakku thamizh konjjam theriyum
214	Do you know English?	உங்களுக்கு English தெரியுமா?	unggaLukku English theriyumaa?
215	Stop always speaking in English, only speak Tamil, otherwise I cannot learn Tamil	Englishல பேசாதீங்க, தமிழ்ல பேசுங்க. இல்லனா என்னால தமிழ் கத்துக்க முடியாது	Englishla peesaadhiingga, thamizhla peesungga. illanaa yennaala thamizh kaththukka mudiyaadhu
216	Speak slowly	மெதுவா பேசுங்க	medhuvaa peesungga
217	Please don't speak fast	வேகமா பேசாதீங்க	veegamaa peesaadhiingga
218	I am learning Tamil, please speak slowly	நா தமிழ் கத்துகிட்டு இருக்கெ, மெதுவா பேசுங்க	naa thamizh kaththukittu irukke, medhuvaa peesungga
219	I don't understand, please slowly	எனக்கு புரியல, மெதுவா பேசுங்க	yenakku puriyala, medhuvaa peesungga

318

220	I don't understand what you are saying	நீங்க சொல்றது எனக்கு புரியல	niingga soldRadhu yenakku puriyala
221	Please repeat again	திரும்ப சொல்லுங்க	thirumba sollungga
222	Please tell me slowly	மெதுவா சொல்லுங்க	medhuvaa sollungga
223	I find learning Tamil very difficult	எனக்கு தமிழ் கத்துக்குறது ரொம்ப கஷ்டமா இருக்கு	yenakku thamizh kaththukkuRadhu romba kashtamaa irukku
224	I find learning Tamil difficult, so it is taking me a long time to learn	எனக்கு தமிழ் கத்துக்குறது ரொம்ப கஷ்டமா இருக்கு அதனால எனக்கு தமிழ் கத்துக்க ரொம்ப நாள் ஆகும்	yenakku thamizh kaththukkuRadhu romba kashtamaa irukku adhanaala yenakku thamizh kaththukka romba naaL aagum
225	Ask me something simple in Tamil, I will try to answer in Tamil	என்கிட்ட தமிழ்ல ஏதாவது Simpleஆ கேளுங்க. நா தமிழ்ல பதில் சொல்றெ	yenkitta thamizhla yeedhaavadhu Simpleaa keeLungga. naa thamizhla padhil soldRe
226	I understood 80% of what your mom said	உங்க அம்மா சொல்றது, எனக்கு 80% புரிஞ்சுது	ungga ammaa solRadhu, yenakku 80% purinjjudhu
227	I don't know what to say	எனக்கு என்ன சொல்றதுன்னு தெரியல	yenakku yenna solRadhunnu theriyala
228	I will try saying 10 sentences, tell me if they are correct	நா ஒரு பத்து வாக்கிய-ம் தமிழ்ல சொல்றெ, சரியான்னு சொல்லுங்க	naa oru paththu vaakkiyam thamizhla soldRe, sariyaannu sollungga
229	How do you say 'book' in Tamil?	Bookனு தமிழ்ல எப்டி சொல்லுவீங்க / சொல்றது?	Booknu thamizhla yepdi solluviingga / soldRadhu?
230	Do you know how to read Tamil?	உங்களுக்கு தமிழ் படிக்க தெரியுமா?	unggaLukku thamizh padikka theriyumaa?

319

231	How do you spell that in Tamil script?	அத தமிழ்ல spell பண்ணுங்க?	adha thamizhla spell paNNungga?
232	What is this called in Tamil?	இது தமிழ்ல என்ன?	idhu thamizhla yenna?
233	Am I saying it correctly?	நா சரியா சொல்றேன்னா?	naa sariyaa soldReennaa?
234	Just answer the question	எனக்கு பதில மட்டும் சொல்லுங்க	yenakku badhil mattum sollungga
235	Please repeat that slowly	அத மெதுவா திரும்ப சொல்லுங்க	adha medhuvaa thirumba sollungga
236	You only said it just now	நீங்க இப்ப தான் சொன்னீங்க	niingga ippa dhaann sonniingga
237	Listen when I tell	நா சொல்லும்போது கேளுங்க	naa sollumboodhu keeLungga
238	Listen to what I'm saying	நா சொல்றத கேளுங்க	naa soldRadha keeLungga
239	I understood / understand what you said	நீங்க சொல்றது எனக்கு புரிஞ்சுது / புரியுது	niingga soldRadhu yenakku purinjjudhu / puriyudhu
240	I don't understand what you said	நீங்க சொல்றது எனக்கு புரியல	niingga soldRadhu yenakku puriyala
241	I am confused / I got confused	எனக்கு குழப்பமா இருக்கு	yenakku kuzhappamaa irukku

Eating / Drinking

	English	Tamil	Literal Translation
242	What do you like to eat?	உங்களுக்கு சாப்பிட என்ன பிடிக்கும்?	unggaLukku saappida yenna pidikkum?
243	I like dosa and chutney	எனக்கு தோசை சட்னி பிடிக்கும்	yenakku dhoosai chatni pidikkum
244	That food is tasty	அந்த சாப்பாடு சுவையா இருக்கு	andha saappaadu suvaiyaa irukku
245	Did you like it?	உங்களுக்கு பிடிச்சுதா?	unggaLukku pidichchudhaa?
246	I liked it	எனக்கு பிடிச்சுது	yenakku pidichchudhu
247	Do you like it?	உங்களுக்கு பிடிக்குமா?	unggaLukku pidikkumaa?
248	I like it	எனக்கு பிடிக்கும்	yenakku pidikkum
249	Do you want more?	உங்களுக்கு இன்னும் வேணுமா?	unggaLukku innum veeNumaa?
250	Enough?	போதுமா	poodhumaa
251	Enough	போதும்	poodhum
252	It's very good	இது ரொம்ப நல்லா இருக்கு	idhu romba nallaa irukku

253	It tastes like a pumpkin, is it?	இது சாப்பிட பூசணிக்கா மாதிரி இருக்கு, இல்லயா?	idhu saappida puusaNikkaa maadhiri irukku, illayaa?
254	I was hungry	எனக்கு பசிச்சுது	yenakku pasichchudhu
255	I am hungry	எனக்கு பசிக்குது	yenakku pasikkudhu
256	I will be hungry	எனக்கு பசிக்கும்	yenakku pasikkum
257	Are you already hungry? (e.g. how are you hungry already, because we eat recently)	உனக்கு திரும்பவும் / மறுபடியும் பசிக்குதா	unakku thirumbavum / maRubadiyum pasikkudhaa
258	What shall we eat?	என்ன சாப்டலாம்?	yenna saapdalaam?
259	Are you eating now?	நீங்க இப்ப சாப்டுறீங்களா?	niingga ippa saapduRiinggaLaa?
260	Why didn't you eat in the morning?	நீங்க ஏன் காலைல சாப்டல?	niingga yeen kaalaila saapdala?
261	I didn't eat because I am not hungry	நா சாப்டல ஏன்னா எனக்கு பசிக்கல	naa saapdala yeennaa yenakku pasikkala
262	I just ate, I am not hungry	நா இப்ப தான் சாப்ட்டெ எனக்கு பசிக்கல	naa ippa dhaan saaptte yenakku pasikkala
263	Please don't give me anything, I am not hungry	தயவுசெஞ்சு எனக்கு எதுவும் குடுக்காதீங்க, எனக்கு பசிக்கல	dhayavusenjju yenakku yedhuvum kudukkaadhiingga, yenakku pasikkala
264	I am hungry because of that I am eating an apple	எனக்கு பசிக்குது அதுனால நா apple சாப்டுறெ	yenakku pasikkudhu adhanaala naa apple saapduRe

265	I am thirsty, so I'm drinking water	எனக்கு தாகமா இருக்கு, அதனால நா தண்ணி குடிக்குறெ	yenakku thaagamaa irukku, adhanaala naa thaNNi kudikkuRe
266	I didn't drink water because I am not thirsty	நா தண்ணி குடிக்கல, ஏன்னா எனக்கு தாகமா இல்ல	naa thaNNi kudikkala, yeennaa yenakku thaagamaa illa
267	I am hungry because of that I am eating	எனக்கு பசிக்குது அதனால நா சாப்டுறெ	yenakku pasikkudhu adhanaala naa saapduRe
268	This is a salad, only for me. Nobody should touch it	இது Salad, எனக்கு மட்டும் தான். யாரும் இத தொட கூடாது	idhu Salad, yenakku mattum dhaan. yaarum idha thoda kuudaadhu
269	Yesterday's leftovers are still there, we shall eat that for dinner	நேத்து மீந்து போனது இன்னும் இருக்கு, அத நாம dinnerக்கு சாப்டலாம்	neeththu miindhu poonadhu innum irukku, adha naama dinnerkku saapdalaam
270	I don't want to eat that food, let's order takeout	எனக்கு அந்த சாப்பாடு சாப்ட வேண்டாம், Parcel வாங்கிடலாம்	yenakku andha saappaadu saapda veeNdaam, Parcel vaanggidalaam
271	Do you want to eat dinner later?	உனக்கு அப்றமா dinner சாப்டணுமா	unakku apRamaa dinner saapdaNumaa
272	Do you like tea or coffee?	உங்களுக்கு காபி பிடிக்குமா இல்ல டீ பிடிக்குமா	unggaLukku kaapi pidikkumaa illa tii pidikkumaa
273	With sugar or without sugar?	சக்கரயோடவா இல்ல சக்கர இல்லாமயா	sakkarayoodavaa illa sakkara illaamayaa
274	With sugar	சக்கரயோட	sakkarayooda
275	Without sugar	சக்கர இல்லாம	sakkara illaama
276	I like coffee with a little milk and no sugar	எனக்கு சக்கர இல்லாம கொஞ்சம் பாலோட காபி பிடிக்கும்	yenakku sakkara illaama konjjam paalooda kaapi pidikkum

277	Can you give me coffee with a little milk and no sugar?	எனக்கு சக்கர இல்லாம கொஞ்சம் பாலோட காபி குடுக்க முடியுமா	yenakku sakkara illaama konjjam paalooda kaapi kudukka mudiyumaa
278	How much coffee do you drink in a day?	ஒரு நாளைக்கு எவ்ளோ காபி குடிப்பீங்க?	oru naaLaikku yevLoo kaapi kudippiingga?
279	I made coffee this morning but it isn't good	நா இன்னைக்கு காலைல காபி போட்டெ ஆனா அது நல்லா இல்ல	naa innaikku kaalaila kaapi pootte aanaa adhu nallaa illa
280	Should I make coffee?	நா காபி போடட்டுமா?	naa kaapi poodattumaa?
281	Shall I make tea?	நா டி போடட்டுமா?	naa tii poodattumaa?
282	When did you make coffee?	நீங்க எப்ப காபி போட்டிங்க?	niingga yeppa kaapi poottiingga?
283	I made coffee (recently)	நா இப்ப தான் காபி போட்டெ	naa ippa dhaann kaapi pootte
284	I made coffee at 7	நா ஏழு மணிக்கு காபி போட்டெ	naa yeezhu maNikku kaapi pootte
285	That tea is cold, don't drink it	டி ஆறிடுச்சு, குடிக்காதீங்க	tii aaRiduchchu, kudikkaadhiingga
286	My coffee became cold	காபி ஆறிடுச்சு	kaapi aaRiduchchu
287	Don't eat that food until it has cooled down	அந்த சாப்பாடு ஆருர வரைக்கும் சாப்டாதீங்க	andha saappaadu aarura varaikkum saapdaadhiingga

Day to day Tamil sentences

	English	Tamil	Literal Translation
288	I am very busy today	நா இன்னிக்கு ரொம்ப Busy	<u>n</u>aa innikku romba busy
289	Today I will not be very busy	நா இன்னிக்கு ரொம்ப Busyஆ இருக்க மாட்டெ	<u>n</u>aa innikku romba busyaa irukka maatte
290	Did you finish work?	வேலைய முடிச்சிட்டீங்களா	veelaiya mudichchittiinggaLaa
291	I finished the work	வேலைய முடிச்சிட்டெ	veelaiya mudichchitte
292	What did you do today?	இன்னிக்கு என்ன பண்ணீங்க?	innikku yenna paNNiingga?
293	What else did you do?	வேற என்ன பண்ணீங்க?	veeRa yenna paNNiingga?
294	I have a meeting now	நா இப்ப meetingல இருக்கெ	<u>n</u>aa ippa meetingla irukke
295	Wake up / Get up!	எழுந்திருங்க	yezhundhirungga
296	How did you sleep last night?	நேத்து ராத்திரி எப்டி தூங்குனீங்க?	<u>n</u>eeththu raaththiri yepdi thuungguniingga?
297	When did you get up this morning?	இன்னிக்கு காலைல எத்தன மணிக்கு எழுந்தீங்க?	innikku kaalaila yeththana maNikku yezhu<u>n</u>dhiingga?
298	What time you get up?	எத்தன மணிக்கு எழுந்தீங்க?	yeththana maNikku yezhu<u>n</u>dhiingga?
299	I got up at 8 yesterday	நா நேத்து எட்டு மணிக்கு எழுந்தெ	<u>n</u>aa <u>n</u>eeththu yettu maNikku yezhu<u>n</u>dhe
300	I woke up early this morning, I don't know why	நா இன்னிக்கு காலைல சீ-க்கிரம் எழுந்துட்டெ, ஏன்னு தெரியல	<u>n</u>aa innikku kaalaila siikkiram yezhundhutte, yeennu theriyala

325

301	What time you slept?	எத்தன மணிக்கு தூங்குனீங்க?	yeththana maNikku thuungguniingga?
302	Yesterday night I slept / lie down at 11	நேத்து ராத்திரி பதினோரு மணிக்கு படுத்தெ / தூங்குனெ	neeththu raaththiri padhinooru maNikku paduththe / thuunggune
303	Yesterday night I didn't sleep because there was lots of noise	நேத்து ராத்திரி நா தூங்கல ஏன்னா நிறைய சத்தம் இரு-ந்துச்சு	neeththu raaththiri naa thuunggala yeennaa niRaiya saththam irundhuchchu
304	I am tired this morning	இன்னிக்கு காலைல நா ரொம்ப Tiredஆ இருக்கெ	innikku kaalaila naa romba Tiredaa irukke
305	Did you shower?	குளிச்சீங்களா	kuLichchiinggaLaa
306	I showered	நா குளிச்சிட்டெ	naa kuLichchitte
307	Did you brush your teeth?	பள்ளு விளக்குனீங்களா?	paLLu viLakkuniinggaLaa?
308	I brushed my teeth	நா பள்ளு விளக்கிட்டெ	naa paLLu viLakkitte
309	Can you come here please?	இங்க வர முடியுமா?	ingga vara mudiyumaa?
310	I'll come there in a minute	ஒரு நிமிஷம், நா அங்க வர்றெ	oru nimisham, naa angga varRe
311	Did you call your mom today?	இன்னிக்கு உங்க அம்மாவ கூப்ட்டிங்களா?	innikku ungga ammaava kuupttinggaLaa?
312	What did your mum say?	உங்க அம்மா என்ன சொன்னாங்க	ungga ammaa yenna sonnaangga
313	Tell your parents I asked how they are	உங்க அம்மா அப்பா கிட்ட எப்டி இருக்காங்கனு கேட்டேன்னு சொல்லுங்க	ungga ammaa appaa kitta yepdi irukkaangganu keetteennu sollungga
314	What did Sanjay say?	சஞ்சய் என்ன சொன்னாரு?	sanjjay yenna sonnaaru?

315	She didn't pick up when I called	நா Call பண்ணப்ப அவங்க Phone எடுக்கல	naa Call paNNappa avangga Phone yedukkala
316	She sent pictures of her house today	இன்னிக்கு அவங்க வீட்டோட Photo அனுப்புனாங்க	innikku avangga viittooda Photo anuppunaangga
317	What are you thinking about?	நீங்க என்ன யோசிக்குறீங்க?	niingga yenna yoosikkuRiingga?
318	I am thinking about work	நா வேலைய பத்தி யோசிக்குறெ	naa veelaiya paththi yoosikkuRe
319	Which one did you like?	உங்களுக்கு எது பிடிச்சிருக்கு?	unggaLukku yedhu pidichchirukku?
320	I only liked that one	எனக்கு அது மட்டும் தான் பிடிச்சிருக்கு	yenakku adhu mattum dhaan pidichchirukku
321	I am going to hit you	நா உங்கள அடிக்க போறெ	naa unggaLa adikka pooRe
322	What happened	என்ன ஆச்சு	yenna aachchu
323	Are you ready to go?	நீங்க readyயா	niingga readyyaa
324	Get ready soon	சீக்கிரம் ready அவுங்க	siikkiram ready avungga
325	Shall we go home now?	நாம இப்ப வீட்டுக்கு போலாமா?	naama ippa viittukku poolaamaa?
326	Let's go early, I need to be back home by 4PM	சீக்கிரம் போலாம், நா நாலு மணிக்குள்ள வீட்டுல இருக்கணும்	siikkiram poolaam, naa naalu maNikkuLLa viittula irukkaNum
327	Shall we go later, I'm busy until 5PM	நாம அப்புறம் போலாமா, நா அஞ்சு மணி வரைக்கும் busy	naama appuRam poolaamaa, naa anjju maNi varaikkum busy
328	Why didn't you tell me earlier?	நீங்க ஏன் முன்னாடியே சொல்லல?	niingga yeen munnaadiyee sollala?

329	Shall we go to the theatre and watch a movie?	நாம theatreக்கு போயி படம் பாக்கலாமா?	naama theatrekku pooyi padam paakkalaamaa?
330	Yes, let's go to the theatre and watch a movie	சரி, நாம theatreக்கு போயி படம் பாக்கலாம்	sari, naama theatrekku pooyi padam paakkalaam
331	At what time shall we go to the cinema?	எத்தன மணிக்கு cinemaக்கு போலாம்?	yeththana maNikku cinemakku poolaam?
332	We shall go to the cinema at 6	நாம ஆறு மணிக்கு Cinemaக்கு போலாம்	naama aaRu maNikku Cinemakku poolaam
332	Shall we go to restaurant and eat dinner?	நாம Dinner சாப்பிட Restaurantக்கு போலாமா?	naama Dinner saappida Restaurantkku poolaamaa?
334	No, let's not go to a restaurant, we shall cook at home	இல்ல, Restaurantக்கு போக வேண்டாம், வீட்டுல சமைக்கலாம்	illa, Restaurantkku pooga veeNdaam, viittula samaikkalaam
335	Shall we go to the park now?	இப்ப Parkஉக்கு போலாமா?	ippa parkukku poolaamaa?
336	First I need to eat, after that only going for a walk	மொதல்ல நா சாப்டணும், அப்புறம் தான் walking	modhalla naa saapdaNum, appuRam dhaan walking
337	When did you come home today?	இன்னிக்கு எப்ப வீட்டுக்கு வந்தீங்க?	innikku yeppa viittukku vandhiingga?
338	I was at the gym, then I came home	நா gymல இருந்தெ , அப்புறம் வீட்டுக்கு வந்தெ	naa gymla irundhe , appuRam viittukku vandhe
339	When did you go to the gym?	gymக்கு எப்ப போனீங்க?	gymkku yeppa pooniingga?
340	I went to the gym at 11	பதினோரு மணிக்கு நா gymக்கு போனெ	padhinooru maNikku naa gymkku poone
341	Please come back / Please come back home	திரும்பி வாங்க / திரும்பி வீட்டுக்கு வாங்க	thirumbi vaangga / thirumbi viittukku vaangga

Weather

Compared to the western world, people in Tamil nadu hardly talk about the weather. Since the climate is tropical, normally there won't be any drastic change in the climate unless there is a huge cyclone or scorching heat during May. So, just be aware of these sentences, but don't depend on them too much for conversations.

	English	Tamil	Literal Translation
342	It rained	மழை பெய்ஞ்சுது	mazhai peynjjudhu
343	It's raining	மழை பெய்யுது	mazhai peyyudhu
344	It will rain	மழை பெய்யும்	mazhai peyyum
345	It rained so it is very cold	மழை பெய்ஞ்சுது அதுனால ரொம்ப குளிரா இருக்கு	mazhai peynjjudhu adhunaala romba kuLiraa irukku
346	It is very sunny / It is hot	வெய்யில் அடிக்குது	veyyil adikkudhu
347	It is cold	குளிரா இருக்கு	kuLiraa irukku

Feelings

	English	Tamil	Literal Translation
348	I am happy	நா சந்தோஷமா இருக்கே	naa sandhooshamaa irukke
349	Are you happy?	நீங்க சந்தோஷமா இருக்கீங்களா?	niingga sandhooshamaa irukkiinggaLaa?
350	Why are you smiling?	நீங்க ஏன் சிறிக்குறீங்க?	niingga yeen siRikkuRiingga?
351	Why are you laughing, what happened?	நீங்க ஏன் சிறிக்குறீங்க, என்ன ஆச்சு?	niingga yeen siRikkuRiingga, yenna aachchu?
352	I am sad	நா சோகமா இருக்கே	naa soogamaa irukkee
353	I am crying	நா அழுறே	naa azhuRee
354	I am scared	எனக்கு பயமா இருக்கு	yenakku bayamaa irukku
355	I am worried	எனக்கு கவலையா இருக்கு	yenakku kavalaiyaa irukku
356	Why are you sad?	ஏன் சோகமா இருக்கீங்க?	yeen soogamaa irukkiingga?
357	Why are you crying?	ஏன் அழுறீங்க?	yeen azhuRiingga?
358	Why are you scared?	ஏன் பயப்புடுறீங்க?	yeen bayappuduRiingga?
359	Why are you worried?	ஏன் கவலையா இருக்கீங்க?	yeen kavalaiyaa irukkiingga?

Taste

360	It is sweet	இது இனிப்பா இருக்கு	idhu inippaa irukku
361	It is salty	இது உப்பா இருக்கு	idhu uppaa irukku
362	It is spicy	இது காரமா இருக்கு	idhu kaaramaa irukku
363	It is sour	இது கசப்பா இருக்கு	idhu kasappaa irukku
364	Sweet, salt, spice, sour	இனிப்பு, உப்பு, காரம், கசப்பு	inippu, uppu, kaaram, kasappu

Hobbies

	English	Tamil	Literal Translation
365	What do you like to do (pastimes)?	நீங்க free timeல என்ன பண்ணுவீங்க?	niingga free timela yenna paNNuviingga?
366	What are your hobbies?	உங்க hobbies என்ன?	ungga hobbies yenna?
367	I like to read books and watch movies	எனக்கு புத்தகம் படிக்க, படம் பாக்க பிடிக்கும்	yenakku puththagam padikka, padam paakka pidikkum
368	What are your favorite movies?	உங்களுக்கு ரொம்ப பிடிச்ச படம் என்ன?	unggaLukku romba pidichcha padam yenna?
369	My favourite movies are	எனக்கு _____ படம் ரொம்ப பிடிக்கும்	yenakku _____ padam romba pidikkum
370	Who are your favorite actors?	உங்களுக்கு ரொம்ப பிடிச்ச நடிகர் யாரு?	unggaLukku romba pidichcha nadigar yaaru?
371	My favorite actors are	எனக்கு _____ ரொம்ப பிடிக்கும்	yenakku _____ romba pidikkum
372	I like Vijay and Kamal Hassan Movies movies	எனக்கு விஜய் கமல ஹாசன் படம் பிடிக்கும்	yenakku vijay kamala haasan padam pidikkum
373	What Vijay movies have you seen?	எந்த விஜய் படம் பாத்துருக்கீங்க?	yendha vijay padam paaththurukkiingga?
374	Why do you like Vijay?	உங்களுக்கு ஏன் விஜய் பிடி-க்கும்?	unggaLukku yeen vijay pidikkum?
375	He is really good in acting	அவரு ரொம்ப நல்லா நடிப்பாரு	avaru romba nallaa nadippaaru

332

VOCABULARY – PART 2

Content:

- Vocabulary

LESSON 4B:
VOCABULARY – PART 2

The Vocabulary sections in this book are divided into two parts:

Lesson 4A: Vocabulary: This part contains the vocabularies used in this book, except for lessons 4B and 4C.

Lesson 4B – Part 2: This part contains the vocabularies which are used in lesson 4B (Tamil sentences for conversation)

Kindly find below table with useful Tamil vocabularies used in lesson 4B (Tamil sentences for conversation). I recommend memorizing these vocabularies in your free time either by using the "my little word land" website or the traditional method of reading and memorizing from the book. Don't spend too much time on it, just 15 minutes a day is adequate.

The advantage of memorizing 'Lesson 4B – Part 2' is you will recollect these vocabulary while learning lesson 4B (Tamil sentences for conversation) and can remember the sentences you learnt in lesson 4B better. It will also assist you in creating new Tamil sentences.

	Vocabulary	Transliteration	Meaning
1	-ல	-la	In, on, at
2	-க்கு	-kku	To, for
3	-ணும்	-Num	Want, must, need to
4	ஒரு	oru	A
5	நிறைய	niRaiya	A lot
6	பத்தி	paththi	About
7	அப்புறம் / அப்றமா	appuRam / apRamaa	After / after that / afterwards
8	மறுபடியும்	maRubadiyum	Again

334

9	திரும்ப	thirumbba	Again / repeat
10	பதில	badhil	Answer
11	மொதல்ல	modhalla	At first
12	வீட்டுல	viittula	At home
13	மணிக்கு	maNikku	At o'clock
14	கிடைக்கும்	kidaikkum	Available
15	ஏன்னா	yeennaa	Because
16	முன்னாடி	munnaadi	Before / in front of
17	நல்லா	nallaa	Being good / tasting good
18	சந்தோஷமா	sandhooshamaa	Being happy (adverb)
19	சோகமா	soogamaa	Being sad (adverb)
20	தாகமா	thaagamaa	Being thirsty (adverb)
21	கவலையா	kavalaiyaa	Being worried
22	புத்தகம்	puththagam	Book
23	ஆனா	aanaa	But
24	என்னால	yennaala	By me / because of me
25	காபி	kaapi	Coffee
26	நாள்	naaL	Day
27	குடிக்கல	kudikkala	Didn't drink
28	சாப்டல	saapdala	Didn't eat
29	தெரியல	theriyala	Didn't knew
30	சொல்லல	sollala	Didn't say
31	தூங்கல	thuunggala	Didn't sleep
32	எடுக்கல	yedukkala	Didn't took

33	புரியல	puriyala	Didn't understand
34	கஷ்டமா	kashtamaa	Difficult
35	குடிக்காதீங்க	kudikkaadhiingga	Don't drink
36	சாப்டாதீங்க	saapdaadhiingga	Don't eat
37	குடுக்காதீங்க	kudukkaadhiingga	Don't give
38	தெரியாது	theriyaadhu	Don't know
39	போடாதீங்க	poodaadhiingga	Don't put
40	பேசாதீங்க	peesaadhiingga	Don't talk
41	வேண்டாம்	veeNddaam	Don't want
42	குடுங்க	kudungga	Drink
43	எட்டு	yettu	Eight
44	பதினோரு	padhinooru	Eleven
45	போதும்	poodhum	Enough
46	வேகமா	veegamaa	Faster (adverb)
47	பிடிச்ச	pidichcha	Favourite
48	குளிரா	kuLiraa	Feeling cold
49	அஞ்சு	anjju	Five
50	சாப்பாடு	saappaadu	Food
51	எனக்கு	yenakku	For me
52	உங்களுக்கு	unggaLukku	For you (formal)
53	உனக்கு	unakku	For you (informal)
54	நாலு	naalu	Four
55	எங்கருந்து	yenggarundhu	From where
56	முடிச்சிட்டீங்களா	mudichchittiingaLaa	Have you finished

57	அவரு	avaru	He (formal)
58	இங்க	ingga	Here
59	வீடு	viidu	House
60	வீட்ட	viitta	House (acc)
61	எப்டி	yepdi	How
62	எத்தன	yeththana	How many
63	எவ்ளோ	yevLoo	How much
64	பசிக்குது	pasikkudhu	Hungry
65	நா(ன்)	naa	I
66	தான்	dhaan	Just / only
67	கத்தி	kaththi	Knife
68	தெரியும்	theriyum	Know
69	கம்மியா	kammiyaa	Less
70	பிடிக்கும்	pidikkum	Like
71	கொஞ்சம்	konjjam	Little
72	கல்யாணம்	kalyaaNam	Marriage
73	நிமிஷம்	nimisham	Minute
74	காலை	kaalai	Morning
75	சாப்டணும்	saapdaNum	Must eat
76	எ(ன்)	ye(n)	My
77	பேரு	peeru	Name
78	ராத்திரி	raaththiri	Night
79	இல்ல	illa	No
80	யாரும்	yaarum	No one

337

81	பசிக்கல	pasikkala	Not hungry
82	இப்ப	ippa	Now
83	மணி	maNi	O'clock
84	சரி	sari	Okay
85	மட்டும்	mattum	Only
86	இல்லனா	illanaa	Or else
87	வேற	veeRa	Other / different
88	வாங்க	vaangga	Please come
89	பண்ணுங்க	paNNungga	Please do
90	கேளுங்க	keeLungga	Please listen / ask
91	பேசுங்க	peesungga	Please talk
92	சொல்லுங்க	sollungga	Please tell
93	வில	vila	Price
94	மழை	mazhai	Rain
95	ரூபா	ruubaa	Rupees
96	உப்பு	uppu	Salt
97	வாக்கியம்	vaakkiyam	Sentence
98	ஏழு	yeezhu	Seven
99	வாங்கிடலாம்	vaanggidalaam	Shall buy
100	சமைக்கலாம்	samaikkalaam	Shall cook
101	போலாம்	poolaam	Shall do
102	சாப்டலாம்	saapdalaam	Shall eat
103	பாக்கலாம்	paakkalaam	Shall see
104	கட	kada	Shop

105	கூடாது	kuudaadhu	Should not
106	மாதிரி	maadhiri	Similar
107	ஆறு	aaRu	Six
108	மெதுவா	medhuvaa	Slowly
109	ஏதாவது	yeedhaavadhu	Something
110	வேறேதாவது	veeredhaavadhu	Something else
111	சீக்கிரம்	siikkiram	Soon
112	சத்தம்	saththam	Sound
113	காரம்	kaaram	Spicy
114	இன்னும்	innum	Still
115	சக்கர	sakkara	Sugar
116	வெய்யில்	veyyil	Sun shine
117	தமிழ்	thamizh	Tamil
118	சுவையா	suvaiyaa	Tasty (adverb)
119	டி	ti	Tea
120	பத்து	paththu	Ten
121	அந்த	andha	That - adjective
122	அது	adhu	That - noun
123	அத	adha	That - noun(acc)
124	அவ்ளோதான்	avLoodhaan	That's it
125	அதனால / அதுனால	adhanaala/adhunaa-la	That's why / because of that
126	அங்க	angga	There
127	அவங்க	avangga	They / she (formal)

128	இந்த	indha	This - adjective
129	இது	idhu	This - noun
130	இத	idha	This - noun (acc)
131	மூணு	muuNu	Three
132	வீட்டுக்கு	viittukku	To home
133	இன்னிக்கு	innikku	Today
134	நாளைக்கு	naaLaikku	Tomorrow
135	ரெண்டு	reNdu	Two
136	புரியுது	puriyudhu	Understand
137	புரிஞ்சுது	purinjjudhu	Understood
138	வரைக்கும்	varaikkum	Until
139	காய்கறி	kaaygaRi	Vegetable
140	ரொம்ப	rombba	Very
141	வேணும்	veeNum	Want
142	பசிச்சுது	pasichchudhu	Was hungry
143	தண்ணி	thaNNi	Water
144	நாம	naama	We (inclusive)
145	என்ன	yenna	What
146	என்னெல்லா	yennellaa	What and all
147	எப்ப	yeppa	When
148	சொல்லும்போது	sollumbhoodhu	When saying
149	எங்க	yengga	Where
150	எந்த	yendha	Which - adjective
151	எது	yedhu	Which - noun

152	யாரு	yaaru	Who
153	ஏன்	yeen	Why
154	பசிக்கும்	pasikkum	Will get hungry
155	என்கிட்ட	yenkitta	With me
156	இல்லாம	illaama	Without
157	மாட்டெ	maatte	Won't
158	வேல	veela	Work
159	நேத்து	<u>n</u>eeththu	Yesterday
160	உங்கள	unggaLa	You (acc)
161	நீங்க	<u>n</u>iingga	You (formal)
162	உங்க	ungga	Your (formal)
163	அவரு செய்றாரு	seyRaaru	He does
164	அவரு பண்றாரு	paNdRaaru	He does
165	அவரு பாத்துக்குறாரு	paaththukkuRaaru	He is taking care of
166	அவரு சொன்னாரு	sonnaaru	He said
167	அவரு பாக்குறாரு	paakkuRaaru	He sees
168	நா(ன்) சாப்ட்டெ	saaptte	I ate
169	நா(ன்) வந்தெ	va<u>n</u>dhe	I came
170	நா(ன்) பண்ணெ	paNNe	I did
171	நா(ன்) முடிச்சிட்டெ	mudichchitte	I finished
172	நா(ன்) போட்டெ	pootte	I put
173	நா(ன்) பாத்தெ	paaththe	I saw
174	நா(ன்) வர்றெ	varRe	I come
175	நா(ன்) படிச்சிருக்கெ	padichchirukke	I have studied

176	நா(ன்) குளிச்சிட்டெ	kuLichchitte	I showered
177	நா(ன்) தூங்குனெ	thuunggune	I slept
178	நா(ன்) படிச்செ	padichche	I studied
179	நா(ன்) எழுந்தெ	yezhundhutte	I woke up
180	நா(ன்) அழுறெ	azhuRe	I cry
181	நா(ன்) செய்றெ	seyRe	I do
182	நா(ன்) குடிக்குறெ	kudikkuRe	I drank
183	நா(ன்) சாப்டுறெ	saapduRe	I eat
184	நா(ன்) போறெ	pooRe	I go
185	நா(ன்) சொல்றெ	soldRe	I say
186	நா(ன்) பாக்குறெ	paakkuRe	I see
187	நா(ன்) படிக்குறெ	padikkuRe	I study
188	நா(ன்) யோசிக்குறெ	yoosikkuRe	I think
189	நா(ன்) போனெ	poone	I went
190	அவங்க அனுப்புனாங்க	anuppunaangga	They sent
191	அவங்க சொன்னாங்க	sonnaangga	They said
192	நீங்க சிறிக்குறீங்க	siRikkuRiingga	You are smiling
193	நீங்க வர்றீங்க	varRiingga	You come
194	நீங்க அழுறீங்க	azhuRiingga	You cry
195	நீங்க செய்றீங்க	seyRiingga	You do
196	நீங்க போறீங்க	pooRiingga	You go
197	நீங்க பாக்குறீங்க	paakkuRiingga	You see
198	நீங்க படிக்குறீங்க	padikkuRiingga	You study
199	நீங்க யோசிக்குறீங்க	yoosikkuRiingga	You think

342

200	நீங்க வந்தீங்க	vandhiingga	You came
201	நீங்க பண்ணீங்க	paNNiingga	You did
202	நீங்க படிச்சிருக்கீங்க	padichchirukkiingga	You have studied
203	நீங்க படிச்சீங்க	padichchiingga	You have studied
204	நீங்க எழுந்தீங்க	yezhundhiingga	You woke up
205	நீங்க போட்டிங்க	poottiingga	You put
206	நீங்க சொன்னீங்க	sonniingga	You said
207	நீங்க பாத்தீங்க	paaththiingga	You saw
208	நீங்க தூங்குனீங்க	thuungguniingga	You slept
209	நீங்க போனீங்க	pooniingga	You went
210	நீங்க பண்ணுவீங்க	paNNuviingga	You will do
211	நீங்க குடிப்பீங்க	kudippiingga	You will drink
212	நீங்க சொல்லுவீங்க	solluviingga	You will say
213	இருக்க	irukka	To be (inf)
214	வர	vara	To come (inf)
215	சாப்ட	saapta	To eat (inf)
216	குடுக்க	kudikka	To give (inf)
217	போக	pooga	To go (inf)
218	படிக்க	padikka	To read / to study (inf)
219	பாக்க	paakka	To see (inf)
220	கத்துக்க	kaththukka	To learn (inf)

343

ROLE PLAY SCENARIOS

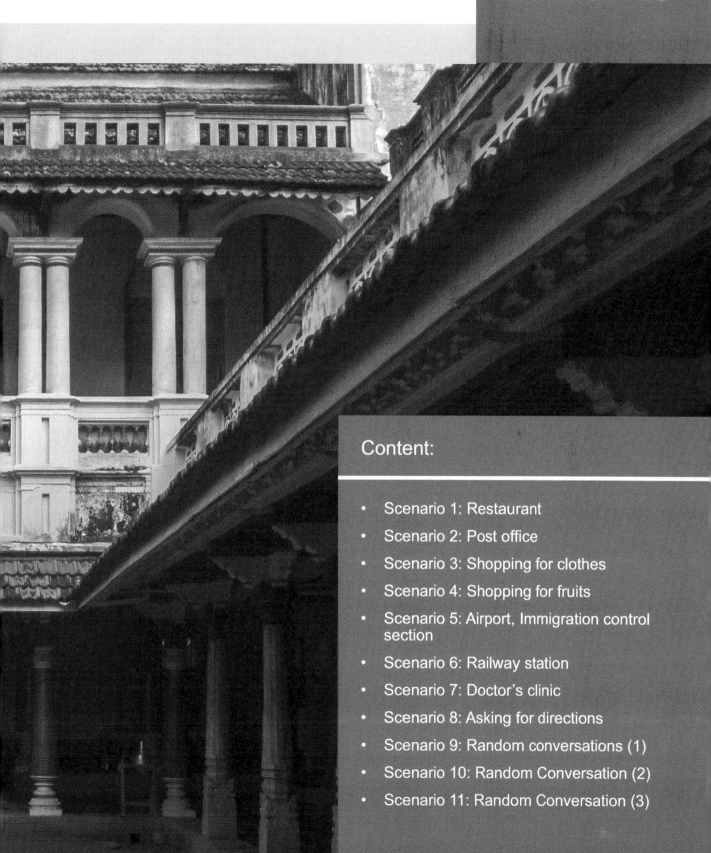

LESSON 4C

Content:

LESSON 4C:
ROLE PLAY SCENARIOS

Note:

- I have created animated videos for role play scenarios in slow and normal speed using my voice. Please use the below link to access those videos in Youtube.

  https://tinyurl.com/roleplay100

- It is advisable for the learners not to concentrate on learning sentences or role-play scenarios before learning other lessons in this book because Tamil grammar is a bit different from English grammar. If you look at the Tamil sentences before learning Tamil grammar, you will get confused and find it difficult to comprehend the Tamil sentences. Whereas, when you learn Tamil grammar and then look at these sentences, then you will be able to understand and learn the sentences well.

The above statement is just a suggestion, as this is the best way to learn Tamil in my opinion. But there are some exceptions as well.

1. You could also learn these Tamil sentences and role-play scenarios simultaneously along with other lessons (Tamil grammar), this would help you to understand Tamil grammar better, and at the same time, your Tamil vocabulary will improve.

2. Some of you might just want to learn a few sentences in the Tamil language to practice it with native Tamil speakers, and you might not be interested in Tamil grammar at all. These tables and role-play scenarios are for you.

Example:

How are you doing?
எப்டி இருக்கீங்க?
tl: yepdi irukkiingga?

In Detail: yepdi - how, irukkiingga - doing (present tense)

Transliteration (tl) - This is the transliteration of the Tamil script; in simple words, this is how a Tamil pronunciation would be if it's written in Tamil.

346

Scenario 1: Restaurant

Let's look at a scenario between friends who want to eat biriyani in a restaurant:

Person A & B are friends, and Person C is a waiter in the restaurant.

A: shall we go and eat in a restaurant today?
இன்னிக்கு restaurantக்கு போயி சாப்டலாமா
innikku Restaurantkku pooyi saapdalaamaa

B: sure, we shall go, but to which restaurant?
சரி, போலாம், ஆனா எந்த restaurantக்கு?
sari, poolaam, aanaa yendha restaurantkku?

A: We shall go to Paradise restaurant.
நாம paradise restaurantக்கு போலாம்
naama paradise restaurantkku poolaam

In Restaurant:

C: Welcome, Sir.
வாங்க, Sir
vaangga, Sir

C: Have you reserved a table?
table reserve பண்ணிருக்கீங்களா?
table reserve paNNirukkiinggaLaa?

B: Yes, we have reserved
ஆமா, பண்ணிருக்கொ
aamaa, paNNirukko

C: Under which name?
எந்த பேர்ல?
yendha peerla?

347

B: Mr. Vincent

A: The restaurant is totally full today.
இன்னிக்கு restaurantல நிறைய பேர் இருக்காங்க
innikku restaurantla niRaiya peer irukkaangga

B: Yes, there are many people.
ஆமா, நிறைய பேர் இருக்காங்க
aamaa, niRaiya peer irukkaangga

C: What would you like to eat?
என்ன சாப்டுறீங்க?
yenna saappiduRiingga?

B: 2 plates Biriyani, please.
ரெண்டு plate பிரியாணி குடுங்க
reNdu plate biriyaaNi kudungga

C: Would you like something to drink?
குடிக்க ஏதாவது வேணுமா?
kudikka yeedhaavadhu veeNumaa?

B: One orange juice and one coffee.
ஒரு ஆரஞ்சு juice, ஒரு காபி
oru aaranjju juice, oru kaapi

C: do you want anything else?
வேறேதாவது வேணுமா?
veeReedhaavadhu veeNumaa?

B: One moment, please.
ஒரு நிமிஷம்
oru nimisham

C: What do you want to eat, Sir?
உங்களுக்கு சாப்ட என்ன வேணும், Sir?
unggaLukku saapda yenna veeNum, Sir?

B: one plate chili chicken.
ஒரு plate chili chicken.
oru plate chili chicken.

C: Anything else?
வேறேதாவது வேணுமா?
veeReedhaavadhu veeNumaa?

B: No, that's all for the moment.
இல்ல, அவ்ளோதான்
illa, avLoodhaan

C: okay
சரி
sari

B: Please hurry.
சீக்கிரமா கொண்டு வாங்க
siikkiramaa koNdu vaangga

C: okay
சரி
sari

Situation: After some time, the waiter provides the food and the two friends enjoy their meal. After they are done eating, the waiter comes back and….

349

C: How was the meal? Do you want anything else?
சாப்பாடு எப்டி இருந்துச்சு? வேறேதாவது வேணுமா?
saappaadu yepdi irundhchchu? veeReedhaavadhu veeNumaa?

B: the meal was delicious; no, we don't want anything else.

சாப்பாடு ரொம்ப நல்லா இருந்துச்சு; இல்ல, எங்களுக்கு வேறெதுவும் வேண்டாம்

saappaadu romba nallaa irundhuchchu; illa, yenggaLukku veeRedhuvum veeNdaam

A: Please give us the bill
Bill கொண்டு வாங்க
Bill koNdu vaangga

C: Here you go, Sir.
இந்தாங்க, sir
indhaangga, sir

A: (pays the bill with a small tip)

C: Thank you very much.
ரொம்ப நன்றி
romba nandRi

Scenario 2: Post office

Let's look at a scenario between a person and a shopkeeper:

Person A is the one who wants to send the post, and Person B is the shopkeeper.

A: Where is the post office?
post office எங்க இருக்கு?
post office yengga irukku?

B: The post office is on the left.
post office இடது பக்கம் / leftல இருக்கு
post office idadhu pakkam / leftla irukku

A: At what time does the post office open?
post office எத்தன மணிக்கு திறப்பாங்க?
post office yeththana maNikku thiRappaangga?

B: The post office opens at 10.00 a.m.
post office பத்து மணிக்கு திறப்பாங்க
post office paththu maNikku thiRappaangga

A: At what time does the post office close?
post office எத்தன மணிக்கு மூடுவாங்க?
post office yeththana maNikku muuduvaangga?

B: The post office closes at 5 p.m.
post office அஞ்சு மணிக்கு மூடுவாங்க
post office anjju maNikku muuduvaangga

A: I want to send this letter by post.
எனக்கு இந்த letter postல அனுப்பணும்
yenakku indha letter postla anuppaNum

A: What is the postage for a letter to Delhi, India?
delhikku அனுப்ப எவ்ளோ ஆகும்?
delhikku anuppa yevLoo aagum?

B: It is 50 rupees.
அம்பது ரூபா ஆகும்
ambadhu ruubaa aagum

A: In how many days will it reach Delhi?
எத்தன நாள்ல delhikku போகும்?
yeththana naaLla delhikku poogum?

B: It will reach in 3 days.
மூணு நாள்ல போகும்
muuNu naaLla poogum

A: Where must I put the letter?
letter எங்க போடணும்?
letter yengga poodaNum?

B: Put it in the mailbox.
mailboxல போடுங்க
mailboxla poodungga

A: Please give me postage stamps.
stamps குடுங்க
stamps kudungga

B: Here you go, 50 rupees, please
இந்தாங்க, அம்பது ரூபா அச்சு
indhaangga, ambadhu ruubaa achchu

A: Where is the head office?
head office எங்க இருக்கு?
head office yengga irukku?

B: It is behind the post office.
post officeக்கு பின்னாடி இருக்கு
post officekku pinnaadi irukku

A: I need 2 postcards as well, please.
எனக்கு ரெண்டு postcardஉம் வேணும்
yenakku reNdu postcardum veeNum

B: Here you go.
இந்தாங்க
indhaangga

Scenario 3: Shopping for clothes

Let's look at a scenario between 2 people in a clothes shop:

Person A is the one who wants to buy clothes, and Person C is the clothes seller.

C: Good morning, sir, what do you want?
வணக்கம், உங்களுக்கு என்ன வேணும்?
vaNakkam, unggaLukku yenna veeNum?

A: Good morning. I want to buy a shirt.
எனக்கு shirt வாங்கணும்
yenakku shirt vaanggaNum

C: What color do you want?
எந்த color வேணும்?
yendha color veeNum?

A: I prefer blue.
blue color குடுங்க
blue color kudungga

C: Light blue or dark blue?
Light blueஆ இல்ல dark blueஆ?
Light blueaa illa dark blueaa?

A: Show me both.
ரெண்டுமே காமிங்க
reNdumee kaamingga

C: Here you go. But what size do you want?
இந்தாங்க, ஆனா எந்த size வேணும்?
indhaangga, aanaa yendha size veeNum?

A: A large shirt.
L size shirt குடுங்க
L size shirt kudungga

C: A cotton or silk shirt?
cotton shirtஆ இல்ல silk shirtஆ?
cotton shirtaa illa silk shirtaa?

A: A cotton shirt. My brother doesn't like wearing silk shirts.
cotton shirt, எ தம்பிக்கு silk shirt போட பிடிக்காது
cotton shirt, ye thambikku silk shirt pooda pidikkaadhu

C: Here you go, Anything else sir?
இந்தாங்க, வேறேதாவது வேணுமா sir?
indhaangga, veeReedhaavadhu veeNumaa sir?

A: Yes, I also want a saree.
ஆமா, எனக்கு ஒரு saree வேணும்
aamaa, yenakku oru saree veeNum

C: The sarees are on the first floor.
sarees, first floorல இருக்கு
sarees, first floorla irukku

A: I want to buy this tie.
எனக்கு இந்த tie வாங்கணும்
yenakku indha tie vaanggaNum

C: Sure, sir.
கண்டிப்பா
kaNdippaa

A: How much is it?
இது எவ்ளோ?
idhu yevLoo?

355

C: It costs 500 rupees.
ஐநூறு ரூபா
ainuuRu ruubaa

A: Oh, but this is too expensive for me. I want to see another tie.
இது வில அதிகம், வேற காமிங்க
idhu vila adhigam, veeRa kaamingga

C: Do you like this tie?
உங்களுக்கு இந்த tie பிடிச்சிருக்கா?
unggaLukku indha tie pidichchirukkaa?

A: Yes, this one is better. How much is it?
ஆமா, இந்த tie நல்லா இருக்கு, இது எவ்ளோ?
aamaa, indha tie nallaa irukku, idhu yevLoo?

C: Only 200 rupees.
எரநூறு ரூபா தான்
yeranuuRu ruubaa dhaan

A: Okay, I will buy this one.
சரி, நா இத வாங்குறெ
sari, naa idha vaangguRe

A: Where should I pay for the shirt and the tie?
shirtக்கும் tieக்கும் எங்க pay பண்ணனும்?
shirtkkum tiekkum yengga pay paNNanum?

C: At the cash counter over there.
அங்க இருக்குற cash counterல
angga irukkuRa cash counterla

A: Thank you.
நன்றி
nandRi

356

Scenario 4: Shopping for fruits

Let's look at a scenario between 2 people in a fruits shop:

Person A is the one who wants to buy clothes, and Person C is the fruit seller.

A: How much do the apples cost?

apple எவ்ளோ?

apple yevLoo?

C: The apples cost 300 rupees per kilogram

apple கிலோ முந்நூறு ரூபா

aapple kiloo munnuuRu ruubaa

A: That's very expensive.

அது ரொம்ப வில அதிகம்

adhu romba vila adhigam

C: The prices are fixed, sir.

fixed price தான், sir

fixed price dhaan, sir

A: Give me half a kilo of apples.

அர கிலோ apple குடுங்க

ara kiloo apple kudungga

C: Anything else?

வேறேதாவது வேணுமா?

veeReedhaavadhu veeNumaa?

A: How much are the grapes?

திராட்ச்ச எவ்ளோ?

dhiraatchcha yevLoo?

357

C: 150 rupees a kilogram.
கிலோ நுத்தியம்பது ரூபா
kiloo nuuththiambadhu ruubaa

A: Are they fresh?
freshஆ இருக்கா?
freshaa irukkaa?

C: Yes, sir.
ஆமா, freshஆ இருக்கு
aamaa, freshaa irukku

A: Okay, then give me 2 kgs of grapes.
சரி, ரெண்டு கிலோ திராட்ச்ச குடுங்க
sari, reNdu kiloo dhiraatchcha kudungga

C: Is that all?
அவ்ளோ தானா?
avLoo dhaanaa?

A: Yes, how much is that in total?
ஆமா, மொத்தம் எவ்ளோ ஆச்சு?
aamaa, moththam yevLoo aachchu?

C: 450 rupees. Will you be paying by cash or credit card?
நாணுத்தி அம்பது ரூபா, cashஆ இல்ல credit cardஆ?
naaNuththi ambadhu ruubaa, cashaa illa credit cardaa?

A: Do you accept debit cards?
debit card வாங்கிப்பீங்களா?
debit card vaanggippiinggaLaa?

358

C: Yes, sir.

சரி, குடுங்க sir

sari, kudungga sir

A: Ah, that's good. Here you go.

நல்லது, இந்தாங்க

nalladhu, indhaangga

Scenario 5: Airport, Immigration control section

Let's look at a scenario between 2 people in the Airport, Immigration control section: Person A is a Tourist, and Person B is an Immigration control officer.

B: How long will you stay here? What is the purpose of your visit?

எவ்ளோ நாள் இங்க இருப்பீங்க / தங்குறீங்க? எதுக்காக india visit பண்றீங்க?

yevLoo naaL ingga iruppiingga / thangguRiingga? yedhukkaaga india visit paNdRiingga?

A: I am here for the holidays.
holidays / vacationகாக

holidays / vacationkaaga

B: Your passport, please.
உங்க passport குடுங்க

ungga passport kudungga

A: Here it is.
இந்தாங்க

indhaangga

B: Do you have anything else to declare?
நீங்க ஏதாவது declare பண்ணனுமா?

niingga yeedhaavadhu declare paNNanumaa?

A: Yes, a small bottle of perfume and a TV.
ஆமா, ஒரு small bottle perfumeமும் ஒரு tvயும்

aamaa, oru small bottle perfumemum oru tvyum

360

B: Do you have any luggage?

luggage இருக்கா?

luggage irukkaa?

A: Yes, a big bag.

ஆமா, ஒரு பெரிய பை இருக்கு

aamaa, oru periya pai irukku

B: Please show me your flight ticket and visa.

உங்க flight ticket visa காமிங்க / காட்டுங்க

ungga flight ticket visa kaamingga / kaattungga

A: Here you go.

இந்தாங்க

indhaangga

B: You will have to pay customs duty for the TV, please fill out this form and pay the money at the counter.

நீங்க tvக்கு customs duty கட்டணும், இந்த form fill பண்ணுங்க, அந்த counterல பணம் கட்டுங்க

niingga tvkku customs duty kattaNum, indha form fill paNNungga, andha counterla paNam kattungga

A: Okay, thank you

நன்றி

nandRi

Scenario 6: Railway station

Let's look at a scenario between 2 people at the Railway station:

Person A is a tourist, and Person B is a worker at the railway ticket counter.

A: What time does the train to Hyderabad leave?

Hyderabadக்கு train எத்தன மணிக்கு கிளம்பும்?

Hyderabadkku train yeththana maNikku kiLambum?

B: At 10:15 AM.

பத்தேகால் மணிக்கு

paththeegaal maNikku

A: And what time does it arrive?

எத்தன மணிக்கு வரும்?

yeththana maNikku varum?

B: At 2:30 PM.

ரெண்டர மணிக்கு வரும்

reNdara maNikku varum

A: Is it a direct train?

direct trainஆ?

direct trainaa?

B: Yes, it's a direct train.

ஆமா, direct train

aamaa, direct train

A: The train leaves from which platform?

எந்த platformலருந்து கிளம்பும்?

yendha platformlarundhu kiLambum?

B: It leaves from platform number 2.
ரெண்டாவது platformலருந்து கிளம்பும்
reNdaavadhu platformlarundhu kiLambum

A: A ticket for Hyderabad, please.
hyderabadக்கு ஒரு ticket குடுங்க
hyderabadkku oru ticket kudungga

B: One-way or return?
one wayஆ இல்ல returnஆ?
one wayaa illa returnaa?

A: One-way.

B: First class or second class?
first classஆ இல்ல second classஆ?
first classaa illa second classaa?

A: First class.

B: Do you want a window seat?
window seat வேணுமா?
window seat veeNumaa?

A: Yes, I want the window seat.
ஆமா, window seat வேணும்
aamaa, window seat veeNum

B: Here, your seat number is 11.
இந்தாங்க, உங்க seat number பதினொன்னு
indhaangga, ungga seat number padhinonnu

A: Thank you very much, sir.
ரொம்ப நன்றி
romba nandRi

B: Here is your ticket and your reservation, 300 rupees.

உங்க ticketஉம் reservationஉம் இந்தாங்க, முந்நூறு ரூபா ஆச்சு

ungga ticketum reservationum indhaangga, munnuuRu ruubaa aachchu

A: Thank you.

நன்றி

nandRi

Scenario 7: Doctor's clinic

Let's look at a scenario between a doctor and a patient:

Doctor: How are you?
எப்டி இருக்கீங்க?
yepdi irukkiingga?

Patient: I have a headache.
எனக்கு தல வலிக்குது
yenakku thala valikkudhu

Doctor: Do you feel tired?
tiredஆ இருக்கா?
tiredaa irukkaa?

Patient: No, but I am unable to sleep well.
இல்ல, ஆனா என்னால தூங்க முடியல
illa, aanaa yennaala thuungga mudiyala

Doctor: Okay, I will give you some medicine to sleep well and something for your headache.

சரி, நா உங்களுக்கு தூங்குறதுக்கும் தலைவலிக்கும் கொஞ்சம் மாத்திர தர்றெ,

sari, naa unggaLukku thuungguRadhukkum thalaivalikkum konjjam maaththira tharRe.

Patient: Doctor, I am also having some eye pain.
எனக்கு கண்ணும் வலிக்குது
yenakku kaNNum valikkudhu

365

Doctor: Please lie down. I will check your eyes.

இங்க படுங்க, நா உங்க கண்ண check பண்றெ

ingga padungga, naa ungga kaNNa check paNdRe

Doctor: Your eyes seem to be fine. Maybe it's because of your headache.

உங்க கண்ணு நல்லா தான் இருக்கு, ஒரு வேல தல வலினால இருக்கும்

ungga kaNNu nallaa dhaan irukku, oru veela thala valinaala irukkum

Doctor: Please take the medicine that I gave you and if you still have a problem with your eyes, please come and meet me again.

நா குடுக்குற இந்த மாத்திரைய எடுத்துக்கோங்க, உங்க கண்ணுல இன்னும் பிரச்சன இருந்தா என்ன வந்து திரும்ப பாருங்க

naa kudukkuRa indha maaththiraiya yeduththukkoongga, ungga kaNNula innum pirachchana irundhaa yenna vandhu thirumba paarungga

Patient: Thank you, doctor. How much is the doctor's fee?

நன்றி doctor, doctor fees எவ்ளோ?

nandRi doctor, doctor fees yevLoo?

Doctor: 500 rupees, and here is the prescription.

ஐநூறு ரூபா, prescriptionஇந்தாங்க

ainuuRu ruubaa, prescription indhaangga

Scenario 8: Asking for directions

Let's look at a scenario between 2 people asking for directions:

Person A is a Tourist, and Person B is a stranger he meets on the road.

A: Excuse me

B: Yes?

A: How do I get to the Castilla Hotel?

castilla hotelக்கு எப்டி போகணும்?

castilla hotelkku yepdi poogaNum?

B: Go straight ahead. Then take the second street. That is Solomen street.

நேரா போங்க, ரெண்டாவது தெரு எடுங்க, அது solomen தெரு

neeraa poongga, reNdaavadhu theru yedungga, adhu solomen theru

A: The second street?

ரெண்டாவது தெருவா?

reNdaavadhu theruvaa?

B: Yes, exactly. Then turn left. The Castilla Hotel will be there

ஆமா, அப்புறம் இடது பக்கம் திரும்புங்க, அங்க castilla hotel இருக்கும்

aamaa, appuRam idadhu pakkam thirumbungga, angga castilla hotel irukkum

A: Thank you very much. Goodbye!

ரொம்ப நன்றி

romba nandRi

367

Scenario 9: Random conversations

Below are random conversations:

A: What is your profession?
என்ன வேல பாக்குறீங்க?
yenna veela paakkuRiingga?

B: I am a doctor.
நா ஒரு doctor
naa oru doctor

A: What does your father do?
உங்க அப்பா என்ன பண்றாரு?
ungga appaa yenna paNdRaaru?

B: He is a dentist.
அவரு ஒரு dentist
avaru oru dentist

A: What does your mother do?
உங்க அம்மா என்ன பண்றாங்க?
ungga ammaa yenna paNdRaangga?

B: She is a housewife.
அவங்க வீட்ட பாத்துக்குறாங்க
avangga viitta paaththukkuRaangga

Scenario 10: Random Conversation

A: I just bought a necklace.

நா இப்ப தான் இந்த necklace வாங்குனெ

naa ippa dhaan indha necklace vaanggune

B: Is it made of gold or silver?

தங்கமா வெள்ளியா?

thanggamaa veLLiyaa/

A: I bought a diamond necklace

நா diamond necklace வாங்குனெ

naa diamond necklace vaanggune

B: Where did you buy this necklace?

எங்க வாங்குனீங்க?

yengga vaangguniingga?

A: I bought it in the Ganesh jewelers

ganesh jewelersல வாங்குனெ

ganesh jewelersla vaanggune

B: It looks very beautiful; shall we go to the jewelry shop together this weekend?

பாக்க ரொம்ப அழகா இருக்கு, இந்த weekend நாம அந்த நகை கடைக்கு போலாமா

paakka romba azhagaa irukku, indha weekend naama andha nagai kadaikku poolaamaa

A: Yeah, definitely.

கண்டிப்பா

kaNdippaa

Scenario 11: Random Conversation

A: I want to go shopping. Where is the market?

எனக்கு shopping போகனும், market எங்க இருக்கு?

yenakku shopping pooganum, market yengga irukku?

B: What do you want to buy?

உங்களுக்கு என்ன வாங்கணும்?

unggaLukku yenna vaanggaNum?

A: I want to buy clothes and fruit.

எனக்கு துணியும் பழமும் வாங்கணும்

yenakku thuNiyum pazhamum vaanggaNum

B: To buy clothes please go to the Ganesh market. To buy fruits please go to the fruit market.

துணி வாங்க ganesh marketக்கு போங்க, பழம் வாங்க பழம் marketக்கு போங்க

thuNi vaangga ganesh marketkku poongga, pazham vaangga pazham marketkku poongga

A: Thank you very much.

ரொம்ப நன்றி

romba nandRi

You have successfully completed the course!

Now, to further improve your fluency level in Tamil, below are the steps you can follow.

Book Classes: You can book classes from me through the link below and I can help you become fluent in Tamil soon.

https://www.italki.com/teacher/3248724

As mentioned earlier, you can watch Tamil movies, listen to Tamil music and practice Tamil with your friends and family to improve your fluency.

Thank you for choosing this book. I wish you all success in becoming fluent in Tamil.

A DAZZLING KALEIDOSCOPE OF TAMIL NADU CULTURE

An Exceptional Guide on Your Trip to Tamil nadu

Footwear

1. You shouldn't wear sandals or boots when one goes inside a house, temple, or clinic. However, do wear shoes when you visit supermarkets, stores, hospitals, and other such places.

2. Many people in this country wear outdoor casual footwear. People find it comfortable to slip into a pair of sandals or flip-flops due to the unpredictable tropical climate.

Bathroom facilities

3. Many places and houses in India have only squat toilets where they use water as in many other countries, for instance, Southeast Asia and the Middle East. Even if there is a Western toilet, it is unlikely to have toilet paper or it may simply be out of it. Therefore, it is appropriate. If possible, you should carry some with you in your purse or bag whenever you leave home

4. At times, public toilets in India are unhygienic. Clean toilets are available only at malls, restaurants, and hospitals. It's a good idea to look for a restaurant or mall if you need to use the toilet.

5. The Indian community often does not have a bathtub or shower in most houses and in some hotels. Instead, they keep a bucket and mug for bathing.

Customs

6. It is a custom that the residents of any locale clean their front door entranceway and draw "Koolam" using rice powder (for the birds to feed on them) or chalk powder. As a symbol of admiration, it would be a nice gesture not to trample it.

7. Because people in India believe education is sacred, you should not walk over or step on paper/ books

8. You should be submissive towards and gracious in the Holy places of worship. It is a religious norm for people of India to avoid non-vegetarian food during their visit to the temple. Avoid eating it and if so, keep it to yourself. Additionally, some functioning Hindu temples do not allow entry to non-Hindus, therefore you should check in advance.

9. The opposite genders maintain distance from one another and do not often mix. Being cordial and warm-hearted, women tend to hug each other, and they frequently keep company and socialize as well. When you visit India, you step into a community that displays tenderness and compassion within their hearts.

10. A culture of ethical values and deep reverence is embedded in this land of ideals. No one utters a mere "How are you" to any random person or if you meet an unknown person for the first time.

Be a good guest

11. Indians are hospitable. It is a common practice for an Indian family to make their guests feel at home. Hence, they serve a variety of eatables as a sign of generosity. Here, a simple "no / enough" is pointless if you don't feel like eating because this only makes them believe that you're being humble despite your appetite. That being the case, keep an exaggerated tone, refuse multiple times, or emphasize that your stomach is full. Just make a big thing of it and suggest that 'I am so full that my stomach is about to burst', or apologetically overstretch, 'I am really full, I cannot eat anymore', and so on.

12. When visiting someone's house for the first time, it is customary to take some fruits (e.g.,1 kg apple) or sweets (250/500 gram Indian sweet) or snacks (e.g., biscuits) as a token of respect. Though not mandatory (as nobody gets offended if one shows up empty-handed), it reflects your immense generosity.

13. Another rule of etiquette you may notice is that people are accustomed to eating with their right hand only. Eating with the left hand indicates disgust because it is used for cleaning yourself in the toilet. Furthermore, if someone gives you a gift or anything, receive it with the right hand only to show reverence to each other.

14. If you get a gift at a birthday party, it is considered proper to open it later rather than in front of everyone. (In contrast, in some Western countries, you're expected to open the gift during the party as a gracious host)

15. As a guest at someone's house, you may be served water (and at times tea or coffee brewed in milk with sugar) along with a tray adorned with delicious treats to enjoy. It is a symbol of warmth amongst the lively people of India.

Taxis

16. In many noteworthy cities of India, apps like Uber and Ola are the most commonly used modes of traveling. These are far more comfortable than a taxi or an auto (tuk-tuk) on the street. If Uber or Ola is not available, discuss the rates with the taxi or auto beforehand.

17. You may observe passengers sitting cross-legged in a taxi. Welcome to India; the land of simplicity and humility! Many drivers and passengers don't like to wear a seat belt, so you will find many drivers not wearing a seat belt while driving and at times there won't even be a seat belt for passengers to use. Grab one if you're ready to go.

18. You may go out shopping, or take a taxi, only to find that the shopkeeper or taxi driver has run out of change. This is not something to fret about. Don't be surprised. It is a common practice in this region to wait while they get change from a nearby shop or the next-waiting cab as to they can hand it over to you in no time.

Food and drinks

19. Indian delicacies are deliciously spicy. The spice level depends on the venue and menu. To opt for less spicy food, grab a seat in an Indo-Chinese restaurant. You'll still be able to satisfy your craving for a flavourful experience of savoury Indian cuisine

20. In every restaurant, people use a wash basin to clean their hands, which is normally not attached to the lavatory. Look around and it will likely be just around the corner.

21. The tap water quality in this region is quite questionable. While traveling, it is advisable to carry bottled mineral water. You can buy bottled mineral water in almost every shop.

22. Being a vegetarian is a cultural norm in India. On this account, India abounds in a phenomenal variety of mouth-watering vegetarian meals that are thoroughly fascinating and appetizing.

Others

23. Along with the scorching heat, you'll likely encounter many bright, sunny days in this beautifully enriching country. Don't forget to have an umbrella for a nice shade as you tread on the vibrant streets of India.

24. If you hear the words "love you" in India, it means that someone likes you very much. However, it does not indicate romance.

25. Some streets in India are littered with mongrel dogs. They are harmless creatures, commonly found lurking around during the day or night. If you find yourself alone and scared on a dimly lit night and they begin barking at you, stand your ground and throw small stones nearby to ward them off.

26. Signboards, hoardings, and road signs are available in English and Tamil language for the convenience and benefit of passers-by. These will help you to travel with ease and reach your destination safely.

27. Metropolitan cities like Chennai, Delhi, and Bengaluru are quite chaotic and have lots of bottleneck traffic. Blaring horns and honking vehicles is a day-to-day convention in this part of Asia in comparison to the West. Trucks even have signs on the back that say "Horn OK Please" or "Sound Horn". This is a commonly painted phrase on commercial automobiles like trucks and buses in India to encourage people to alert the drivers from behind of approaching vehicles.

28. India is known for extending unheard-of hospitality. The degree of cordiality towards foreigners is immeasurably instilled within the local inhabitants. Warm greetings and taking photographs with tourists are quite conventional traits.

29. People are carefree and easy-going; therefore, time is not a virtue in India. Do not expect people or things to be on time. Lighten yourself up.

30. Be more alert when you cross any street in this country than you would be in a Western setting.

31. Be light-hearted about things that might upset you. People almost never mean offense. India is a land of beauty and goodwill.

Universally Celebrated Hindu Festivals in Tamil Nadu, 2023

Numerous festivals are famous in Tamil Nadu. To mention a few, I will throw light on the major rituals celebrated with zeal and zest in the specific region and draw a picture of how people commemorate the arrival of these colourful, happening days every year.

January 14, Bhogi

In the wake of the day, as the sun rises, residents collect used, worn-out belongings, gather in the streets, and burn down every item. This is a symbolic representation of the start of a new year. With a forgotten past, they look forward to a new horizon, enthusiastically willing to paint new memories.

January 15, Pongal

On this day, people buy 2 sugar canes along with fancy organic articles made out of leaves. With thrill and excitement in the air, they decorate their houses. In addition to this, they cook chakkara pongal (made out of jaggery and rice), payasam (made out of rice or vermicelli, sugar or jaggery and milk), and vadai (made out of lentils and fried rice). Everyone offers homemade food to God as a symbol of reverence, showing gratitude for the peaceful year gone by and raising a hand in prayer for a prosperous year to follow. The land farmers especially celebrate this eventful day to show their devotion and appreciation to God for the sound cultivation overflowing in plenty.

January 16, Maattu Pongal

The citizens brush and groom their farmland cows. The day is spent praying to offer thanks to the cow for the ample provision they have been bestowed with in the days gone past.

February 18, Shiva Rathri

According to Hindu mythology, there is a belief that if you do not sleep on this holy night, once the soul departs, it will be in the heavens above. Thereupon, people stay up the whole night, eating, chatting, and watching television.

September 6, Krishna Jayanti

As stated in Hindu mythology, this day marks the birth of lord Krishna. On the advent of this day, people offer full-flavored, fit-for-a-king food to lord Krishna. To pay homage, families dress up their young children as lord Krishna. Besides this, the devotees dip the children's feet in thick rice powder water and make them walk inside the house, signifying that the lord has descended in their fine abode.

September 19, Vinayagar Chaturthi:

In the spirit of Hindu mythology, this day marks the birth of lord Vinayagar. As the day unfolds itself, every family makes an earthen clay Vinayagar statue, decorates the statue, and drapes the house. In reverence, cooked "kozhukattai" (steamed rice bun with coconut, jaggery, or sesame and jaggery including other fillings) along with a range of refreshments is presented to lord Vinayagar. The day rolls by furnished with heartfelt prayers and wishes. The family will worship the Vinayagar statue for days in their house, offering him food, and living with the thought that the lord lives in their house as an esteemed guest. As the holy ritual reaches its last moments, the statue is placed in a pond/well as a send-off.

October 23, Ayudha Pooja / Sarasvathi Pooja

On this special occasion, the whole house is cleaned and decorated. The members of the family place books and hardware equipment or working tools like knives, hammers, and screwdrivers in front of the Holy Divinities. The blessed day rolls on, and families offer food and pray to God for a better education, a successful business, or success at work. Each person seeks prayers in accordance with the profession he intends to thrive.

November 12, Deepavali

This day is in commemoration of when Lord Ram killed Raavanan. Everybody loses themselves in prayers. All and sundry, cook delicious meals in honour of the lord. To add a final touch to the day, people burst crackers to celebrate the killing of Raavanan by the courageous lord Ram.

379

BIBLIOGRAPHY

R. E. Asher and E. Annamalai 2002. Colloquial Tamil, The complete course for beginners. Routledge New York.

Vasu Renganathan 2011. Tamil Language in Context: A comprehensive approach to learning Tamil. Departnment of South Asia Studies. University of Pennsylvania.

Vasu Renganathan 2011. Tamil Language in Context: A comprehensive approach to learning Tamil. Departnment of South Asia Studies. University of Pennsylvania.

Kesavaram P H. 2017. A Practical Course to Learn Tamil For Absolute beginners.

Jeyapandian Kottalam 2014. Learning Tamil by yourself

Made in the USA
Las Vegas, NV
05 November 2024

11202566R00231